China's Superbank

Since 1996, Bloomberg Press has published books for financial professionals as well as books of general interest in investing, economics, current affairs, and policy affecting investors and business people. Titles are written by well-known practitioners, BLOOMBERG NEWS® reporters and columnists, and other leading authorities and journalists. Bloomberg Press books have been translated into more than 20 languages.

For a list of available titles, please visit our Web site at www.wiley.com/go/bloombergpress.

China's Superbank

Debt, Oil and Influence—
How China Development
Bank Is Rewriting the
Rules of Finance

Henry Sanderson
Michael Forsythe

WILEY | **Bloomberg**
PRESS

Other Wiley Editorial Offices

John Wiley & Sons, 111 River Street, Hoboken, NJ 07030, USA

John Wiley & Sons, The Atrium, Southern Gate, Chichester, West Sussex, P019 8SQ, United Kingdom

John Wiley & Sons (Canada) Ltd., 5353 Dundas Street West, Suite 400, Toronto, Ontario, M9B 6HB, Canada

John Wiley & Sons Australia Ltd., 42 McDougall Street, Milton, Queensland 4064, Australia
Wiley-VCH, Boschstrasse 12, D-69469 Weinheim, Germany

ISBN 978-1-118-17636-8 (Cloth)
ISBN 978-1-118-17639-9 (ePDF)
ISBN 978-1-118-17637-5 (Mobi)
ISBN 978-1-118-17638-2 (ePub)

Typeset in 11.5/14pt, Bembo by MPS Limited, Chennai, India
Printed in the United States of America.

10 9 8 7 6 5 4 3

Contents

Preface

Hugo Chávez, resplendent in crisply pressed fatigues and paratrooper boots with red shoelaces, had a very special guest. Meeting him that mid-September day in Caracas was the world's most powerful banker, who had lent Chávez's government at least $40 billion over four years, or about $1,400 for every man, woman, and child in Venezuela.

The guest, stooped and looking older than his 66 years, drank chrysanthemum tea, staring across the table at Chávez, bald from his chemotherapy treatments. He handed the president of the Bolivarian Republic of Venezuela a 600-page book filled with recommendations on how Chávez should run, manage, and build ports, roads, and railroads.

What bank in this day and age can lend so much money to one of the world's riskiest regimes, a nation with two centuries of credit defaults, and then tell its debtor how to spend the proceeds of the loan?

Not Goldman Sachs. Chávez's banker had governmental ties that the legendary New York firm, incubator to US Treasury Secretaries Hank Paulson and Robert Rubin, could only dream of. The man sitting across from Chávez was the Chinese equivalent of royalty. His father was one of the founding fathers of the People's Republic of China. His company was banker to China Inc.

Not the World Bank. That Washington-based product of *Pax Americana* had a loan book only a fraction of the size of this man's company, the world's biggest policy bank. Chávez's Chinese bank had bragging rights over the World Bank as well, having been front and center in crafting the biggest and arguably most successful poverty-reduction program in history that saw hundreds of millions of Chinese peasants become city dwellers. In Africa, the bank has funneled billions of dollars into the continent, stoking Ethiopian exports and reviving Ghana's railroad network after decades of neglect.

Not the Fed. The Federal Reserve Bank might have trillions of dollars at its disposal, and it might rightly be credited with staving off a depression in the wake of the 2008 financial meltdown. But when it comes to results, Chávez's bank arguably has an even more impressive record. The bank devised a system to fund local infrastructure projects that is credited with helping China sail through the global financial crisis while the United States and Europe stumbled.

Chávez's guest was Chen Yuan, chairman of China Development Bank (CDB), the world's most powerful banker.

You can't buy shares in CDB: It is wholly owned by the Chinese government. But it would be a mistake to call it a government bureaucracy that is at the state's beck and call. It is a bank, claiming the lowest nonperforming loan rate of any major Chinese lender and a reputation for hardball negotiations with both domestic and foreign clients. While other countries have long formed development banks to help fund their national companies and bolster economic growth to catch up to more advanced powers, the scale of CDB and the amount it can lend makes it a different animal.

But the world's most powerful bank? Yes. Let us count the ways.

Exhibit 1: China. The bank wrote the manual for the biggest economic and urbanization boom in history, pioneering a system of lending to local government-backed companies that funneled more than $2 trillion across China to build roads, bridges, subways, and stadiums and was later used to stimulate growth when the world economy was crippled by the global financial crisis. The turnkey system it set up, beginning in 1998 in Anhui Province, meant that Chinese growth barely registered a hiccup while the United States went into the deepest economic crisis since the Great Depression. CDB's recently retired vice president, Gao Jian, is regarded as the father of China's bond market. CDB in one year sold more bonds than China's Ministry of Finance.

Exhibit 2: Africa. CDB lending is starting to move ahead of that of the World Bank and other international organizations, focused on building industry and infrastructure for the next stage of Africa's growth and harnessing its biggest clients, China's elite state-owned companies, to do much of the work. While much of Chinese lending in Africa is focused on the extraction of oil and metals to fuel China's insatiable thirst for raw materials, in part driven by the bank's funding of the nation's urbanization, that is only part of the story. The bank's private equity arm, the China-Africa Development Fund, is spurring the continent's manufacturing as labor costs rise at home, helping transform Ethiopia into an exporter of leather and Chinese companies such as Chery Auto to open factories. In Ghana, CDB is financing roads, railroads, and an oil terminal and pipeline network with a $3 billion loan, the biggest in that country's history, and guaranteeing Chinese companies will win most of the contracts.

Exhibit 3: Latin America. CDB's massive and unprecedented lending to Chávez's government has helped secure access for its state-owned oil companies to long-term supply in the competitive global oil market as China's demand continues to rise. It has also been good business for a host of Chinese companies. Chen's point man for Venezuela, a buzzcut and rail-thin man named Liu Kegu, with the booming voice of a Marine Corps gunnery sergeant, is affectionately called "brother" by Chávez. The opposition frets that Chinese influence is eroding the country's sovereignty and drawing it into a risky alliance of dependence. The bogeymen of twentieth-century Yanqui imperialism often were US companies. Is CDB taking that role for China?

Exhibit 4: Clean Energy and Telecommunications. CDB has funneled more than $92.4 billion in lines of credit to China's leading wind, solar, and telecommunications companies, which have used the cash to overwhelm global competitors, securing loans because lenders know the companies have the backing of the world's most powerful bank. Huawei Technologies, the biggest single recipient of the credit lines, has transformed itself into the world's second-largest telecommunications equipment maker over the past decade, using CDB credit to help its vendors in Latin America, Africa, Asia, and Europe buy its gear. Chinese solar companies continue to ramp up production even as losses mount, backed by CDB lines of credit that dwarf the US government loans to the bankrupt Solyndra LLC, which became a campaign issue in 2012. The CDB loans are helping cement Chinese domination in an industry of the future and helping to drive US and European companies to insolvency. Many Chinese companies have debt loads and quarterly losses that should have driven them to bankruptcy as well, but for the CDB loans and, in one case, a local government bailout. CDB financing has helped spark US and European Union trade action against China.

■ ■ ■

In one decade, CDB has become the financial enabler of both China's global expansion and domestic boom. This book tries to explain that importance. It is a book about that bank.

But it is not a book about a bank.

It is a book about China. China's rise as a global economic superpower and the success of its top companies is intricately tied to CDB, run since 1998 by Chen Yuan, the son of Chen Yun, one of the "eight immortals" of the Communist Party. Understand CDB and you understand the core of China's state capitalism, a system of government-controlled banks and companies that many developing countries see as an alternative to a more free market–focused system.

A few fundamental themes shape this book and the bank. Like other development banks in history, CDB has helped create markets and offers financing where no other banks would be willing to lend, allowing China to catch up in its economic development despite a backward financial system. The bank believes in combining the functions of the market with government strategic priorities. This can be seen in its efforts to help local governments set up companies to raise funds and in the progress of the Three Gorges, the world's largest hydroelectric dam, from a project that most Chinese and international banks refused to lend to, to a company that would in 2011 sell bonds and buy a stake in Portugal's biggest utility, EDP (Energias de Portugal).

Second is Chen Yuan's belief in urbanization. Over the past decade, China has seen an expansion of infrastructure like never before, from expressways linking mountainous provinces, to hundreds of new airports, as well as mammoth engineering projects such as the east–west gas pipeline and the south–north water diversion that will bring water to the parched North. Infrastructure created the need for long-term funds that CDB in many cases learned to secure against proceeds from land sales, a model it would use with oil sales in Latin America and Africa. The bank prides itself on working closely with borrowers to improve their ability to pay back loans, enabling it to lend to countries the West considers extremely risky by selecting projects that will provide a return. In many cases, the money goes straight to Chinese contractors and does not enter the host government. Lastly, the vast sums that CDB can raise from China's bond market, where interest rates are controlled, means it can offer attractive financing in the form of equity or loans that few banks can match.

This book charts CDB's rise on the world stage. As European and American banks have faced government bailouts and downgrades to their debt ratings, the world's locus of financial power has shifted. Now China, led by CDB, has the capital to spend in developing countries in Africa and Latin America, much like foreign banks in the 1980s, as well as in the developed markets of Europe and the United States. China's outbound investment is expected to reach hundreds of billions of dollars this decade as its industries move up the value chain and consumer demand for raw materials continues to rise. While its international lending in most cases is at commercial interest rates and follows the oil-for-loans deals that Western banks like Standard Chartered have pioneered in the past, it is the ability of CDB to lend long term and the amount that makes it an important and different player rather than the common notion that it provides "cheap loans." So is the way it can bring Chinese contractors and oil firms together into one deal. The same is true of sectors from telecommunications to renewable energy. Development banks in other countries just do not have the same scale of funds. CDB's combination of government backing and commercial principles is a powerful one. It will have a lasting impact on China's ability to source supply in the global commodity markets and help Chinese firms to grow by tying access to the money to contracts.

China's financial landscape remains state dominated. While economists in the West before the financial crisis believed that the best way to prosperity is to reduce government involvement in the economy and let the private sector do the work, CDB and its chairman grew up in a different world, where there were no markets, no stocks or bonds, and an almost nonexistent private sector. There were shortages of goods and inadequate pricing mechanisms. CDB later went on to create markets and funds where there were none. At the same time as CDB has grown to be the world's largest policy bank, the Chinese state has not only kept full ownership but also continues to set the lending rates banks have to base their loans on. It is no different in the oil, power, or commercial banking sector, where the state has kept a controlling share of China's largest firms in an effort to build over 100 so-called national champions. Memory of the failure of free markets on such a massive and costly scale in 2008 offers little incentive for China to reduce state ownership in the banking system, at the same time as its banks have expanded onto the world stage. As CDB competes head-on with Western banks for global lending in overseas markets in Hong Kong and elsewhere, many will have to come to terms with a competitive bank that serves both sovereign wishes as well as those of the market.

But this is not a book only about China's triumphs. The good-news story also comes with a dark side. What CDB has wrought also has potentially disastrous consequences. The system of local-government financing—triumphant as it was in boosting Chinese growth in recent years—has led China's heretofore quickly commercializing financial system back into the twentieth century, saddling the banking system with potentially bad debt from trillions of yuan in projects with questionable economic value, such as an Olympic stadium complex in farmer Li Liguang's hometown of Loudi, a place that will never play host to the quadrennial event, to bronze statues of winged-warrior princesses sitting atop faux Corinthian columns guarding a mountain forest on the Russian border.

CDB's local-debt finance system is also, in the words of political scientist Victor Shih, an "engine of inequality," depending on the exploitation of poor villagers and farmers to generate revenue from land sales. It has upended the lives of millions of people like farmer Li, who lost his land to a local government-funded stadium project and got inadequate compensation. The system has helped to send China's income-inequality level so high that the government has stopped publishing the globally recognized income-inequality index. No less an authority than former premier Zhu Rongji, speaking at Beijing's elite Tsinghua University in April 2011—the shared alma mater of Zhu, Chinese leaders Hu Jintao and Xi Jinping, and Chen Yuan—said: "The money is like plundering people and has lifted up land prices by so much."

■ ■ ■

This book combines on-the-scene reporting and interviews from across the world with number-crunching from Chinese bond prospectuses to tell the story of the world's most powerful bank. The bank is not an easy nut to crack, with lack of transparency one of the main concerns about its increasing dominance across the globe. CDB often works with international organizations, foreign governments, and foreign banks, yet it is not keen to answer questions: Despite annual performance and sustainability reports, it officially has no public relations department. So at times we adopted a Maoist method to get access: We used guerrilla tactics.

We are both Chinese-speaking accredited journalists working in Beijing. As such, we have access to conferences and political events. That includes the annual meeting every March of China's legislature, the National People's Congress, at the Great Hall of the People on Tiananmen Square. CDB officials who also took part in that meeting were prime targets. There we had impromptu interviews. Sometimes, as in the case of Liu Kegu, we secured long sit-downs to talk about everything from Venezuela to the origins of local government financing. Beijing must have more conferences than any city save Las Vegas, and when CDB officials showed up, we were there.

And Chen Yuan has scores of acquaintances the world over. Many of them, including J.P. Morgan's Jacob Frenkel, were happy to talk to us, as were former CDB employees, who gave candid accounts of their time at the bank. Scholars, including Erica Downs at the Brookings Institution in Washington, are also starting to focus on CDB. We drew heavily on her research on CDB's oil-for-loans program.

We did this without taking any time off from our daily routines, attempting to integrate our daily reporting with our book project. It was not easy, but it was worth it, because when we say CDB is the world's most influential bank, we mean it. If you want to understand China both at home and how it is influencing the world, examining China Development Bank is a good place to start.

We organized the book into six chapters.

Chapter 1 explores CDB's hallmark innovation, the system of local government finance that has transformed China's landscape in just over a decade, pumping trillions of yuan into projects as varied as the world's newest expressway system and China's answer to Manhattan, a city complete with a Lincoln Center and Twin Towers rising on the shores of the Bohai Gulf. Starting in the Yangtze River city of Wuhu in 1998, CDB bankers devised a way to unlock China's household savings to feed the model, and leverage the rising price of state-owned land. Money to cities fueled a surge in urbanization as millions moved from the countryside. China's GDP shot up, fueled by investment and the resulting gains in productivity. The system was in place nationwide by 2008 and took in the lion's share of more than 4 trillion yuan in stimulus money and new bank lending that allowed China to continue its growth spurt through the global financial crisis.

Chapter 2 profiles Chen Yuan, chairman of the bank since 1998. Chen has been instrumental at reasserting the party in China's economy through its lending to state-owned companies and to the country's most successful firms. Chen's lineage as son of one of China's founding revolutionaries makes him a princeling, prominent among a class of leaders, including incoming leader Xi Jinping and former Politburo member Bo Xilai, whose fathers helped unite China under the Communist banner in 1949. Studying economics in the 1980s as the country was caught up in heated debates on how best to reform its ailing Soviet-style system after decades of poverty, he began to develop his unique views that called for a strong role for the state at the same time as the market expanded. Taking the helm at CDB, he created a theory of development finance to guide the bank, determined to make it both profitable and serve the government's goals. He managed to reduce its nonperforming loan ratio from over 40 percent to less than 1 percent in the space of a decade, and turn it into the largest overseas lender.

Chapter 3 looks at CDB's China-Africa Development Fund, China's largest private equity fund investing in Africa, and its attempts to stimulate manufacturing in Ethiopia as well as CDB's lending to Ghana just after it had discovered oil for the first time. We travel to leather, shoe, and glass factories in Addis Ababa, learning the mixed success of China's attempts to seed manufacturing projects on the continent. Africa's poor transportation network has meant difficulties for a CDB-funded glass factory. Yet a Chinese state-owned company is helping to build a railway to the nearest port in Djibouti on the Red Sea that promises to turbocharge exports. China is reviving an infrastructure and manufacturing-focused approach to development finance that is creating jobs across the continent, helping stoke its economic upturn after decades of war, kleptocracy, and failed international development programs and philosophies.

Chapter 4 focuses on the company's work to secure a steady flow of oil and gas to China through loans-for-energy deals around the world. It particularly focuses on Venezuela, destination of almost half of these loans. The goal: Support the state's mission to ensure access to a steady supply of oil to feed a growing economy. In Venezuela, which passed Saudi Arabia at the end of 2011 as the country with the largest proven oil reserves, China wins twice: securing oil though its loans and then winning business for its state-owned companies from the Venezuelan government. Across the world, CDB drives a hard bargain, wrestling for years with Russian negotiators over a $25 billion oil-and-pipeline deal and hiring scores of international lawyers from such firms as New York's White & Case and Washington's Hogan Lovells. By all indications, it is a model that works, allowing China to expand its financial presence in countries where Westerners, from a young Benjamin Disraeli in the 1820s to Citigroup in the 1980s, have lost fortunes. After Ecuador defaulted on $3.2 billion of international debt in 2008 and 2009, CDB moved in, lending $1 billion backed by oil. The danger for China is that local resentment over Chinese loans, such as in a post–Chávez Venezuela, will lead to demands for renegotiation or even default. If that happens, it will be an expensive lesson for a rising financial power.

Chapter 5 looks at CDB's lines of credit to Chinese new energy and telecom firms. CDB has provided China's top telecom firms Huawei and ZTE with a combined $45 billion line of credit to help the companies' customers finance purchases. The chief financial officers of telecom makers América Móvil in Mexico and Brazil's Tele Norte Leste Participacoes say that international competitors just could not beat CDB's terms to buy Huawei network equipment. The loans have helped propel Huawei, a Shenzhen-based company run by a former People's Liberation Army officer, to second place in the world in the telecom gear market behind Sweden's Ericsson AB.

CDB is also providing lines of credit to China's biggest alternative energy companies, including solar panel makers Yingli, Trina Solar, and LDK. The Chinese companies ramped up capacity in 2010–2011 even as the global solar and wind industries experienced a slump, leading German and US companies to file for bankruptcy. Chinese companies, thanks to the overwhelming backing of CDB, may do what Nikita Khrushchev could only dream of and truly "bury" their Western competitors.

The chapter also looks at how China Development Bank, the handmaiden of state capitalism, is developing a new form of private-equity financing. Call it public equity. CDB Capital, funded by 35 billion yuan in seed money from the bank, is investing in an array of projects around the country. Armed with a monopoly among banks for direct investments, CDB is attracting an array of global partners, including TPG Capital, whose cofounder Jim Coulter passed by the bronze busts of Chen Yun, Mao Zedong, and the late paramount leader Deng Xiaoping at CDB Capital's Beijing headquarters in May 2011 before inking a cooperative deal.

■ ■ ■

And that is China Development Bank in a nutshell. If the Communist Party is God, CDB is its prophet, extending the power of the Chinese state across the globe and cementing its power at home.

Acknowledgments

Henry Sanderson

Thanks to my parents, my sister Vanessa, and Gu Bo for their support and encouragement during this project as well as for reading drafts. To Jenny Xu for helping with translations throughout, pointing me in the right direction, and finding new source material on CDB. In Ethiopia, many thanks to Fannie Gong. I've learned a lot from discussions with Victor Shih, Carl Walter, Fraser Howie, and Deborah Brautigam, whose own books were an inspiration. The excellent work of Zhang Yuzhe at *Caixin* magazine was also helpful. At Bloomberg, thanks to Ken Kohn, Chris Collins, and Shelley Smith for allowing me to do this project, as well as to Neil Western for supporting the local government stories. The Beijing bureau colleagues and bureau chief John Liu have also provided many stimulating discussions on the world of Chinese finance. At Wiley, many thanks to Nick Wallwork for taking on this project. In Beijing, thanks too to Matt Weitz and Lauren Johnston.

Mike Forsythe

Thanks to my wife, Leta, for being the source of inspiration and encouragement. To my supervisors at Bloomberg, Peter Hirschberg, Chris Anstey, and Dan Moss, for being so understanding in giving me some time during busy workdays to focus on this project. A big hat-tip to Neil Western and John Liu as well. Thanks also to the many Bloomberg News reporters around the world who contributed to this story. Charlie Devereux in Caracas provided invaluable color to the story, including the opening anecdote. Edmond Lococo in Beijing and Crayton Harrison in Mexico City were invaluable in putting together the story of Huawei and ZTE. Thanks to scholars such as Erica Downs at Brookings and Douglas Paal at Carnegie for their research and insights. Fred Hu and Victor Shih also lent us their wise insight.

Chapter 1

Let 10,000 Projects Bloom

While our national government enjoys virtually unlimited credit, the initiators of urbanization projects, local governments, have little. Public faith in the economic success of governmental undertakings in the area of urban renewal and revitalization is not yet to the point that significant securities issues of pending or completed projects can be floated on capital markets.

—*Chen Yuan, governor of China Development Bank, on CDB Web site, 2005*

L oudi is one of countless cities with millions of inhabitants that few outside of China have ever heard of. Its economic mainstay is a state-owned steel mill that lost 2 billion yuan (about $300 million) in 2010.[1] (One dollar is around 6.38 yuan.) Of course, it's booming. A two-hour drive west of the Hunan capital, Changsha, via a new expressway, its streets are lined with karaoke parlors and new apartment complexes featuring palm trees and pastel tones. One complex, called "Wealthy City," is surrounded by billboards showing pictures of Caucasian women strolling through shopping malls featuring brands like KFC and

Microsoft. At the edge of the city on what used to be farmland is a brand-
new, shiny 30,000-seat steel stadium and an aquatic center, where
workers chisel out the Olympic rings by night years after the Beijing
Olympics has ended more than 800 miles to the north. Loudi has had its
own party: Land prices tripled in the city from 2007 to 2010, and a high-
speed rail line will soon stop here. China Railway Construction Corp.
mixes cement day and night to make that a reality. Sitting on top of it all
and somehow mysteriously controlling the trigger, local government
officials come and go in black Audis from an imposing compound that is
complete with white-colonnaded façades and domed arches, nicknamed
"the White House" by locals. The tinted windows don't reveal whether
they're proud or worried: The whole country is on the move, and
growth is the mantra.

Li Liguang, a young married man in a vest top with a hoarse laugh
and short cropped hair, one of the first generation to move off the farm
in this hilly city where beans and rice are farmed. A subsistence farmer
for most of his life, he's building a new house on the 750-square-foot
plot of land the government gave him after taking his old land for the
new stadium. He hauls bricks all day long to construction sites in his
cobalt-blue East Wind truck. With all the new apartment complexes
going up, there's enough work. At night, he settles down in his
makeshift, tarpaulin-covered home that he shares with his wife, two
children, and stooped mother. The only light in the surrounding
darkness is the gleaming work site across the road for the new sports
complex. He has bigger dreams. Once he finishes the house, he hopes to
rent part of it out to earn money to help pay the medical insurance that
comes with being a new urban citizen. "After we were moved everyone
had to depend on themselves to make money," Li said nearby, drinking
a hot, fiery liquor one hot and humid summer night, as fireworks cel-
ebrating a marriage lit up the sky in this city in the middle of Mao
Zedong's home province of Hunan. "Without land we had to find our
own work."

From Li's dreams and hundreds of millions more like it come the
building blocks of China's economic miracle. The urbanization of
the country is the secret sauce of its success. Until 2009, Li lived on his
almost half-acre of land and was happy to use whatever extra money he
had to buy his favorite White Sand brand cigarettes. Now, instead of

dealing with tens of yuan, he's thinking in units of tens of thousands, if not hundreds of thousands. Farmer Li has become *Homo Economicus.*

Multiply Li's experience by 400 million and you begin to see why China's economy has not grown by a respectable 5 or 6 percent a year but at extraordinary rates, averaging about 9 percent a year for the last three decades. In 2011, China became a predominantly urban country for the first time in its 5,000-year history. The process of transforming farmers into city dwellers—maybe working in construction, maybe at a factory—ignites an economic alchemy that adds about 3 percentage points a year to China's economic growth as people move from low-productivity agrarian jobs to high-productivity urban jobs.[2]

Li's experience also has a dark side. Although he has big ambitions, he really should have already arrived on Easy Street. Property records show that land he once farmed is worth millions of yuan, many times more than the 280,000 yuan he says his family of nine received in compensation when a city-owned company forced him to sell his land. Nationwide, at least 50 million farmers have lost their land as cities expand, often receiving a fraction of the fair market price.[3] It's a reversal of one of the core principles of the Communist Revolution, when Mao redistributed land from rich landlords to penniless peasants. Powerful local officials have snatched it back, sometimes violently, to make way for apartment blocks, bullet trains, malls, "development zones," and sports complexes in a building binge that has been financed by more than 10,000 so-called local-government financing vehicles (LGFVs; 地方融资平台), companies set up by local governments to allow them to spend beyond the limits of their budgets. These hidden and unregulated companies have been the unseen hand pushing China's investment-led economic growth over the past decade, which has so impressed foreign visitors. No city, from the skyline of Shanghai to the western mega-city of Chongqing, has been without one, or sometimes handfuls, and they have been the main conduit through which the savings of the Chinese people have been channeled into investment and construction. But the result has led the state banking system to hold trillions of yuan of questionable debt with little accountability for its repayment. Even the authorities don't know how much debt is out there. What does all this investment have to do with China Development-ment Bank (CDB)? Everything. The bank invented the secret sauce.

The Wuhu Model

Deng Xiaoping, the short, squat, chain-smoking paramount leader of China in the early 1990s, decided that the country needed to accelerate growth and build momentum for reform just over a decade after China had started to open up its economy and as it faced international isolation for killing student demonstrators in Tiananmen Square. His famous southern tour to what would become the manufacturing heartlands of China urged local officials to "be bold" in tackling problems. Local governments spent wantonly on hotels, villas, golf courses, and stock market speculation, getting around difficulties in borrowing money by setting up trusts and selling bonds in Japanese yen overseas. A Bloomberg headline in 1995 summed up the mood: "China Says Central Governments in Order, Provinces Not."[4] In 1992, bank lending for investment grew by almost 50 percent, and two years later, inflation was over 20 percent. Local governments set up over 8,000 developmental zones, and by the end of 1992, there were over 12,000 real estate companies. Who could keep track of it all? Since branches of the central bank were under local control, getting approval for funds from the supplicant banking system wasn't difficult. China's Communist Party structure reaches right down to the county level, but local governments had started a long game of cat-and-mouse with central authorities.

The crackdown swiftly followed. Rampant inflation led China's financial czar and later premier Zhu Rongji to cut local governments off from direct borrowing in 1994, with a strict budget law that forbade them from running deficits or selling bonds. The central government would take the lion's share of tax revenue and transfer some of it to local governments; as one newspaper put it at the time: "The central government eats a rising loaf and the local government eats a stale loaf."[5] Local governments couldn't introduce their own taxes or change tax rates, yet they still had the same requirements to spend and provide infrastructure and services.

The reforms were in part political, based on centuries-old fears by the central government that it was losing control to the provinces, exacerbated by the collapse of the Soviet Union only three years earlier. China's central government had been losing its share of tax since 1978, with its share of revenue falling to less than 15 percent of gross domestic product (GDP). Central government revenues jumped in the years after

1994 as a result, while local governments saw their share of revenues fall from 78 percent in 1993 to 45 percent in 2002. The Japanese "samurai" bonds did not end well, and in 1998 and 1999, international investors were losing millions of dollars with the collapse of a local investment trust, Guangdong International Trust and Investment Corp., in southern China. It was the first default since the Communists came to power in 1949, and shocked foreign investors out of their notion that the central government would bail out every local government debt. At the same time, the country's banks were saddled with dud loans to state-owned companies. The Asian financial crisis in 1998 that started in Thailand and spread throughout the region couldn't have come at a worse time.

For CDB, though, the Asian crisis was an opportunity. The founding of these special-purpose vehicles, which came to be known as local-government financing vehicles, or LGFVs, had its roots in the restrictions imposed on local governments. Just as in 2008, it required spending to stimulate the economy and China was entering its golden period of urbanization, but local governments were strapped for cash. Commercial banks were insolvent and being reformed to list overseas. The country was entering a fundamental change from a largely agricultural economy laced with Soviet-era heavy industry to the China you see today: the glitzy skyscrapers, expressways, ports, and apartment complexes. Gao Jian, who sports severe Germanic glasses and a full, vertically growing head of hair, is a Harvard-educated vice governor of CDB who is widely credited as the father of China's modern-day bond market. In a 2010 article[6] he recalled that local governments had 30 percent of the coun-try's tax intake, but they still needed to "eat" and to build, and their tax intake could cover only the basic eating part. They had no property tax, as municipalities in America have, and couldn't sell bonds directly or run a deficit. So CDB bankers headed to the Yangtze River city of Wuhu in Anhui—home province to then–vice president Hu Jintao—where they helped the city get around limits on direct borrowing set up only a few years earlier. As Gao explained in his essay, CDB was used to provide the "seed money" that no commercial bank would be willing to provide.[7] At that time in China, there were few sources of long-term funds. CDB, unique among Chinese banks, is financed by bonds instead of deposits, most with maturities of ten years or more that are bought by China's commercial banks. That gave it an advantage in funding long-term infrastructure projects that might not generate a return on investment for many years. The bank was simply "the best match" for LGFVs, Gao wrote. And after the chaos of the early 1990s, the central government needed and began to take control of China's economy.

The new urban focus in China in the late 1990s unleashed a wave of state capital boosted by growing Chinese savings. The money stayed inside the system; this time there was no money from foreign investors or foreign banks. CDB, as a policy bank, could not take people's deposits directly. So the cycle went something like this: the country's commercial banks used people's savings to buy bonds sold by CDB on the nation's bond market where they, the banks, were the main investors. CDB would then help local governments set up companies to borrow, and give them initial long-term loans. Thus dressed up and empowered, the LGFVs were free to go on a further borrowing spree seeking short-term loans from the commercial banks or selling bonds themselves on the bond market to banks and securities companies. If the central government wanted to stimulate the economy, it could send money flowing down this cash waterfall. The risk in the end came back to their front door. The model was unique and relied on CDB's view of itself as creating markets—it was supposed to put local government funding on a market basis by setting up independent companies that could finance construction and raise funds, thus improving the credit and market discipline of the local government. But that discipline quickly broke down. The companies could be stuffed with whatever assets were needed: equity, land, stakes in local state-owned companies, and city banks. More assets meant more borrowing. Many assets benefited the public only: parks, hospitals, and schools.[8] Since the assets often generated no money themselves, local governments could provide subsidies to "beautify" the balance sheet, and companies could count it as profit. CDB could bring in the other commercial banks, private lenders such as trust companies, and set up myriad different companies handling different projects. The model sounded good in theory: It would combine public benefit with capital market finance. It would turn fiscal revenue into equity. Projects that would not generate a return on investment could be combined with those that did. Gao saw it as part of the evolution of the Chinese economy ever since it had started up reforms in 1978: "Since reform and opening, China's industrial focus has changed from heavy industry to light industry, and again from basic industries (coal, electricity), and so bank credit will also migrate," he wrote in 2010. "Urbanization has become the new main driving force of the new round of economic growth and bank credit will gradually shift to urban construction. Since public utility investment is led by the government, objectively speaking you need to set up local financing vehicles."[9]

But why would banks lend to companies with such weak credit and little history of earnings? Chen Yuan's overriding belief was in urbanization. "Urbanization is the most important and enduring motive force in stimulating consumption and investment in China's domestic economy today," he said in 2005.[10] And in 1998, Chen foresaw that the property market and urbanization would cause land prices to rise, according to Yu Xiangdong, a scholar at a CDB-affiliated think-tank in Shanghai who works closely with Chen. He saw that China could stoke half a century of development with urbanization at its core, Yu said. The state had an advantage over the private sector: It owned all the land. Land revenues are also extrabudgetary revenue and don't have to be included on the central government's accounting of local budgets, meaning there is little oversight on their use. Local governments were sitting on one of the world's most valuable resources with virtually no requirement to be accountable about how it was used. CDB set the stage by devising a system to leverage the future value of land into large up-front loans, such as one it gave the port city of Tianjin in 2003. As more infrastructure was built, land values could only ever go up, as would housing prices. All the bank needed was to work with the local government to create a system that worked. And now was the chance: Between 1996 and 1997, as the Asian crisis started, spending on infrastructure in China doubled, and by 2002, it had risen by nearly three times, according to a book written by CDB and Renmin University.[11] China and local officials became addicted to investment. What was better than an ever-rising state-owned asset that could be used as collateral?

A photo shows Chen Yuan, the new head of CDB, wearing braces and a white shirt on a hot August night in 1998, four years after Zhu's reforms, clinking sparkling wine with the then-governor of Anhui Province, Hui Liangyu. Wu Keming, who was the deputy mayor of Wuhu at the time, also played a key role. In the background is Chi Jianxin, who would later go on to run the bank's African investment fund. CDB provided 1.08 billion yuan in loans to Wuhu that year for urban infrastructure, and by the end of 2010, it had lent a total of

5.39 billion yuan. CDB executives put together a slide-show that featured how what they called the "Wuhu Model" managed to transform a sleepy city into a bustling metropolis that today is home to one of China's most prominent carmakers. The company, Chery Automobile Co., just happens to be owned by one of the first LGFVs. In Wuhu in 1998, a single platform designated by the government was used, the Wuhu Construction Investment Co., to mobilize land sales and bank loans to fund infrastructure investments. As Figure 1.1, taken directly from a CDB presentation, shows, land expropriation and the transfer of land rights are central to making the machine work, used for paying back the loan. "The city had land but no way to turn it into cash, so the government couldn't get money," researcher Yu says. "At that time, no one realized what Chen Yuan knew: that once the land price goes up, you have a second source of income." But the Wuhu government had also promised to use its future fiscal revenue to pay back the loan after ten years if it couldn't sell the land, he said.

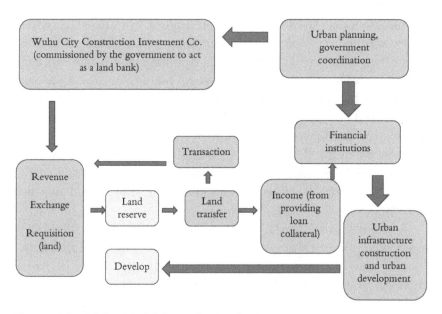

Figure 1.1 Wuhu Model Operating Method

Source: CDB slide on the Wuhu Model from June 20, 2008 (translated from Chinese).

Wuhu officials bypassed the central government for approval of their pioneering plan, turning to the local People's Congress—China's answer to a town council—for approval. The city was greatly aided by Chen's prestige. As Chen and the Wuhu officials saw it, they were creating a virtuous cycle. Public works like roads would boost home prices, which in turn would boost land prices. Higher land prices would mean more local government income, hence more spending. CDB built Wuhu Construction into a giant; eventually its assets grew from 319 million to 21.4 billion yuan, and it bought equity stakes in 21 local companies, including Chery, which is now using CDB backing to expand into every corner of the developing world, from Africa to Latin America. "From then on, the Wuhu Model was extensively applied across the country," the bank's official history says, boosting urbanization, leaving a "precious legacy in the field of financing for urban infrastructure construction."[12] But what on earth had it started? CDB's lending to local governments did not crowd out other lenders of capital, as some say state-owned development banks can do. Instead, it sucked them all in. The model's success in Wuhu was replicated across the country, with CDB lending money to LGFVs in Shanghai (home to former president Jiang Zemin) and Tianjin (home to Premier Wen Jiabao) as well as the canal city of Suzhou. In the central city of Wuhan, it consolidated all the local government financing companies into one large company. Getting a CDB loan was like obtaining the government's Good Housekeeping Seal of Approval. Then—like the Pied Piper—CDB loans led the ostensibly commercialized "big four" banks—Industrial & Commercial Bank of China, China Construction Bank, Bank of China, and Agricultural Bank of China—to make their own loans. The rest of the national banks and the local "city" banks followed suit. Every province in China—even Tibet—has now set up such companies to finance infrastructure investments.

The Chongqing Model

Long before Bo Xilai, the charismatic former Communist Party boss of Chongqing, became famous because of his wife's alleged murder of a British citizen, Huang Qifan, a portly man with pockmarked cheeks, arrived in the hilly southwest city that sits aside a muddy stretch in the Yangtze in 2001 to be deputy mayor. He had previous experience creating the Pudong district in Shanghai, which had grown from a cabbage patch into the city's financial center, where now the towers of Bank of China, HSBC, and Citibank overlook the colonial Bund across the river. A keen talker and proponent of the city's reforms, his press conferences have been known to go on for hours. He was helped by the arrival of Huang Zhendong as Chongqing party secretary; Huang had moved from the position of transport minister, where he'd learned a thing or two about roads. But before they could start spending on infrastructure, they needed funds and to deal with the problem of the ailing state-owned companies that littered the city's landscape and were making huge losses but providing the bulk of employment. So they turned to CDB. In 2004, they set up Chongqing Yufu Asset Management Group, which would later become known as China's Temasek, after the Singaporean sovereign wealth fund. Yufu went on to buy bad loans off of commercial banks' books so local companies didn't have to shut down and fire workers, which could have threatened the Communist Party's desire for stability. Yet Yufu needed funding, and who would lend them money to buy a whole lot of questionable debts? Yufu took CDB loans to buy 15 billion yuan of bad assets from the Industrial and Commercial Bank of China Limited (ICBC), now the largest listed bank in the world.[13] The model, of course, involved land. Many of the bankrupt local state-owned companies had their factories on valuable city-center land; Yufu sold this land for them, moved them out to the suburbs, and used the money to buy their bad loans from ICBC. It was a perfect example of how CDB had worked closely with a local government to sort out their finances, cleaning the slate for investment-led urbanization to begin and making sure state-owned firms would still be around to benefit.

CDB had done a similar move in Tianjin, where it had worked with the local government to eliminate 2 billion yuan of bad loans to automaker Tianjin FAW Xiali Automotive Co., which was almost bankrupt, transforming it in a decade into a company with a market capitalization of almost $2 billion in mid-2012. A commercial bank would have no way of resolving the problem, Chen said. But CDB was not a commercial bank. So it negotiated with the mayor and party secretary, proposing that CDB could lend 10 to 20 billion yuan to redevelop old parts of the city. CDB stepped up with the money, as long as the government got rid of the bad loan. After two years of efforts by the city, the bad loan disappeared. "The story stunned some foreign investment banks, but I told them it was possible in China," Chen said.[14]

In Chongqing, CDB sent an advisor from the bank to Yufu to help the company buy up nonperforming loans from local state-owned enterprises (SOEs). Yufu helped Chongqing Machinery, a local SOE, with a debt restructuring that would have made the financial alchemists in New York or London proud.[15] In 2003, the company was reporting 80 million yuan of losses; by 2005, it was recording profits of 200 million yuan. After itself having had its bad loans taken off its books by the central government in 1999, as we will see in the next chapter, CDB was now helping Chongqing to do the same. It helped restructure a local bank, securities companies, and a rural credit cooperative. Without foreign investors, losses could be moved within the system, allowing the state to take increasing control of resources and avoid bankruptcies and defaults. By 2008, Chongqing's state-owned companies had grown their assets some four times over, to 700 billion yuan. Yufu was an embodiment of the rise of the state in the city, and CDB had funded it.

While in the 1990s the city had borrowed in Japanese yen to finance expressways, LGFVs became the key to accessing China's growing domestic funds that were piling up in the nation's state-owned banks. The year after Huang had arrived, Chongqing set up eight LGFVs with the help of CDB funding. Its GDP grew by an average of 11 percent between 2001 and 2006, and infrastructure investment grew by 200 percent.[16] It was an unparalleled building boom. Now the city's hills are littered with new apartment blocks, its riverbanks are ringed with highways, and a metro system snakes along the tops of the hills. The size of the city's LGFVs drew the World Bank's attention and made the city an early poster-child for this type of funding. The first funding source that the World Bank named in an article on the city's funding[17] was CDB soft loans, loans with a favorable and below-market interest rate which accounted for the bulk of lending to the city's LGFVs. CDB accounted for 64 percent of loans to Chongqing Expressway Development Corporation, one of the largest such companies, which built the city's biggest motorways. Such companies could also set up endless subsidiaries and funnel money any which way they liked. By 2006, they had assets of 191.9 billion yuan, or 42.5 percent of the city's state-owned assets. Once the market became stronger, then this state-owned capital could gradually withdraw, the city's mayor, Huang, said in a March 2006 speech.[18] Yet that did not happen. In May 2012, CDB and its chairman, Chen Yuan, pledged further funding for the city as it faced a political crisis: Its former party secretary, Bo Xilai, had been suspended from the Politburo. Finding private capital would prove harder than first thought. The city became an emblem for China's investment-led state capitalism, a model that was based on CDB loans that could create extraordinary growth rates in a short amount of time. China no longer needed to bother with the delays of market capitalism or the demands of foreign lenders. LGFVs had allowed local governments to borrow beyond what they had dreamed possible.

Cities like Wuhu, Tianjin, and Chongqing were pioneers in using the CDB-invented LGFV model. The system spread across the country, and came into its own in 2008 when it helped shield China from the worst effects of the global financial crisis, this time from across the Pacific Ocean from California's overindebted housing buyers.

Global Financial Crisis

The global financial crisis of 2008 made its way to China from the office towers of New York and the stucco homes of southern California with vicious speed. As the Chinese New Year dawned in February, the government put the number of jobless migrants at 20 million as demand for the exports they produced in coastal factories collapsed along with the US housing bubble fueled on home-equity loans. Many migrants would go home for the holidays and not return to their jobs. China faced the prospect of its exports falling off a cliff as the worst downturn since the Great Depression hit its biggest customer. The global financial titans were bleeding cash and would create $1 trillion of losses related to subprime debt, according to the International Monetary Fund.

On November 5, 2008, China announced a 4 trillion yuan stimulus, equivalent to 12.5 percent of 2008 GDP.[20] The news was broadcast around the world, with China receiving praise for its authoritarian decisiveness. But the central government would fund only 1.18 trillion yuan of the stimulus; where would all the other money come from, and where would it all go? China decided to fund its program through its state-owned banking system. CDB took center stage and provided a ready-made model to push Chinese growth back on track: the LGFVs. The secret sauce invented by CDB was about to help China sail through the global economic slowdown fomented by the financial crisis. While Goldman Sachs, Citigroup, and Lehman Brothers were all central to the financial crisis that paralyzed the United States in 2008, CDB showed why it was the world's most important bank. The relative advance of China as the big Western economies faltered put the nation in its strongest position in at least two centuries, back to the height of the Qing Dynasty, when the Qianlong emperor could spurn Lord George Macartney's 1793 mission and address Britain and the other European powers as lesser states.

While CDB had been the pioneer in lending to these companies, now all of the banks started to issue loans. Total bank lending to the companies rose from 1.7 trillion yuan of outstanding loans at the beginning of 2008 to nearly 5 trillion yuan just two years later.

Local governments could not have been more willing beneficiaries. In China, there are only so many opportunities for free money, and this was one of them. Now, favorite local projects could be built. Within a month of the document's publication for the stimulus, 18 provinces had proposed projects with a total budget of 25 trillion yuan, over 80 percent of annual GDP.[22] The vast majority of the money did not go toward health and education or to households but to infrastructure projects and railways. Nationwide, fixed-asset investment grew 28.8 percent year on year in the first quarter of 2009. In particular, new urban construction projects nationwide rose 87.7 percent year on year, after declining 4.4 percent a year earlier.

In two years, 2009 and 2010, China increased its total government debt at the same speed that America did in the five years before the housing market bust in 2007.[23] By the end of 2010, local governments were strapped with 10.7 trillion yuan of debt, according to a national audit released in the summer of 2011, nearly a third of the country's GDP, and analysts were predicting nonperforming loan (NPL) rates at banks of over 10 percent or more for the major state-owned lenders, levels not seen since the days of the state-led bad loan binge in the late 1990s, when NPLs hit 25 percent in 1997.[24] Of that total 10.7 trillion, almost half was debts borrowed for new projects since 2009. What was worse, most of these were short-term loans maturing in just a few years. There were 360 companies backed by local governments when the World Bank did a survey in 2007; by the end of 2010, there were over 6,000, according to a national audit. The central bank estimated there were more than 10,000 such vehicles. It was a nice round number; in truth, no one knew the exact amount of debt that was out there.

Since 1995, China's local government debt had risen fivefold compared to GDP, and more than 80 percent had gone to infrastructure. Like subprime debt in the United States, these off-balance-sheet vehicles have infected the balance sheets of all China's major banks. Local governments had cashed in and not worried about the consequences. As long as their GDP grew, they could be assured of a promotion. For the banks, they had been told to lend, so were just following orders. The problem was, now the money needed to start providing some returns.[25]

While there is little transparency with the bulk of the lending, which was done via bank loans, LGFVs also started to sell bonds in the domestic bond market in 2009, which generated hundreds of Chinese-language bond prospectuses. They detail—some more than others—how at least 10.7 trillion yuan was borrowed on shaky or nonexistent collateral to companies that often have cash flows running at a trickle. Local officials knew that the central government would never stop the flow of credit once projects were started, and the bigger the debt, the more they would be helped. When investors turned to the bond market, they believed that the companies were backed by local governments and implicitly by the bureaucrats in Beijing, as did the ratings agencies, whose reports endlessly detail accounts of zero cash flow and little profit but AAA or AA ratings. Above all was the belief that as long as China's economy grew, there would be no problem.

CDB's imprint on the companies is indelible. In the three years from 2009 to 2011, among 422 bond prospectuses issued by 341 LGFVs as they turned to the bond market, some 147 said they had received bank loans from CDB, had CDB as their bond underwriter, or had their bonds guaranteed by a CDB-funded guarantor. In all, the 147 companies reported loans and lines of credit from CDB amounting to 928.6 billion yuan.[26] It is important to note that this is a very small subset of total LGFVs—as low as 3 percent of the total—and that many bond-issuing companies that disclosed they had loans from CDB didn't say how much they were. Disclosure in bond prospectuses in China—a Leninist authoritarian country where transparency is not a way of life—is spotty at best. The LGFVs that issue bonds are usually among the biggest in the country, such as provincial expressway companies.

One item few prospectuses omit: homage to CDB. Tianjin Binhai Construction and Investment Group, which was set up in 2005 in an agreement between the city and CDB, said it "relied on CDB from the outset." Huainan Urban Construction Investment Co. in Anhui, which won a 7.1 billion yuan loan from CDB at the beginning of 2008, said it relied on CDB loans to finance most of its projects. In Jiamusi, an Amur River city near the Russian border in Heilongjiang, a 2010 prospectus bragged that the local investment company, Jiamusi New Era Infrastructure Construction Investment Group Co., was "among the top 100 cities that get CDB support."[27] In the South, on the border with Myanmar, Yunnan Highway Development Investment Co. was created in 2006 through an agreement with CDB.

A Town Called Loudi

In Loudi, the stimulus was akin to dropping cash from the sky; it allowed the city to create a new idea of itself. It would no longer be only a town where nothing happened in the middle of China with a loss-making steel producer. It brought work for farmer Li Liguang, as the city boomed from government-funded infrastructure projects, including the stadium and the high-speed rail line. CDB underwrote the LGFV's 1.2 billion yuan bond sale, which was sold in China's domestic bond market in early 2011, with the bank listed first among a parade of lenders that had already provided financing to the city. The LGFV, Loudi City Construction Investment Group, was set up in 2000 and injected with land and other assets to borrow money for construction. In 2009, the government gave it more assets than ever before: The company was incorporated with eight subsidiaries, including a tap-water company, a musty government-run hotel, and a series of construction companies. It was handed 20 percent of state-owned equity in a local gas company. All told, during the year of the stimulus, its assets increased by 50 percent, with landholdings increasing by 394 percent. Documents show that the highway into town was paid for by an expressway company using borrowed money, a lot of it. A June 2011 prospectus reveals that Hunan Provincial Expressway Construction Group had lines of credit with Chinese banks totaling 205.1 billion yuan. CDB led the pack with a 73.1 billion yuan credit line, followed by China Construction Bank, ICBC, and Bank of China, plus credit lines from many smaller banks. Debt is increasing at a much faster clip than toll collections, which come to 4 mao (6.2 cents) per kilometer for cars on the Changsha–Loudi expressway.

A stadium was paid for in part of the bond offering underwritten by CDB, plus bank borrowing. How would the company pay for all of this? The answer lay in land sales. Eighteen tracts of land valued at $1.5 million an acre were the collateral, according to the January 2011 prospectus. That's the price recently offered for an acre of land adjoining a private golf course on Indian Hill Road in Winnetka, Illinois, one of the wealthiest towns anywhere in the world. Average family income in Winnetka: $250,000 a year. In Loudi, average yearly take-home pay is $2,323. And yet the bond was rated AA by Beijing-based Dagong Global Credit Rating Co., one level higher than the same company rated US sovereign debt in 2012. The company that gave the land appraisal was in the same office as the city government's land bureau. "The income from selling land is a reliable guarantee for the timely payment of interest on this bond," the bond's prospectus said. Loudi City Construction's debt has exploded, a story that is repeated across the country. Total liabilities have grown from 1.43 billion yuan at the end of 2007 to 3.02 billion yuan in the first half of 2010, according to its bond prospectus, even as the company bled money, posting negative operational cash flows every year, as shown in Figure 1.2.

"The debt isn't a problem as Loudi is not a developed place," Yang Haibo, an official at Loudi City Construction, said as he sat with colleagues in a smoke-filled meeting room under a No Smoking sign one early June day. "It's an emerging city."

Yang is a small, gruff man, who carries his mobile phone in a leather case on his belt and has swept-over hair, as do many officials. After he tried to call the local propaganda bureau for permission to speak to a foreign reporter, he agreed to lunch in a busy new restaurant opposite his office, where he and his colleague were more interested in drinking

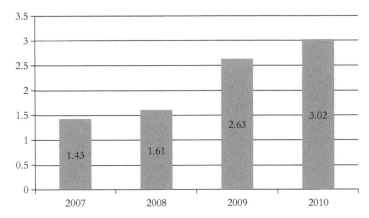

Figure 1.2   Loudi City Construction's Total Liabilities (billion yuan)
Source: Loudi City Bond Prospectus, January 2011.

beer than talking about how they would pay their debt. He said the company has around 800 million yuan in loans from CDB, or around a third of its total debt. Every year CDB invites him for training in the provincial capital of Changsha. "I know Chen Yuan, but I don't think he knows me," he said, laughing. "Their loan rate is much lower than other banks," Yang said.

Yang's office was in one of the most imposing buildings in town, next to a traffic circle where an ugly, twisted metal sculpture is supposed to be the logo for the money-losing state-owned steel company. But the prize was the local government office, the White House, which had been built right on the edge of town as far away from the population as possible, a trend popular in China as it leaves valuable city-center land available to sell. Looking like the US Capitol, it opened in 2006 at a cost of 500 million yuan,[28] its construction caused the Communist Party secretary of the day to be detained and charged with "sloppy management of city finances."[29] Hundreds of yards from the main entrance to the building, a small door has a gold plaque that says petitioners can be received there. Petitioning is a practice dating from imperial times by which people take their complaints either to local officials or directly to the capital. For the mandarins in Loudi, public infrastructure like the stadium may not be a great cash generator. The city has no major sports teams, few bands and pop singers ever put Loudi on their tour list, and swimmers at the pool pay 20 yuan every morning for a dip, 30 yuan if they're extravagant enough to swim in the afternoon. But in China, focusing on that kind of return on investment is missing the point. A stadium boosts the value of the surrounding land, and that means more money for the local government, which can sell that land to developers of apartment blocks. But first of all, the city needs to acquire that land and bring it into its control so it can count it as an asset, as most of it is classified as rural. That's where the farmers of Dawu enter the picture.

Li's Story

The plot Li Liguang's family farmed for generations still lies empty, weeds sprouting from the red earth, just behind the stadium. It is surrounded on all sides by new pastel-colored apartment blocks. The land where the family lived was countryside until the city simply took it a few years ago. By rezoning the land as urban, officials could incorporate it into their development plan, which allows them to sell the land for a wider range of uses than agricultural, according to its bond prospectus. Villagers initially were relocated to the alleyway, where they built shanties with tarp and corrugated-tin roofs. The sports bureau took about 47 acres of land in Dawu where the stadium is and another village, issuing notices—and verbal threats—in 2006, saying the land was needed for the stadium. "They told us if we didn't move, they would send a lot of people to destroy our house," Li says. "If you didn't agree, they would detain you." The only bright notes in his new place are the red scrolls bearing the Chinese character for good fortune that adorn some front doors. And the only beans the family grows now are cultivated by Li's mother on a 43-square-foot plot behind the temporary home, where the stench of a putrid bright-green stream hangs in the air. Stooped, with gray hair, she recalls the clear well water they had access to before that was so clean she could wash with it.

They are convinced that the city has sold the land to developers, even though they can't prove it. "They flattened the land and still haven't used it," Li, a wiry man, says as he sits inside his house, cradling his baby. "If the government gives you a million yuan to buy the land, only 80 percent will go to the farmers. And us ordinary folk don't know where the missing money's gone." Li said he didn't worry about feeding his family of nine—including his wife, first child, parents, and brother's family—in his old place, and he was able to pay for extras by selling vegetables a couple of times a month in the city and doing odd jobs. Now he makes about 100 yuan on a good day driving his beat-up, cobalt-blue East Wind truck hauling bricks to construction sites, wages that are almost all spent on groceries. "It was a reliable income," he says. "Before we had food to eat. Now if I don't work as a laborer we don't have anything."

Li's story is replicated across China, in a nationwide urbanization drive that economists credit with boosting China's productivity and sociologists and political scientists blame for widening the country's already yawning wealth and income gaps and fomenting unrest.[30] Nationwide, income for local governments from selling land-use rights totaled 7 trillion yuan from 2006 through 2010, according to China's Land Resource Bureau. In 2010 alone, local governments took in 2.7 trillion yuan by selling land rights of farmland for nonagricultural use.[31] A survey that Landesa, a Seattle-based nongovernmental organization, conducted with Beijing's Renmin University, found that 60 percent of China's farmers were not satisfied with their compensation.[32] "The next generation will face bigger problems, as they have no land," Li said.

While Zhu Rongji's 1994 reforms centralized tax collection, they perversely allowed local governments greater control over the usage rights of land, allowing them to keep all land-leasing revenues. This growing, valuable state-owned resource was now totally in the hands of local governments, and they had no obligation to publish their budgets to the public. As CDB has done overseas with oil, land-revenue streams can be used to secure loans, with the debt service paid off by land sales whose value is supposed to increase thanks to the infrastructure financed by the loans, meaning projects have to cover operating costs only. CDB has also been more innovative than other banks in finding means to collateralize loans, using many different local-government revenue streams. In Shanghai, it funded a river cleanup project using the drainage assessment charge from affected users of the river as collateral. As Chen Yuan said in 2005, "Unlike many commercial banks, CDB doesn't sit back and just review data when loan requests are presented."[33] Tying many projects together into packages backed by land means that some projects can subsidize others. But relying on land, a finite resource, to repay loans, means that new land has to constantly be found and sold, and the costs of kicking people off the land has to be kept lower than the market price.

Those costs are apparent in the village. The compensation that Dawu villagers say they received works out at about 6 percent of what the city was selling land for in 2008, a year after they were evicted. Dawu natives said they received 38,000 yuan per mu, a Chinese measure of land that is about one-sixth of an acre. That's less than half the average of 85,420 yuan the Loudi city government says it paid, according to a notice on the Web site of its State Land Resources Bureau. The land is worth many times even the higher figure. Loudi city in 2008 sold its land to developers for 600,000 yuan per mu, according to the bond prospectus. Around the stadium, land earmarked for high-rise apartment blocks can fetch 2 million yuan per mu, according to one real estate agent. At those prices, it would take Li 92 years to earn enough to buy back his still-vacant plot, based on his current wage rate.

China's LGFVs are the unseen hand that has created anger among citizens at widening inequality as the administration of President Hu Jintao and Premier Wen Jiabao strives to create a "harmonious society." A total of 60 percent of all large-scale protests in China are due to land grabs and compensation disputes.[34] Loudi is one of 186 local authorities, from Guangxi on the Vietnamese frontier in the south to Heilongjiang on the Russian border in the north, that issued bonds or short-term notes through financing vehicles in the first nine months of 2011. Some 105 of them said they engage in *chaiqian*, according to their pro- spectuses, a word that has come to mean the heavy weight of the state's hand when it takes away your home and tosses you out. Normally the character is painted in clear red on your wall. Across China, compen- sation given to farmers is at least 15 times lower than prices sold for development, according to Landesa. That way, local governments, through their LGFVs, can make payments on the bank loans and bond coupons that financed the stadiums, roads, and "White House." "Without suppressing land compensation, local governments can't make the margins to pay back the banks," says Victor Shih, the US scholar. "In essence, they [LGFVs] are the engines of inequality in China.

There's more to come. Some 60 million farmers will be uprooted over the next two decades as China's urbanization gathers speed, according to an estimate by the Chinese Academy of Social Sciences in Beijing.[36] In many cases, officials take land they don't use, an August 2011 report from the academy said. The inequality in some cases has led to violence, far away from the confines of the state-banking system. That was certainly the case in Fuzhou, a city in Jiangxi Province, just to the east of Hunan. There, a land dispute with the government was central to a May 2011 bombing that killed three people. Qian Mingqi allegedly set off three blasts at or near government buildings in the city amid a dispute over compensation he had been offered in a resettlement, according to reports by the official Xinhua News Agency. Qian died in one of the explosions. He had been asking for more compensation after being resettled in 2002 to make way for a highway.

Three months before the bombings, Fuzhou's investment vehicle went to the country's bond market for the first time, raising 800 million yuan. In its prospectus, in which it said it received CDB loans, the company said its main business included construction, land development, and "resettlement."

"Manhattan" in China

The CDB-led stimulus-induced lending boom that spawned Loudi's stadium was supposed to slow down as China's economy recovered, which it quickly did as 2009 gave way to 2010. Instead, it's becoming increasingly clear that China is addicted to the infrastructure, capital-intensive growth perfected by CDB's Wuhu model. In 2011, the total debt reported by some 231 LGFVs that sold bonds that year rose by about 20 percent, according to a Bloomberg study of all bond prospectuses issued by the banks that year.[37] Nowhere is the Wuhu model being taken further and the promise of endless urbanization greater than in the city of Tianjin, where China is building a Manhattan.

Tianjin Binhai New Area Construction & Investment Group Co. is a creature of CDB. Tianjin itself is a Lebanon-size municipality of 13 million people and Binhai is its heavily industrialized port region on the Bohai Gulf, where ships appear to be sailing through fields amid the countless channels cutting through the land. It is there, within sight of the ruins of imperial-era forts stormed by French and British troops in 1860 during the Second Opium War, that Tianjin Binhai and other financing vehicles have embarked on what may be the most grandiose project in a nation of grandiose projects.

Two years ago, planners began leveling the old center of Tanggu—home to China's oldest railway station—to make way for China's version of Manhattan, complete with a Rockefeller family–invested building and office towers developed by New York real estate developer Tishman Speyer Properties LP. The East River and Hudson are there, too, with water bounding three sides of the planned financial center, which lies on an oxbow of the Hai River. So is Lincoln Center, which is advising the local government on setting up a new arts center in the development, called the Yujiapu Financial District.

Tianjin's history with CDB goes back to 2003, when the bank signed the biggest loan agreement in China at the time with the city's land bank, a loan of 50 billion yuan, which was later handed over to the financing vehicle. At the beginning of spring of that year CDB vice governor Yao Zhongmin held talks with newly arrived Mayor Dai Xianglong, who had beaten out Chen for the top job at the central bank five years earlier. Yao proposed using revenue from land sales to guarantee the loans from CDB. The Tianjin delegation said CDB was too slow to approve finance for a previous subway line. So Yao upped the stakes. He said quickly, "We can improve our efficiency." Dai asked how quickly they could do it. "One month, we can complete the appraisal in one month," Yao replied solemnly. Dai was very happy and promised to give any materials to CDB that they wanted.

CDB was the panacea that allowed expansion based on leverage and allowed the city to spend beyond the limits of its fiscal funds. Before the bank turned up, Tianjin had been able to afford maintenance of its existing infrastructure only, not new building, according to a book on the case published by CDB and Renmin University.[38] From 1999 to 2003, Tianjin's average fiscal funds every year for city infrastructure were a measly 6.3 billion yuan, which was hampering its development as a port. Setting up the financing vehicle put the infrastructure funding on a "market basis." Under CDB's loan deal, the land bank had the rights to sell the land in the central city and would pay back the proceeds straight into its account at Tianjin's CDB branch before being transferred to the city's account in the same bank. CDB could thus automatically take the money it was owed and could supervise the process of funds transfer. The loan was split into a 24 billion yuan soft loan with a more favorable interest rate and 26 billion yuan hard loan, with a total maturity of 15 years. For the first five years the city only had to pay back interest on the soft loan. The interest rate was 10 percent below the benchmark rate for the duration of the soft loan and 10 percent below the benchmark rate for the hard loan for the first five years: In total, it was 8 percent cheaper than normal loans at the time.

The key to getting the funds was that Tianjin could use 15 years of land usage rights sales to secure the loan, both to act as collateral and as a source to pay back the funds. The city also had to promise to use its own infrastructure fund to pay back the money if land sales ran into difficulties. The bankers forecast that the land sales income would increase every year by 10 percent. That turned out to be a conservative bet: In reality, the income increased by 20 percent. By 2006, land income was 10.3 billion yuan, up from 2.4 billion yuan in 2004. By 2009, it was a different story: China Index Academy estimated the city's land sales revenue was 73.2 billion yuan, a 67 percent increase over 2008.

While the outbreak of severe acute respiratory syndrome (SARS) in early 2003 in Beijing intervened and prevented Chen Yuan from visiting Tianjin to sign the deal, it was eventually signed in June of that year. The original loan contract was signed with the city's land bank; in 2004, the city set up an LGFV with four subsidiaries to handle the different projects, including two subway lines, greening of the city, and riverside infrastructure development. The income from the subway projects only needed to cover operating costs; it didn't need to pay back the loan; the money to pay back the loan for all the projects would nearly all come from government income from selling land rights. The investment that CDB started helped bring in the property developers too and attract further funds: The riverside construction project saw 10 billion yuan of investment in infrastructure over three years but drew a total of 80 or more billion yuan of property investment.

Yet there's a point where ambition and enthusiasm becomes reck-lessness and hubris, and Tianjin may have crossed that line. There's no better place to witness the physical manifestation of hubris than Yujiapu, Tianjin's planned Manhattan.

There, Xu Fei, an official at the Tianjin Binhai New Area Central Business District, stands in front of a brightly lit model of the future city, and says the total planned investment in the project, plus parks, resi-dential towers, and the twin city across the river called Conch Bay, is 200 billion yuan. The first phase opens up in 2013 with the inauguration of a high-speed rail station. Both cities are under construction simulta-neously, with 14 of a planned 122 buildings being erected in Yujiapu, plus all 48 of the planned Conch Bay skyscrapers as of the end of 2011. Construction cranes crowd the field of vision on both sides of the river, and thousands of workers are teeming about the work sites. The cities will be serviced by five subway lines, Xu says.

The area is meant to attract banks, brokerages, and other investment companies, with a planned 164 million square feet of office space for Yujiapu and Conch Bay. That's more than one-third of the 450 million square feet in Manhattan, a city that took more than three centuries of organic growth to build out its skyline. That includes a 1,930-foot-high tower, taller than the 1,770-foot-high 1 World Trade Center currently under construction in the real Manhattan. Tianjin officials are employing the philosophy of the 1989 movie, *Field of Dreams*: If you build it, they will come.

Tianjin isn't headquarters to a world-class bank, let alone a leading Chinese bank that could occupy those offices, as Goldman Sachs, Citigroup, and J.P. Morgan Chase fill Manhattan buildings. Xu mentions local banks Tianjin Rural Commercial Bank and Bohai Bank—minnows in the world of Chinese banking, let alone global banking—as future tenants. Yujiapu also must compete with financial centers in Tianjin proper, which is building one of the world's tallest buildings, and Beijing, with its own financial district and another one under construction. "It's a difficult question to answer," Xu says when asked what companies will fill up the new city.

Xu says the buildings in Yujiapu are all being occupied by state-owned companies, including a steel company and a mining company turned real estate developer that is putting the finishing touches on

Tianjin's answer to Rockefeller Center. Asked if any private companies were setting up shop there, she pointed to a hotel. A giant billboard in Conch City—red background with white characters—quotes Chinese president Hu Jintao, who visited the area in April 2011, as saying "Put all your strength into storming the fort to win the battle of developing and opening the Binhai New Area, work hard to become the lead soldiers in the battle to realize scientific development." Not words you'd find in Adam Smith's *Wealth of Nations*.

To build Yujiapu, Tianjin officials are piling onto borrowing that was already half a trillion yuan by the end of 2011—equivalent to half the annual per-capita income of the city's 13 million people. More than 5,000 people were moved out of the area starting in 2008 to make way for the project, among the millions nationwide evicted from homes to make way for China's urbanization projects. Tianjin Binhai New Area Construction & Investment Group Co. sold 10 billion yuan worth of bonds in December 2011, earmarking 1 billion yuan from the sale to fund the construction of the district's transport hub, which includes a high-speed rail line that will cut travel time to Beijing to 45 minutes. In the first half of that year, its debt, mostly from bank loans and led by CDB, rose 11.9 percent from the end of 2010 to 71 billion yuan, according to a bond prospectus. To finish all the projects, more money is needed, said Tianjin's vice mayor, Cui Jindu.

In 2011 one of the LGFVs building Yujiapu was the most indebted in the country to disclose its finances. Not only are Tianjin's debts rising, but its ability to pay them through land sales—the foundation of CDB's Wuhu model—is vulnerable to downturns in the real estate market, such as one that hit in 2011 as the government put curbs on home buying and revenues from government-run land sales plummeted. Land provided 41 percent of the city's income in 2009, according to the China Index Academy. "Our local-government backed financing vehicles in Tianjin have no risk," Tianjin's mayor, Huang Xingguo, said during a meeting at China's National People's Congress in 2011. "CDB has given a lot of support to Tianjin. We are very thankful." Sounding a confident note in the hot stuffy room full of journalists, he put the total amount of CDB loans at around 80 billion yuan and said Tianjin's property market is controllable, brushing away fears of a crash in property prices that could affect land sales and therefore repayment of loans.

Credit Risk in a One-Party State

In China, no bond has ever publicly defaulted, making investment in local governments akin to a one-way bet. Even though the cities and counties turned to the bond market, fulfilling Chen Yuan's belief in shifting infrastructure investment to a market-based system, banks and ratings agencies overlooked details on collateral and cash flow, believing in the backstop of the local government. With ever-rising land and property prices, there was little incentive for transparency. When CDB lent to an LGFV this, too, acted like a "credit guarantee" from the center, further reducing the need for investors to look at details of collateral or credit risks. At the bottom were the LGFV assets, often in the form of land. Once the LGFV could be dressed up with land assets or local government subsidies for bond issuance, investors like the state-owned banks could buy the bonds. In turn, the bonds could be packaged into so-called wealth-management products, high-yielding short-term investments that banks could sell to clients, offerings that have boomed in China over the last few years as depositors seek to beat inflation.[39] Having got the stamp of approval for selling a bond, which acted as another credit guarantee, LGFVs could then guarantee credit and borrowing for other LGFVs from the same area, so they, too, could join in. In theory, the companies should have a record of three years of profit and outstanding bonds to net assets of below 40 percent to sell debt in China. But who has been in charge of approving these bond deals? Most LGFV bonds have been approved by the powerful economic planning agency, the National Development and Reform Commission. Among other jobs, it also approves China's investment projects, from power stations to highways. So why would it deny funding to its own projects? Was the market really providing any checks and balances?

In the smoky port of Huanghua, the answer is a firm *no*.

The city occupies a tiny slice of Hebei Province wedged between Tianjin and the border with Shandong Province. Somewhere out in the salt marshes is the collateral for Hebei Bohai Investment Co.'s bond. Hebei Bohai is in the business of expanding a port where one really isn't needed. New port terminals line the Bohai Gulf, especially in neighboring Tianjin, the biggest port in north China. Huanghua Port is the terminus for state-owned China Shenhua Energy Co.'s coal railroad.

Hebei Bohai is helping to build the port and is majority owner in the marine fuel services company. Stacks of what look like massive concrete jacks, the building blocks for marine jetties, litter the ground on the side of the dirt road leading out to one of the piers. Shenhua's facility is something out of Dante's *Inferno*. More than a dozen smokestacks belch soot into the air. The land seems to just give up, eventually becoming the heavily polluted Bohai Gulf.

The city has seen the mega-port projects and grandiose infra-structure plans of its northern neighbor and has collectively cried out "Me, too!" CDB made it possible. Tianjin at least has an existing port—and an industrial base that includes some of China's biggest steelmakers. That's not the case in Huanghua, a place dominated by smokestacks of a coal-receiving station and surrounded by desolate, drained marshes studded with piles of salt. There the LGFV cannot even identify the land collateral it uses to borrow money on the bond market. Its LGFV, tasked with expanding the port and building roads, parks, and other "green projects," sold 1 billion yuan worth of bonds in May 2011 guaranteed by five tracts of land the company says is valued at more than 1.54 billion yuan, or 462 yuan per square meter. That's more than three times what it paid the local government in December 2009, according to the company's land use permits. Its debt surged during the 2009–2010 stimulus and CDB gave Hebei Bohai a 5.6 billion yuan line of credit in 2007. Other banks lending to the company include ICBC, China Construction Bank, and Bank of Communications. The company's debt is so big that it swamps the local government's total reve-nue. According to the bond prospectus, Hebei Bohai borrowed 5.08 billion yuan in 2010 alone, a sum almost equal to total local govern-ment revenue. The company's debt is equal to about one-third of the local GDP.

Go across town to ask Lu Chunjiang, a Communist Party member and head of the company's asset management department, where his assets are, however, and he can't say. The local state land office (国土资源局) at first was unhelpful when we asked to see the land transaction records identified in the prospectus. Workers eventually gave us more details on the plots than were available in the prospectus, providing cross streets, purchase prices, and lot sizes. "I don't know where that land is exactly," Lu told us when we dropped by, unannounced and uninvited, to his office. "Somewhere north of town. But it is land just like you saw driving into the port area, you know, the fields with the piles of salt."

Some LGFVs even managed to borrow without any collateral at all. That's the case in Yichun, a Maryland-size area of about 1.3 million people. The city raised 1.2 billion yuan through a bond sale in 2009 offering investors a yield of over 7 percent, at the peak of the stimulus. Yichun is a poor city in a poor province. Income of its residents was little more than half the national average in 2010. That hasn't stopped the government from going on a spending spree. The new local police headquarters has a miniature dome reminiscent of that on the Vatican's St. Peter's Basilica. Its LGFV, which gets CDB bank loans, sold the bond backed only by a pledge from the local government and possible future land sales. China International Capital Corporation gave it the lowest debt rating of any city financing vehicle. In contrast, Dagong rates the bonds two levels higher than US debt. Money raised from the sale is being used for the destruction of what the prospectus calls "shantytowns."

Single-floor traditional Russian-looking wooden homes in the valley are being demolished to make way for thousands of low-income apartments. The company also has financed a new reservoir, an airport terminal, and parklands, one featuring faux Corinthian columns topped by winged warrior princesses and bronze sculptures of chariot-riding local gods. Wang Zhongbing, a retired factory worker who spends summer days chatting with friends in a park next to the Yichun River, says the economic development is passing his family by. Only one of his three adult sons has a job, he says. He came to Yichun in 1962 when he was 28 years old to work in a state-run factory.

"I miss Chairman Mao," says Wang, sitting on a red plastic chair in front of a billboard for newly built Pinaster Town, featuring a picture of a woman in high heels stepping out of a Rolls-Royce. "The common people cannot afford these houses." Wang says the advertisement doesn't give an accurate picture of Yichun, which, like much of northeastern China, was hit by layoffs at its state factories in the 1990s and never fully recovered. His own work unit closed.

The Yichun financing vehicle, which supplies the city's heat and therefore has a guaranteed source of income in a place where temperatures are below freezing for much of the year, would have lost money every year from 2006 to 2008 except for direct government subsidies. Its prospectus promised that land from the city "will provide a more substantial cash flow." Two years on, that hasn't come to pass, according to Wu Liangguo, the head of the Yichun City Bureau of Land and Resources and its Communist Party secretary. "The land market in Yichun isn't that great," says Wu, born in 1961, who jogs even in the minus-22-degrees-Fahrenheit chill of the Siberian winter. "The local government financing vehicle may get land in the future but it isn't a certainty."

Cracks in the System

CDB's lending to local governments stems from the failure of Zhu Rongji's 1994 reforms, which left local governments with huge spending burdens—everything from providing water to roads—but few ways to raise funds apart from leasing out state land. The prohibition set on borrowing by local governments was a rule observed only in the breach, just pushing the borrowing off the budget and into the arms of the state banks. Without any transparency, and with all of the capital from the state-owned banks rather than private institutions, the market has added no discipline. It had all the hallmarks of an experiment with capitalism but with none of the checks and balances. In one case, a Shanghai LGFV borrowed 2 billion yuan of loans for a high-speed railway project, but ended up using half the money for property projects. After the experience of the late 1990s, when many local government and state-owned enterprise loans were bailed out, the commercial banks were supposed to look after themselves, yet many of the projects they piled into led by CDB had poor returns. An HSBC analysis by Hong Kong–based analyst Zhang Zhiming showed that 33 percent of the local government financing vehicles generated insufficient cash flow to make their debt payments and about 68 percent reported return on capital less than the benchmark lending rate—meaning the banks make a loss. But the nonperforming loan rate at China's banks continued to edge downward from 2010 to 2011, especially at CDB. What was going on?

In the summer of 2011, as land prices fell, some of the first cracks started to appear in the system that CDB had created and helped build, showing how reluctant authorities would be to tolerate a default that could threaten the banking system, eroding years of efforts to make the country's banks more commercial. In April 2011, one of the biggest LGFVs, Yunnan Highway Construction, which had outstanding loans amounting to 90 billion yuan, sent a letter to bankers saying it was unable to pay principal on a bank loan and would pay only interest, according to the influential *Caixin* financial magazine. Such a note would normally send a chill down the spine of any banker. Another Yunnan LGFV, Yunnan Investment Group, which according to a November 2008 prospectus had borrowed at least 15.4 billion yuan from CDB, had its bonds put on a watch list by China Chengxin International Credit Rating Co., one of China's best credit ratings agencies, after it announced an asset transfer. Sichuan Expressway Construction & Development Corp., which has at least 49 billion yuan in loans and lines of credit with CDB, was cited for violating rules in June after it transferred its stake in a Hong Kong–listed arm to another company without informing bondholders. The market for bonds sold by local government financing companies plunged and the powerful National Development and Reform Commission stopped approving them in August 2011. The front page of *Caixin* asked: "Are the defaults starting?"

Not so fast, was the answer. CDB is an arm of the central government. It has leveraged that status to lend to local governments across the country from Tibet to Heilongjiang. Should its bad loan rate rise, it will reflect on China's own creditworthiness. CDB has a reputation as China's best-run major bank with the lowest reported nonperforming loan rate of any lender. The recognition of nonperforming loans will be a political process as it was in the late 1990s. And CDB is likely to be the last bank they default on, since it prides itself on having more analysis of local government projects than commercial banks and on doing more to structure the loans. "I'm not worried about them defaulting, because CDB has a special relationship with the government," Chen said in a short interview in 2011 in Hainan. "CDB has been financing local governments from the outset." Yet what did that say about Chen's ambition to create a global international-standard bank?

In China, the Yunnan letter would have just meant another arm of the state (the banking system) taking the losses, which it wasn't going to do lightly. Yunnan Highway Construction had borrowed 20 billion yuan from CDB to crisscross the mountainous southern province with roads. So the Yunnan government stumped up the cash and agreed to inject 300 million yuan in capital to the company and lend it 2 billion yuan. That summer the government hit back at investors, saying they had "no need to worry" about bonds sold by LGFVs, according to a statement on August 29 by the National Development and Reform Commission, the ministry that approved the bonds. The intention was to bring a touch of the market to local government financing, and Chen had defined development finance as a bridge linking the government and the market.[40] But now the government was saying that couldn't happen, that indeed there was no risk as there was a firm backstop by the government.

With most of the stimulus debt lent on short-term maturities, toward the end of 2011, after receiving the green light from the China Banking Regulatory Commission, banks began rolling over their LGFV loan debt, giving borrowers more time to pay back. Just as in the 1990s, the "commercial" banks had been rescued by the central government. As a result, that debt won't be repaid at maturity and realized as cash flow at banks, and it means more money for China's state sector and less for private companies. It's also risky for banks: The LGFV loans essentially become illiquid loans, constantly rolled over into the future, the opposite of deposits, which are highly liquid and can be withdrawn at a moment's notice. It is also a failure of the market that CDB had created in order to value risk and capital correctly, much like the credit-default swap products the United States had invented to insure against losses in subprime debt. The risk had been passed from the local governments to the banks, and then back onto the central government. That gave the central government little choice but to force banks to resolve the debts, pushing them out into the future rather than letting the market function. Had CDB really created a market or was it a market to be manipulated and arbitraged by local governments for their own benefit when no one was looking?

From the beginning, CDB got more deeply involved with local governments than any other Chinese bank. The bank's creation of LGFVs was the key that unlocked the motor of local government development, becoming the force that has created China's economic growth. Up to half its loan book in 2011 could be local government lending, according to analysts, accounting for one-third of all the local financing vehicle loans and larger than that of all four of the top commercial banks put together. (See Table 1.1). CDB started the platform, the LGFV, that allowed other commercial banks to follow, allowing an unleashing of credit in 2008 that had little oversight. As Liu Kegu, an advisor to CDB, put it in March 2012, in comments that were later deleted online, "The backlog of projects from 30 years of reform were nearly all approved, they rushed to projects, with projects that had been killed in the past coming out."[41] With fixed lending and deposit rates and a guaranteed spread between the two, the commercial banks didn't need to worry about making a profit from good projects and felt they were following orders to stimulate the economy. "The main problems in local debt occurred when everybody scrambled to lend in a bid to boost domestic demand during the global financial crisis. They broke the boundaries set by us," CDB's vice president, Wang Yongsheng, told Bloomberg at the March 2012 National People's Congress in Beijing.

There was a fundamental mismatch: The debts and the companies themselves were left off local government budgets, even as investors,

Table 1.1 Top LGFV Recipients of CDB Loans[*]

Company	Loans and Lines of Credit (billion yuan)
Fujian Provincial Expressway	81.5
Hunan Provincial Expressway	73.1
Beijing State-Owned Assets Operation	58
Tianjin Binhai Construction and Inv.	50
Sichuan Expressway	49
Wuhan Urban Construction	45.9
Shanghai Chengtou	43
Guangxi Communications	41.5
Chongqing Expressway Group	39.4
Tianjin Infrastructure Construction	37.1
Chongqing City Transportation	30.6

[*]Local government exposure at China's banks in billions of yuan.

Source: Bond prospectuses issued 2009 to 2011.

banks, and ratings companies viewed them as having the implicit guarantee of local governments. Today, the LGFVs have dozens of subsidiaries, cross-holdings, and cross-guarantees, making it impossible to tell how much one local government is on the hook for if one link in the chain is broken. Some LGFVs have also turned into lenders, passing on money to property companies. While China wanted to further develop the institutions and infrastructure of a bond market, at the same time as it expanded, banks did their best to hollow out the integrity and effectiveness of those same institutions. Ratings agencies gave bonds sold by local government-backed companies high ratings because they believed in the implicit back stop of the local government; investors took the yield as free money. At least the ratings agencies themselves were self-conscious enough to recognize the self-destructive behavior. "Whoever gives them the better rating gets the business," Dagong's fiery chairman, Guan Jianzhong told us. "This is very dangerous."

While there is no way of telling what quality of assets CDB was left with, the experience of cities like Chongqing, where GDP growth was 16.4 percent in 2011, showed that for all its problems, there is sheer genius behind the model. Chen Yuan of CDB had realized in 1998, before other banks, the force of urbanization and its role in economic growth. China long ago decided that the key to GDP growth is boosting productivity, and few economic events boost the productivity of a populace than moving them from life on a farm to life in the city. And that's exactly what happened in Dawu village to Li Liguang.

Li has been busy creating a new life for himself as a city resident, complete with the coveted urban residence permit (户口) that can grant access to better schools and healthcare. In Li's old place he grew most of his food and spent the rest of his money on groceries. Now he's entered the local economy. Ironically, he wishes officials would start building on his land, giving him the chance to pick up some work. But such moves are never easy: Unlike local government officials, Li can't get bank loans. So he's borrowed 100,000 yuan from family and friends. That still wasn't enough, putting Li in a Catch 22: Without a loan, he can't finish his house, and without a house, he has no collateral for a loan. "The renminbi is appreciating everywhere in the world, but in China it's depreciating," Li said one late August evening, overlooking paddy fields.

Other villagers say people are borrowing money from underground banks at a rate of up to 40 percent interest.

The use of land as collateral and as a source of income to repay loans means local governments have to acquire it cheaply and sell it at a profit. Local governments have become land monopolists, trying to acquire as much land as possible by expanding cities into rural areas, such as in Loudi. The lack of compensation given to farmers has not helped China to boost consumption. In 2011, China's investment-to-GDP ratio was 49 percent, below only that of Mongolia, Sierra Leone, and São Tomé and Principe, according to the International Monetary Fund. Over the past ten years, about 90 percent of China's fixed asset investment has been at the local government level,[42] while since 2003, China's savers have enjoyed a negative real interest rate on savings they put in commercial banks, which then use that money to buy CDB bonds. If the infrastructure buildout is not efficient, it wouldn't be a stretch to say China's savers have been robbed.

The reliance on LGFVs and the low rates paid to Chinese savers has also created one of the world's biggest property bubbles: Nationwide, housing prices in China have risen at least by 140 percent since 1998. And unlike the welfare, health, and pension expenses that have crippled Europe, China's forced urbanization has left a lot of debt before it even begins to deal with these expenses. By 2011, Standard Chartered was predicting that China's debt levels were in reality around 71 percent of its 2010 GDP, approaching US levels.[43] No one knew how far the debt extended, who else had lent to the companies, and who was liable. There was only one way that China would pay for this debt, and that would be through China's savers, through higher tax, or through more inflation. "China's making a big bet on infrastructure raising growth and that raises incomes and part of those incomes pay for the building of the infrastructure. The big bet is on how efficient this buildout of infrastructure is," Stephen Green, head of China research at Standard Chartered said.

The creeping power of the state at the expense of private companies since the 1990s has meant that debt-addled state companies building infrastructure projects that won't generate cash flow for years, if ever, get preferential loan rates from 6 to 8 percent a year. In the meantime, private companies that want to expand their workforces, such as one drugstore owner in Zhejiang's Wenzhou city, pay about that much every month. Local governments could get banks to lend to projects with even the smallest amount of revenues, as the central government knew that projects had to continue. After all, you cannot leave a metro system half built. "The local government financing platforms aren't designed for one-off deals," and CDB has "set rather long terms," CDB's vice president, Wang Yongsheng, said. "A project, if stopped halfway, would become a problem." Had local governments won the game in the end?

By July 2012, as China reported its sixth straight quarterly decline in economic growth, it was becoming clear that the country was addicted to the easy stimulus provided by the LGFV model. Official after official in the year previous had pledged to slow down growth in local lending. In March of that year, Premier Wen Jiabao proclaimed in his annual policy speech—China's answer to the US president's State of the Union Address—that the nation would control its lending to local governments and set up an early-warning system to detect problems. Four months later, banks were again being told to boost their lending to LGFVs.[44]

For officials in Loudi, this means the party—and the Party—will continue. In the "White House," the central government building on the outskirts of town, officials sat with their iPads in a room lined with red banners with Communist slogans and a large gold hammer and sickle. The colonnades that linked the white buildings with high domes were cool in the afternoon heat. They had built a park opposite the building that was a small symbol of misdirected infrastructure: It was empty and concreted over. No office worker would dream of spending a lunch break there. It was a park designed without one single consideration of those who would use it. It was top-down park designing and it hadn't worked.

■ ■ ■

CDB's lending to local governments has helped unleash a wave of infrastructure construction, from expressways to local government stadiums, metro lines, and apartment complexes, helping China become an urban nation at a speed never before seen in history. Intended to bring a touch of the market to local governments and let them get money despite restrictions, it has ended in a borrowing spree that has left trillions of yuan of debt and millions of farmers without land and with inadequate compensation. Based on the hefty savings of the Chinese people that have been placed in state-owned banks, it's also created a daunting property bubble. The model has been driven by the foresight of one man, Chen Yuan, who recognized the potential of the country's urban drive. How did the bank gain so much power?

Notes

1. Hejuan Zhao, "Disassembling a Steel Giant," *Caixin*, July 1, 2011, http://english.caixin.com/2011-07-01/100275151.html

2. Yukon Huang, former chief representative for the World Bank in China, interview, February 13, 2012.

3. Interview with Zhu Keliang, lawyer at Landesa, August 2011.

4. Dodge, Laura, "China Says Central Government in Order, Provinces Not," Bloomberg News, March 23, 1995.

5. Hendry, Sandy. "China's Central Government to Boost Tax Revenue to 60%," Bloomberg News, December 3, 1993.

6. 《中国金融》杂志: 高坚: 关于地方经济发展的金融机制问题. (Gao Jian, "Concerning the Structural Financial Problems of Local Economic Development," *China Finance*, June 17, 2010.)

7. Ibid.

8. As with many things in China, you can tell what went wrong by the rules that later prohibit it. In 2010, the State Council issued an edict forbidding local governments from injecting schools, hospitals, and other "public benefit" assets as capital into local government financing vehicles.

9. 《中国金融》杂志: 高坚: 关于地方经济发展的金融机制问题. (Gao Jian, "Concerning the Structural Financial Problems of Local Economic Development," *China Finance*, June 17, 2010.)

10. Chen Yuan, "Development Financing and China's Urbanization," China Development Bank, 2005, www.cdb.com.cn/english/NewsInfo.asp?NewsID=1174

11. China Development Bank and Renmin University, *Development Finance in China: Case Studies* (Beijing: Renmin University Publishing House, 2007).

12. Research Academy of China Development Bank, "*China Development Bank, Practice and Achievements of Development Finance*," 民主与建设出版社, Beijing, October 2011.

13. This section is based on: China Development Bank and Renmin University, *Development Finance in China: Case Studies* (Beijing: Renmin University Publishing House, 2007).

14. "陈元：做一个真正的银行家" 经济观察报, October 31, 2009. "Chen Yuan: Being a Real Banker," *Economic Observer.*

15. "国企债务重组的" "重庆经验"

16. World Bank Report, China, "The Urban Development Investment Corporations (UDICs) in Chongqing, China," Technical Assistance Report, Washington D.C., 2009 n.d. http://siteresources.worldbank.org/INTCHINA/Resources/318862-1121421293578/1429963-1235543628658/Chongqing_UDIC_en.pdf

17. Ibid.

18. Ibid. Speech is Annex 7. "With the background of an urgent public demand, weak market signals, and inadequate market mechanism, the government-authorized investment makes the first move in the construction sector, which helps with initiating the involvement of social investments. When the market signal becomes stronger and market mechanism is established, the state-owned capital then gradually withdraws."

19. Authors' spreadsheet on CDB loans.

20. Barry Naughton, "Understanding the Chinese Stimulus Package," *China Leadership Monitor* 28 (Spring 2009). http://media.hoover.org/sites/default/files/documents/CLM28BN.pdf

21. Central Bank and Audit Office estimates.

22. Ibid.

23. GaveKal Dragonomics, presentation in Beijing, March 2012.

24. Yoshiaki Azuma and Jun Kurihara, "Examining China's Local Government Fiscal Dynamics," *Cambridge Gazette: Politico-Economic Commentaries*, no. 5, January 3, 2011.

25. Société Generale, *The Economic News*, June 28, 2011.

26. Authors' spreadsheet on CDB loans.

27. Bond prospectuses issued on Chinabond, www.chinabond.com.cn

28. "City Image Building Lines Official Pockets," *Caijing*, October 30, 2011, http://english.caijing.com.cn/2008-10-30/110024617.html

29. Ibid.

30. He Qinglian, "Why Have Peasants Become the Major Force in Social Resistance?" Human Rights in China Web site, http://www.hrichina.org/content/3790

31. Zhang Monan, "Balancing Wealth Distribution," *China Daily*, April 25, 2011.

32. Landesa survey on land rights in China, February 24, 2011, http://www.landesa.org/wp-content/uploads/2011/02/Landesa-17-province-survey.pdf

33. Chen, "Development Financing and China's Urbanization."

34. 中国改革, *China Reform* 3 (2012).

35. Victor Shih Interview, August 2011.

36. Chinese Academy of Social Sciences, 中国城市发展报告, 2011.

37. Authors' research and spreadsheet on 2011 bond issuances.

38. China Development Bank and Renmin University, *Development Finance in China.*

39. Wealth Management Products reached an estimated 10.4 trillion yuan in 2012, or 11.5 percent of total deposits in the banking system.

40. Chen Yuan, "Enhancing the International Competitiveness of Financial Systems," *International Finance News*, May 19, 2005, www.cdb.com.cn/english/NewsInfo.asp?NewsId=1014

41. 国开行原副行长刘克崮: 万亿是严重错误万亿拉动方案的出台没有充分听取政协的见，因此导致改革30年积压下来的很多项目几乎都批了，急着上项目，把过去毙了的项目翻出来，箱底都扒出来了，严重的错误. Posted online in March 2012.

42. J.P. Morgan, "China Banks: A Revisit to Local Government Debt and the Sector's Resilience Against Asset Quality Risks," Asia Pacific Equity Research, July 15, 2011.

43. Stephen, Green: "China: Build It, and Someone Else Will Pay for It," *On the Ground*, 29 June 2011.

44. "部分银行明确支持地方平台贷款," *China Securities Journal*, July 31, 2012, http://www.cs.com.cn/xwzx/jr/201207/t20120731_3432288.html

Chapter 2

Turning a Zombie Bank into a Global Bank

Chinese banks can be operated as soundly as American banks. China Development Bank is aiming to become a sound top-ranking international bank.

—*Chen Yuan, quoted in Li Luyang,*
"Impressions of Chen Yuan," 2000

C hen Yuan, vice governor of the People's Bank of China (PBOC), was in his room at the tony Carlyle Hotel on New York's Upper East Side. Faxes were coming in from banks of the likes of Goldman Sachs and Morgan Stanley, all wanting to offer their services in helping Chen to invest China's foreign exchange reserves.[1]

It was the mid-1990s, and Chen was the international face of Chinese finance. Fluent in English and a regular at meetings of the International Monetary Fund (IMF) and World Bank in Washington, he was considered by many to be a shoo-in for the central bank's top job. Jacob Frenkel, then-governor of the Bank of Israel, said Chen's role was to be the "interlocutor between the Chinese financial market and the world financial market." It was the perfect match between avocation and vocation for Chen, a serious man with a passion for global finance and economics, who had studied at the Bank for International Settlements in Switzerland.[2]

It wasn't to be. The PBOC governor's job stayed with Dai Xianglong, an apparatchik who had worked his way up through China's decrepit state banking system in the 1970s and 1980s. Chen was given the task of running China Development Bank (CDB), an institution created in 1994 from a hodgepodge of Soviet-style investment companies and sporting a stratospheric nonperforming loan (NPL) rate.

Chen wasn't part of the group of acolytes of incoming premier Zhu Rongji, who had reorganized the banking system in China. Wang Qishan, Dai Xianglong, and Zhu Xiaohua, known as Zhu's "three carriages," all served as deputy governors of the central bank. Dai had been head of the Shanghai branch of Bank of Communications when Zhu was in charge of the city. Chen's character was fundamentally different from Zhu's; Chen liked to take his time and consider things and was more passive. Zhu, who had the fiery temper often ascribed to fellow natives of Hunan Province, including Chairman Mao, liked men of action who were willing to act straightaway.[3] Still, Zhu respected Chen and the head of CDB came with ministerial rank, so he asked Chen to take the job. At the central bank, his high family status as the son of economic planner Chen Yun had made him a slightly awkward person to give orders to; now he could take charge.[4] At CDB, he had the opportunity to practice what he preached. The central bank had been in charge of issuing guidelines for lending risk. It had told banks what to do, allocating an annual credit quota to the heads of the large banks. Chen, who had done a lot of research while at the central bank, could now act on his long-term vision for the Chinese economy. "I bore a lot of responsibility when I went to CDB," he told the *Economic Observer*, a Chinese financial newspaper.[5]

As a disastrous financial crisis in Asia unfolded that saw South Korea, Thailand, and Indonesia go cap-in-hand to the IMF for assistance and housing prices collapse in Hong Kong, China's banking system was insolvent. In the four years CDB had been in existence, it had made lending decisions so bad that nearly one in two of its borrowers weren't repaying the money. The East Asian crisis showed the importance of banking reform. Yet as the IMF and World Bank recommended that those countries open their banking system to competition and close sick banks, China took a different approach. Its state-controlled banking system funneled people's deposits into CDB bonds that allowed it to grow from a bank with one branch and three offices into a bank that in 2011 had assets of over 6 trillion yuan—almost $1 trillion—and a loan book bigger than that of J.P. Morgan Chase & Co. At the same time, foreign banks in China still have less than 2 percent of assets. CDB can sell bonds into the global market at a fraction of the cost of other global banks, and it has expanded into every conceivable area of China's financial universe: It owns a securities venture, a private equity division, a leasing arm, and a credit guarantee company, all of it lending with the state's implicit backing. When the financial crisis hit in 2008, it was CDB and China's state banks that could provide the money to keep the economy going as Europe and America's private banks tottered on the brink of collapse and needed to be bailed out using taxpayer money.

Although its original purpose was to take on the policy lending from China's commercial banks and loans to state-owned enterprises (SOEs) that the government previously had handled directly, under the Soviet model, CDB—according to its own reckoning—now has a lower NPL ratio than those banks, all of which have listed on the Hong Kong stock market and are now among the biggest banks in the world by market valuation. Chen has bested them at their own game, including expanding overseas more aggressively. Indeed, the Hong Kong branches of the mainland commercial banks view CDB as a serious competitor for overseas loans. But unlike them, it is debt based, leaving the state with trillions of yuan of liabilities outstanding. Even more than for Fannie Mae and Freddie Mac in the United States, the Chinese government stands behind these debts and the lending they back up. Why would the state want such an unwieldy animal? (See Table 2.1.)

A Life in the Party

You cannot understand the rise of J.P. Morgan in the nineteenth century without understanding the life of its eponymous namesake. Likewise, the history of CDB's emergence as the world's most influential bank is closely linked with its longtime leader, Chen Yuan. And that story begins with his father.

Table 2.1 Global Development Banks (USD, billions)

Bank	Assets $billion	Total Loans $billion
China Development Bank (2011)	991	876
China Exim Bank (2011)	190.34	143
Asian Development Bank (2011)	113	
World Bank (Including IBRD, IDA, IFC, June 2011)	545	327
Inter-American Development Bank (2010)	87.22	129
Korea Development Bank (Sept. 2011)	132	73
Brazilian Development Bank (2010)	306	208
KFW Bankengruppe (Germany, 2011)	606	153
FMO (Netherlands)	6.56	3.35

Note: World Bank loans IBRD and IDA only.

Source: Bloomberg, annual reports.

On a hot and humid mid-June day in 2005, China's leaders came to the Great Hall of the People in central Beijing, an imposing Soviet-style building where foreign dignitaries are received in hushed rooms below paintings of Chinese landscapes. They had come to pay respect to the hundredth anniversary of the birth of Chen Yun, a thin and reserved man whose decisions held great sway over the country's economy under two of the most powerful and determined leaders of the twentieth century, Mao Zedong and Deng Xiaoping. Chen Yun was called a "late proletarian revolutionary" by state media, and President Hu Jintao said he had devoted his life to the establishment of the socialist system. Chen had exerted control over China's economy for most of the Communist Party's first 40 years in power, believing above all in the stability of the economic system, both when it changed from a market-based model to a Soviet-style planned model in the 1950s and when it did the opposite in the 1980s. His struggles first against Mao's rush to move to a planned system overnight and later against Deng's efforts to move quickly the other way were the defining and decisive issues of the Communist Party's traumatic first decades in power. Although his son Chen Yuan would inherit much of his father's character and outlook on economic problems, his life couldn't have been more different.[6]

Chen Yun grew up without parents in a poor county outside Shanghai and experienced the capitalist heyday of the cosmopolitan city in the 1920s Shanghai as a shop clerk and labor organizer at the Commercial Press. He took only one recorded foreign visit in his life, to Moscow, and lived in the same old house in western Beijing for 30 years, which he refused to get repaired despite its leaky roof.[7] His early memories of Shanghai and the inequalities it embodied stayed with him for the rest of his life and influenced his view to slow down the opening of China's economy to the market in the early 1980s, with worries that the new special economic zones would allow foreign capitalists back in and spread corruption.[8] Unlike other top leaders, Chen never visited the zones, and opposed the opening of one in the now-quiet city of Shanghai despite its long history of industry.[9] One of the few times he became visibly angry was when he heard about a huge scandal in the southern province of Guangdong, where China's manufacturing boom would emerge from the economic zone of Shenzhen.[10]

As the elder Chen retired in the early 1990s and China followed a path of greater openness and economic growth thanks to a final push by the aging patriarch, who had stressed that markets were not the same as capitalism and could exist under socialism, his son Chen Yuan began to court international financiers. He became both Communist and modern; he had a sense of ownership, having grown up in the party system. But he didn't need to display a reverence for the strictures of Marxism espoused by his father. At Washington's exclusive Cosmos Club in the mid-1980s, Chen was queried about the contradictions between China's market-focused economic reforms and communism. Chen's response: "We are the Communist Party and we will decide what communism is," he told the gathering, according to American academic Steven Levine, who was at the meeting.[11]

Where Chen Yun had little experience of the West, his son embraced it, becoming one of the few officials at the central bank in the early 1990s who could speak fluent English. While some of the reason for his familiarity is a product of the different times and the far more prosperous China that the younger Chen inhabited, he and his family savored the best of the West to an extent very few Chinese—even rich Chinese—can attain. The Carlyle in New York, where he stayed as a PBOC vice governor, is rated by Condé Nast as the city's best hotel. Chen Yuan's son attended the elite Concord Academy in Massachusetts and went to work in private equity. His daughter, Chen Xiaodan, was a star attraction at the 2006 Bal des Debutantes in Paris, wearing a plum Oscar de la Renta gown. Count Edouard du Monceau de Bergendal from Belgium was her partner at the dance, according to the ball's website.[12] Chen Yun's descendants are recreating the Chinese moneyed and privileged class that and his fellow Communist revolutionaries fought to overthrow.

Chen Yuan's taste for the good life, however, is not matched by a flamboyant personality. While his classmates at Beijing's Tsinghua University joined the Red Guards in the early days of the Cultural Revolution of 1966 to 1976, Chen stayed indoors, studying English.[13] People who know him describe him as anything but politically attuned, much happier to be reading a paper on economics than plotting a political rise. "He's very introverted. He's not very talkative. He's the polar opposite of Bo Xilai. He speaks very softly, he doesn't engage in small talk. He always talks about technical issues," says Fred Hu, the former head of Goldman Sachs in China, who has known Chen for about 25 years. Chen Yun's son also inherited the low-key reserve of his father. Chen the younger speaks softly—almost inaudibly, almost mumbling. His posture can best be described as hunchbacked, folding into himself. For much of his life he too lived in a modest courtyard home in central Beijing, recalled Douglas Paal, former vice chairman for Asia at J.P. Morgan.

Like his father, Chen's passion is the economy, and in that he inherited similar ways of viewing the world. This includes seeing to the root of a complicated problem; the belief in stability and slow economic transformation rather than overnight transition; and seeing things from a long-term position, according to CDB-affiliated scholar Yu Xiangdong.[14] The depth of his economic knowledge and foresight has long been praised by those who have worked with him. In early July 1997, on a visit to Hong Kong before the handover to Britain, Chen told Liu Zhiqiang, who was working there for the People's Bank of China, that something bad was going to happen in the region. "You should pay attention to Asia's markets. I think there will be a problem," Liu remembered Chen told him.[15] A month later, the Asian financial crisis started after Thailand depreciated its currency.

And in a Communist Party where twentieth-century historical legacies matter and play out in twenty-first-century intraparty political jostling, Chen Yuan fiercely guards his father's reputation. Still, he would retain a lifelong reverence for his father, handing out coffee-table books of his photos to foreign bankers as he turned to making CDB into the world's largest policy lender. When Yu met us in June 2012, he startled us by starting the conversation 80 years in the past, discussing Deng Xiaoping's actions during the Communists' first large-scale territorial administration in Jinggangshan, an area in southern China on the border between Jiangxi and Hunan provinces. It was the opening salvo in an argument to show how Chen Yun, labeled by many as a conservative hard-liner in the 1980s, was really a force for moderation, in contrast to the more rash and hot-headed Deng, whose expertise was more in military matters than the economy.

In China's hierarchical system, where the party controls the state and all the levers of power, birth matters, and it has allowed Chen Yuan to amass power through CDB. His blood—as a former CDB employee puts it—is purple. Just how purple was evident in 2007 when China's next president, Xi Jinping, made an official visit to Australia. Chen was treated as an equal to Xi, who, like Chen, is the son of one of the revolutionary founders of the People's Republic and therefore a so-called princeling, by the Chinese delegation at Parliament House in Canberra, recalls Geoff Raby, Australia's ambassador to China at the time. "It was as if all the princelings were on the same level," Raby recalled.[16] At a meeting between German Chancellor Angela Merkel and Premier Wen Jiabao in the southern city of Guangzhou in early February 2012, Chen sat next to Wen, in the prime position for the Chinese delegation that included some of the country's largest and most prominent firms, such as Lenovo and China Southern Airlines.

Although often low profile, the sons and daughters of the Communist Party's founding fathers, generals, and cadres have built up powerful control over the economy and finance. Chen Yuan's sister, Chen Weili, help found China's first venture capital firm, China Venturetech Investment Corp., hoping to make it the Merrill Lynch of China in the 1980s, though it went bust in 1998. "I felt a responsibility to come back to help change China," she said.[17] She had returned to China after two and a half years at Stanford University, where she was drawn to Silicon Valley.[18]

The family of former premier Li Peng is involved in the energy sector, and Levin Zhu, son of former premier Zhu Rongji, heads China International Capital Corp., the socialist state's first investment bank. Of the elder Chen's five children, only Chen Yuan, the older son, moved into a position of power. Chen Yuan's sister, Chen Weihua, was sent out to teach in the countryside by the Great Wall during the Cultural Revolution for ten years and became a history teacher. Chen Yuan became the longest-serving Chinese financier to run a big bank, his status enabling him to build up a powerful fiefdom in a system where the party regularly shuffles around the heads of the banks so that they do not establish a power base that could challenge the system. And he continued into the job past the age of 65, when most top leaders holding ministerial rank retire. How has one man managed to head such a large bank for so long?

■ ■ ■

Chen Yuan was born in the revolutionary capital of Yan'an in northeast China in early 1945, as the Communists entered the final stages of a civil war following the Japanese surrender at the end of World War II. His father had arrived there in late 1937, becoming the head of the party's Organization Department, a body that to this day selects officials for all the powerful positions in the country, including the heads of the biggest state-owned businesses, such as China Mobile.[19] The elder Chen had already gained a reputation for solving economic problems with Mao that would last for the rest of his life. In Yan'an he sorted out the Communists' own currency, known as a frontier currency, or *bianbi*. In 1935, the ruling Nationalist (Kuomintang) Party had launched a currency reform and created a new currency, *fabi*, which became so popular it had driven out the Communists' own currency. By the early 1940s, the Communists had printed so much *bianbi* that the result was hyperinflation. Chen Yun arranged for the local salt companies to issue notes using salt as the reserve, which was one of Yan'an's main assets, so they could help soak up the excess currency.[20] Chen Yun also established a unified tax system and created the first annual plans of the Communist Party.[21] Chen Yuan remembers an early life moving across China, as his father was dispatched to the Northeast as a Central Committee member to help prevent the Nationalists under

Generalissimo Chiang Kai-shek from reasserting control over the industrial heartland following the Japanese surrender and withdrawal. "As far as I can remember we were always moving," he told the *Economic Observer* in an interview.[22] After the Communist victory in 1949, the family settled into the life in Beijing, which once again became the capital, as the country closed itself off to the outside world that Chen Yuan would later embrace. His father, in charge of the economy, became the fifth-highest-ranking party leader a year later.[23]

Chen Yuan entered the Beijing No. 4 Middle School in 1958, the best middle school in the capital, situated near the calm imperial lakes in the center of the city. Two years later, Mao launched the "socialist high tide," an attempt to boost economic development and create a leap in agricultural output and steel.[24] Not for the last time in his life, his father tried to curb Mao's excessive plans, but the elder Chen's calls for an end to this quick advance failed, leading to the disastrous Great Leap Forward, in which Mao hoped to catch up with Britain in 15 years. Chen Yun had said that catching up with developed countries would take 50 years[25] and warned that a too-quick move to the planned economy would lead to shortages of things that the market provided.[26] Instead, as agricultural production was moved into communes and backyard furnaces used for steel, there was a devastating famine that caused the deaths of tens of millions of people.[27] Chen Yuan remembers that, during this period, his father stopped walking in parks. "People have nothing to eat," he remembered his father telling him, so he felt ashamed to see them.

Chen Yun escaped the persecution of other high party members whom Mao turned against for critiquing his plans for constant revolution at the outbreak of the Cultural Revolution, although he was sent to a sanatorium in Nanchang in eastern Jiangxi Province for over two years with only his cook, his guard, and a secretary.[28] Mao had asked at a conference in January 1962: "Why is it that only Chen Yun can solve economic problems?" But by 1966, Chen Yun had lost his influence with the Chairman. As Harvard professor Ezra Vogel wrote, Chen "appeared to be a good judge of Mao's mood, sensing when and how it was possible to speak out and when there was no choice but to withdraw temporarily."[29]

His son, Chen Yuan, did not participate in the frenzy that went on around him while at Tsinghua University in Beijing, China's top university, in the late 1960s. "I was never actively involved in the Cultural

Revolution," he told the *Economic Observer*. From an early age, he had been interested in world news through his father's newspapers, the old *Reference News* that summarized foreign newspaper reports. But before he became interested in economics he wanted to be an engineer, and in 1965 he had entered Tsinghua to study automation. That was the very university where the Cultural Revolution began two years later, with mobilization rallies on campus, battles between factions, and the first group of Red Guards forming at the attached middle school across the street from the Old Summer Palace.

Despite the family's pedigree, however, Chen didn't escape the turmoil of the period. Like Gao Jian, who later became vice governor of CDB and handled all of its bond sales, he lost a decade of his youth. Because of the chaos, he graduated a year later than planned, in 1970 and was sent to a factory in central China's Hunan Province. It took him eight years to go back to graduate school. But he was luckier than his younger sister, Chen Weihua. She was about to enter university just as the Cultural Revolution began and was sent straight to the countryside. It wasn't until 1977 that she took the university entrance exams. By the early 1970s, the family was split, Chen Weihua remembered in a September 2011 interview with the *China Youth Daily*: "Seven people in our family were spread all over the country, my mother was sent down to a cadre school, my brothers and sisters were each sent to separate places," she said.[30] When her father's cook became sick, her elder sister, Chen Weili, visited him in Jiangxi to look after him for ten months. Her father Chen Yun requested that she not take a salary during that period since she hadn't been serving the country, so Chen Weili returned the funds to her work unit.[31] In 1970, in Hunan at the cadre school, their mother, Yu Ruomu, was branded an "active counterrevolutionary element," put in solitary confinement, and subjected to public abuse.[32] During this time Chen Yuan wrote a letter to his father in neighboring Jiangxi Province, mentioning that the Gang of Four—a group including Mao's wife that spearheaded much of the Cultural Revolution—was criticizing his view that productivity was the most important thing. Chen Yuan asked, "Where are they not right, where are they mistaken?"

It was the right question to ask as the Cultural Revolution started to quiet down and the army was brought in to restore order. By the time

Chen Yuan returned to Beijing in 1973, he had become interested in economics, through the newspapers that his father had left him. While reading Marxist-Leninist classics, he came across the concept of the US Federal Reserve for the first time. "I wanted to know what the Americans were thinking and doing, that's how I became interested in economics," he told the *Economic Observer*.[33] But the country had no real banking system. Chen was assigned a job as a technician in the third research institute of the Aero-Space and Aeronautics Ministry in Beijing before he could finally make it back to graduate school at the age of 33, entering the Chinese Academy of Social Sciences where he studied under economists Ma Hong and Yu Guangyuan. He had spent his twenties without any indication of his future life at the helm of Chinese finance.

But just as he started to study economics properly for the first time, the country put the turbulent Cultural Revolution behind and began a long process of reform. There was debate about whether to move quickly, via so-called shock therapy, or to take the gradualist approach, in which many of the state-controlled planning institutions were kept in place while only a very few economic zones were opened to foreign investors. Many Chinese were for the first time trying to work out how the Chinese economy actually operated. And in some cases, the real economy moved ahead of the planners. "There was very heated debate," Chen Yuan remembered.[34] During the 1980s, banks and other financial institutions sprang up, and inflation surged to nearly 20 percent.[35] His father Chen Yun, who still had extraordinary influence over the party, was not against the market but wanted to move slowly so as to curb inflation. He had coined the famous phrase that China should advance by "crossing the river by touching stones," meaning that growth should be stable with reforms based on experimentation. "One should first take small, measured steps," he had said in December 1980.[36] His birdcage theory held that economic zones and capitalism should be tightly controlled within the overall command economy, like a bird in a cage. At the time, Premier Zhao Ziyang and Chen Yun had a good relationship, but Deng Xiaoping, who had a military background, and party general secretary Hu Yaobang wanted to accelerate the pace of economic reform and opening, and gradually split with the elder Chen.

The Princeling Party: The Beginning of State Capitalism

As small private businesses started to open up in the country for the first time and the communes were abolished, Chen Yuan moved into Beijing politics, becoming party secretary of western Xicheng District in Beijing in 1982, an area dominated then as now by centuries-old courtyard homes and narrow alleyways. Later he was minister in charge of commerce and trade for the Beijing government as well as deputy director of its Economic Reform Commission. Li Luyang, a Chinese journalist at the time, remembers Chen Yuan as being different from other officials. "He likes to do things, and likes to do difficult things," he wrote in 2000 about Chen's time as Xicheng's Party Secretary.[37] This was when Chen started to organize research groups on China's economic history, alongside others such as Justin Lin Yifu, later chief economist of the World Bank, and future vice premier Wang Qishan. Chen focused on longer-term problems than did other groups and was influenced by the Hungarian economist János Kornai, who had written about shortages in economies under transition. In the 1980s, Chen also wrote about this problem, which he labeled literally "tight operation" of the economy, 紧运行.[38] No socialist country had moved to a market-based system before without considerable difficulties. "In the transition from a planned economy to a market economy there is this condition called insufficient supply of resources," Shanghai academic Yu said. "Because China's economic system was a closed one at the time, there's very limited resources. But people's demands and desires are limitless because the market economy just opened people's eyes." So Chen Yuan wanted to find out how these shortages affected China's economy and how to resolve them, Yu said.

In 1987, according to Tufts professor Joseph Fewsmith, Chen Yuan failed in his bid to be elected to the Beijing Party Committee, in one of the first uses of local elections, due in part to the resentment of his status as a princeling.[39] Zhao Ziyang, who was then premier, gave him the post of vice governor of the central bank, in part to placate Chen Yun, with whom he was having disagreements about reform of the economy. In one fell swoop, in part because of his connections, Chen Yuan was placed at the center of Chinese finance. The central bank was a weak government body and was dominated by the provincial offices controlled by local party officials. China's interest rate policy always has been decided by the ruling State Council, China's cabinet, with the central bank even now playing a more advisory role. The bank set credit targets and reserve requirements and acted mainly as a lender to ailing SOEs and banks, which could borrow directly. Before the founding of China's policy banks in 1994, including CDB, the central bank lent directly to banks to finance policy projects it needed to get funded. Indeed, direct central bank lending to financial institutions grew heavily while Chen was there, from 225 billion yuan in 1985 to 1.15 trillion yuan in 1995, contributing up to 53 percent of Bank of China's loan portfolio in 1991.[40] Basically, the state-owned banks were on life support from the central bank.

By the end of the decade, China's economy was overheating. Inflation was one factor driving student protests that broke out in the capital in the spring of 1989, having reduced the value of growing savings in Chinese banks. A decade after the Communist Party had started its reforms, the protests had a deep effect on the party, both politically and economically, resulting in the ouster of Zhao as the general secretary and leading cadres to assess where they had gone wrong. This crisis in the reform program was further heightened by the collapse of the Soviet Union in late 1991. For the first time since the party came to power it was threatened with loss of complete control, and for many leaders, the 1989 protests could have plunged the country back into the chaos of the Cultural Revolution. Chen Yuan stepped into the limelight at this time as part of a faction that became known as the princelings' party, a neoconservative clique that published a manifesto in the *China Youth Daily*, a newspaper associated with the China Communist Youth League. Titled "Strategic Choices and Practical Responses after the Collapse of the Soviet Union," it called for the transformation of the Communist Party from a revolutionary party into a ruling one, called for more party involvement in the economy, and advocated that the party take control of state assets.[41] "The Communist Party should not only hold the barrel of the gun, it should also take control of financial assets and the economy," it said.[42] Thus were born the ideas that would come to dominate Chen Yuan's brand of state capitalism.

How much was this Chen's ideological manifesto? At first, the princelings' birth hampered them in politics. Chen Yuan and others fared poorly at the fourteenth party congress in 1992. (Congresses take place once every five years to pick new leaders.) Chen was not even selected to the congress, and no princelings made it onto the Central Committee, a smaller group picked from congress members that in turn chooses the ruling Politburo. Although the paper was associated with Chen and some said he had signed it, it might have been written by Pan Yue, then at the *China Youth Daily*, who would go on to be environment minister. Still, Chen's views at the time can be gleaned from a paper published in his name in March 1991 that touched on many of the same points, which was subtitled, "Are we moving forward to revitalization, or are we moving backward to disintegration?"[43] The paper, which came out of a seminar in late 1990 and was later published in the party journal, *Qiushi* (Seeking Truth), marked a step forward from his father's cautious conservatism. It focused on how to strengthen political control and the power of the central government without derailing the dynamism of market-driven growth. Some conservatives wanted to go back to the planned economy, but Chen suggested a new type of centralization that would avoid the "feudal economy" of local fiefdoms that threatened the country and would strengthen central government control over key assets.

The slowing of central government fiscal revenue posed the biggest challenge to the economy, and the 1980s had seen an easing of central government control in the wrong areas, ceding control to local governments, he wrote. Further decentralization would result in social and political collapse and "what we will see is a weak central government and a lot of fiefdoms that work for their own interests. And this disunity will spread into all areas of society and the socialist mansion that we've spent years to build will collapse. Let alone a unified socialist power, not even a modern capitalist power should allow such decentralization." It was nothing less than a moment of crisis. "If we let the fiefdoms to their own devices, the economy will disintegrate, followed by political disunity and secession," Chen wrote. The overtones of what happened in the Soviet Union are not hard to miss.

In the West, believers in the free market were in the ascendant following the 1980s tenures of President Ronald Reagan in the United States and Prime Minister Margaret Thatcher in the United Kingdom. The IMF and the World Bank were telling developing countries to open up their markets and reduce the role of government. Despite the storyline told at the time by foreign pundits that China's state-controlled economy was going the way of the dodo, the reality was far more complex. Chen Yuan was busy thinking through the foundation of what we know today as China Inc., the state-led capitalism that many believe poses an existential challenge to free market liberalism.

The way Chen saw it, at China's stage of development, the market could not create the right industrial structure or satisfy shortages in the economy. Instead, the government needed to take up that role; otherwise, there would be inflation and growing unrest. "The market can function on its own but its needs certain interventions, for example, industrial policies and control on aggregate demand," he wrote. "Those people who think the market is the invisible hand and can perfectly allocate resources is what I call 'market utopia' or 'market omnipotence.'" The "recentralization" he called for meant that the state needed to exert influence in strategically important areas and let go of non-strategic areas where enterprises could have more power. To be a strong country, China needed to develop its own system, and the experience of all industrial countries showed they had first developed with the backing of a strong state. "China must develop as an economic great power that is not dependent on any other country or group of countries," Chen wrote. What better way to combine the planned economy impulses of his father with his more modern economic outlook that embraced the market? The state kept control, but the economy was efficient and the market helped drive the state's efficiency.

Chen was right about the state's role in industrial policy, and this would have a lot to do with development banks, which have long had a role in industrial policy as countries seek to catch up to more developed countries. The United Kingdom, the first country to industrialize, didn't need a development bank, as its process of industrialization was gradual. The rest of Europe did catch up, although it needed capital up front for transport and production facilities. In France, in the mid-nineteenth century, two new development finance institutions emerged, the Crédit Foncier and the Crédit Mobilier, as recounted in William Diamond's 1957 book on development banks.[44] Crédit Foncier was a mortgage bank whereas Crédit Mobilier was to finance investment in utilities and industry, just as CDB would in China. The founders of Crédit Mobilier "believed that industrialization was a means of improving the welfare of the masses and that banking had a special missionary role to play in the process," Diamond wrote, a view similar to CDB.[45] Although it was a private enterprise concerned with profits, it had close ties to government policy, similar to Chen's views that CDB must make a profit while serving the state. It lent long term, participated in the equity of companies, and underwrote securities, helping to produce the institutions of a capital market. Crédit Mobilier became a model for similar banks in Germany, Austria, Belgium, Netherlands, Italy, Switzerland, and Spain. Asia later followed. Japan set up an industrial bank in 1902 as it began industrializing that was deliberately built along the lines of the Crédit Mobilier. "These banks were designed at one stroke to relieve the shortages of capital, entrepreneurship and managerial and technical skills which face countries seeking to develop rapidly," Diamond wrote.[46]

Still, Chen Yuan was not a Communist in the old mold, and he read Keynes and other Western economists. While at the central bank, he traveled the world, and the international influence started to show, with contributions to IMF publications and talks in world capitals. Although he was for the planned economy, he obviously admired the American capitalist model, too. As a sign of his admiration, in the late 1980s, he managed to get his son into Concord Academy in the United States, an elite prep school. Douglas Paal, who served as China director on Reagan's National Security Council, helped secure the visa. "I said, sure, talked to the embassy. And then discovered just how much the staff within the embassy, especially the Chinese, hated seeing princelings getting benefits back then," Paal recalled. "We had to really delicately steer that through, but eventually the kid came to Concord Academy. They were all headed to the US for school in those days if they could."

His time at the central bank had made Chen aware of the decrepit state of China's banking system, with a huge amount of NPLs piling up. As William Rhodes, former senior vice chairman of Citigroup, said about meeting him: "I guess it was probably 2000, I was here on a trip with Sandy Weill. I wanted to meet Chen Yuan because he had just moved over from the People's Bank to the Development Bank. He had been very realistic on the problems that the state-owned banks were going to face. He said they were going to have to put a major input of capital. When I think of Chen Yuan, I think of all the officials I talk to in China, he is the most realistic."

Taking Over a Basket Case

In China, the state-owned banks *are* the financial system. Even traveling in the remotest mountain village in China after days of bumpy roads or in the poorest farming town, you will likely see a branch of one of China's four main state-owned commercial banks or at the very least an outpost of the postal savings bank. These banks work because the central government gives them a guaranteed spread of 3 percentage points or more between the rate of interest they must pay to China's prodigious savers and the rate they lend out, much of it to state-owned companies. But what happens when one side of the family doesn't want to pay back the other? In the late 1990s, that's what happened: The system where the state lends to its other half was beginning to crumble. China's leaders had worked out how to use household deposits that had risen 280 times in 1999 compared to 1978, when China started reforms, but without risk controls, banks had just shoveled the money out the door to any state project the government wanted. Not only CDB but the whole banking system in China was basically insolvent, with a stock of loans to SOEs that were being downsized and dud real estate projects. Despite the emergence of new banks and other financial institutions after China started to reform its economy in 1978, the big four banks—Agricultural Bank of China, Bank of China, Industrial and Commercial Bank of China (ICBC), and China Construction Bank—continued to dominate lending. To understand how bad it was, in the late 1990s, NPLs in the Chinese banking system made up 40 percent of total lending. Globally, having less than 5 percent of lending nonperforming is considered good health.[47] By the end of 1999, loans outstanding from all financial institutions were 9.4 trillion yuan, over 110 percent of gross domestic product and more than twice the 50 percent lending-to-GDP ratio of 1978.[48] Although a host of reforms in 1994 supposedly had made commercial banks responsible for their profits and losses, it would take until 2008 for the Chinese government to remove all the legacy bad loans from its banking system, before the last major bank, Agricultural Bank of China, listed in Hong Kong in the biggest initial public offering in the world at the time. In total, China spent some 4 trillion yuan to restructure and recapitalize China's banks, equal to 22 percent of China's 2005 GDP.[49] In a developing country, that was a lot of money.

The man in control of the financial system in the 1990s and tasked with sorting out the mess was Zhu Rongji, who would stop at nothing to centralize the financial system. In the spring of 1993, he held an emergency meeting at the Fengtai Hotel in Beijing, announcing himself head of the central bank, to the astonishment of local officials. He later took charge of the entire economy as premier the same year, 1998, he asked Chen Yuan to go to CDB. He had the unenviable task of closing hundreds of state-owned companies and turning employees out of jobs while reforming the monster of the banking system. Nicholas Lardy, a senior fellow at the Peterson Institute for International Economics in Washington, DC, pointed out in his 1998 book, *China's Unfinished Economic Revolution*, that for the first quarter of 1996 China's state-owned industrial sector was in the red for the first time, with losses exceeding profits. He cited Zhou Tianyong, a member of the Economics Department of the Central Party School, as saying that as of the end of 1994, SOEs would have needed to write off 1.2 trillion yuan in loans to state banks just to be able to pay interest on their debt at their current levels of profitability. It looked as if China's combination of capitalism and heavy state ownership was tottering.

Faced with an insolvent financial system, Zhu had a unique chance for financial reform. Instead, not for the first time, the state waded in and sorted out the mess, leaving a legacy of government interference that has endured to the present day. Zhu ended up engineering a bailout that involved recapitalizing the whole banking system, taking bad assets off bank books by creating a series of "bad banks" that would try to get what they could from the loans. Modeled in part on the successful Resolution Trust Corporation, which disposed of bad debt from defunct US savings and loan institutions, the asset management companies were supposed have a limited life, fading away after the ten-year bonds used to buy up the bad assets matured. Instead, the bonds were rolled over, and the asset management companies (AMCs) live on, with Huarong AMC opening a new glass office tower in Xicheng—the district once run by Chen—in 2011 and Cinda AMC, which took bad debt from China Construction Bank and CDB, considering a stock market listing in Hong Kong in 2012.

In all, four of these companies were set up to take the bad loans, with the Ministry of Finance putting 10 billion yuan into each one and the AMCs issuing bonds to banks. The 1.4 trillion yuan of bonds were supposed to give the banks good income-producing assets that yielded a return as compared to their dud lending. Of course, to do that, they had to have the implicit backing of the central government. In reality, the bonds are very hard to value, and they weren't even listed on the official budget, eventually disappearing into the system.

The AMCs acquired some 1.4 trillion yuan in loans from the big four banks at face value, paying the full original amount of the loan *plus* accrued interest. The AMCs paid full price for bad assets because they knew the Ministry of Finance would pick up the tab. In an investigative research note in August 2004, John Caparusso, a Hong Kong–based Citigroup banking analyst, estimated the total recovery rate on the loans to be only 26.8 percent, including real estate.[50] He estimated that ultimate losses on bad debts generated in the 1980s and 1990s by the big four banks alone totaled 2.7 trillion yuan, or about 23 percent of 2003 GDP. About 1.66 trillion yuan remained within the banks as of 2004, he wrote. CDB itself had managed to get rid of 100 billion yuan. The commercial banks were cleared to list on the Hong Kong stock exchanges and given a clear mandate to become profitable to avoid another bailout, but CDB has never listed. Why did the state take policy loans out from a policy bank that was *supposed* to lend to policy projects?

The Asian financial crisis gave China's leaders a chance to centralize their banking system and increase Communist Party control to promote their ever-desired political stability, the exact opposite of what the IMF and the World Bank were recommending for the rest of Asia. Zhu did not liberalize interest rates or legalize private banks, and saw the crisis in terms of weakening central power.[51] The biggest reform was the establishment in all the banks of party committees that had power over local officials and also gave intelligence to the party. Taking the bad loans off the books and pushing the burden out to the future also allowed the government to report low levels of government debt and a strong balance sheet at a time when countries around the region were suffering a crisis of confidence. Chinese banks were only allowed to properly write off less than 1 percent of all loans in any given year, so that the central government and the Ministry of Finance didn't bear the burden. No one wanted to take the immediate cost.

Of course, even today China faces the costs of pushing out that debt. The AMCs haven't closed but flourished, and the bonds on the bank balance sheets have been extended. But Zhu's reforms were an immediate blessing for the banks and for CDB, offering a cleaner balance sheet overnight. Critically, with all the banks coming under increasing central party control, the differences between CDB and the so-called commercial banks were unclear and remain so to this day, even though the commercial banks went on to global equity offerings, to the delight of foreign investment bankers. All of them did policy loans. Cleaned of its dud loans for free and not subject to the strict banking regulations that commercial banks were, CDB would be the only bank that could challenge the dominance of China's big four banks, both domestically and overseas, as they went on to become the biggest banks in the world.

Transforming CDB from an ATM Machine

In the early days, the bank still functioned as little more than a government department. As its official history notes, its projects were designated by government departments and bonds were purchased by other banks by administrative orders. "Basically it was a bank with only the cashier function," said a person who used to work at the bank who did not want us to use his name.[52] Staff members spent lavishly and carried cash around on business trips, sometimes as much as 100,000 yuan, Chen Yuan told the *Economic Observer*.[53] Many of them came from the Soviet-style state planning commission or SOEs. "They were engineers and administrative people and former officials. They didn't know anything about banking," the former employee said. To many borrowers, the largest policy bank was like a second Ministry of Finance, Chen said. "They feel like it's a free lunch, you can borrow and you don't have to pay back," he said.

Chen Yuan inherited a basket case. Always ambitious, from day one he was determined to change CDB from a bureaucracy to a proper international bank. "Before that the governor was just a typical official, just sitting there, not doing anything big," the former employee said. "The bank was in distress, and the NPL ratio was higher than [that of] the Big Four. That was what a policy bank was supposed to do, like a branch of the National Development and Reform Commission [China's Soviet-style economic planning body]. It was mainly financing the state, they were not supposed to be profitable, and the bank was not profitable. So Chen Yuan came to the bank and decided to launch a big transformation."[54] He faced serious obstacles, since many staff believed the bank *should* be lending to whichever state-owned client wanted it. Its NPL ratio in 1997 had been 42.7 percent, so almost half of all loans it had lent out had failed, a total of 170 billion yuan.[55] Chen had to convince many of the state-owned borrowers again and again that if their bad loan ratio went too high, they couldn't function at all.[56] "The first objective that I set for myself as well as CDB is to become a real bank and not just an ATM machine of the government," Chen said in the interview he gave to the *Economic Observer*. On first seeing the bank's huge and mounting stock of NPLs, the mild-mannered banker said he "felt a big headache."

He introduced the idea of choosing projects, doing official credit appraisals and internal credit ratings, as well as many complicated procedures many in the bank apparently did not understand. Before he had arrived there, the loans were simple: The audit department looked at projects; if it approved them, the loans were provided. Chen required loan officers to carry out risk review processes for all new loans, with four rounds of reviews. Every six months the computer randomly picked someone whose books were looked into. A loan committee rotated bank vice governors, to avoid relationships with borrowers. Then the loan would arrive on Chen's desk. He had the right to approve or deny the review result, not the actual loan itself. In a rare step for a bank that had been formed out of the old planning commission, he vetoed some of the National Development and Reform Commission programs and some local government projects. "This was very difficult, especially at the beginning. All these project managers including government agencies, believe the policy banks should provide loans. . . . We had a very difficult job. We have to tell people over and over again. If the bad loans accumulate then one day we won't be able to lend, so that will be bad for everybody. And gradually they began to accept," Chen told the *Economic Observer*.

The bank went through three so-called credit reforms, according to its official history, that helped reduce its bad loans. The first, in April

1998, established an internal risk control mechanism for new loans; one in January 1999 resolved bad debt; and the reform in November 2000 moved CDB to international standards. Chen tightened up internal rules. Those suitcases of cash? He made everyone repay funds they were carrying around, or else it was deducted from their salaries. In two months, everyone had returned all the money.

Chen wasn't a leader who could rally the troops, but his status as the son of Chen Yun gave him heft. "His blueblood background created a sense of respect by people in the bank, even though he wasn't a charismatic leader, or made any attempt to charm staff or motivate them," the person who worked there said. "Internally he had influence. People respected him and feared him so people started to work hard to evaluate the process rather than just issue the loans to everyone." Chen's status also allowed him to cut ties to local government officials and enterprises.

The bank was aiming to become "one of the big guys" and even hired Boston Consulting Group to point out the problems between CDB and international banks. By 2003, Chen was becoming increasingly confident that NPLs were a thing of the past: "China's banks are not machines for producing nonperforming assets," he said; rather, they were capable of reaching an international first-class standard.[57] In fact, CDB was not far behind international banks, he said. That same year, the bank started to back SOEs in overseas acquisitions. A year earlier, the NPL ratio had been reduced to below 3 percent. How did he do it? (See Table 2.2.)

At first, Chen was given some help from the state. Cinda Asset Management, the first of the AMCs set up by Premier Zhu Rongji, took a total of 100 billion yuan of bad loans off CDB's books in December 1999, out of its total of 170 billion yuan of bad debt it had amassed. In return, CDB got a 100 billion yuan ten-year bond on its balance sheet that paid interest amounting to 2.25 percent per year tax free with

Table 2.2 CDB's Drop in Nonperforming Loans

Year	NPL Ratio %
1998	32.63
1999	18.66
2000	8.78
2001	3.91

Source: CDB.

payment of the principal guaranteed by the Ministry of Finance.[58] We don't know what loans these were, but the Cinda bonds made up 10 percent of the bank's assets as of 2002. When CDB was formed into a joint stock company in 2008, with shares issued to the Ministry of Finance and Huijin, which holds the state's share of financial institutions, the bond interest CDB had received was set against the principal of the bonds.[59] The Ministry of Finance took the remaining amount of money in the form of a receivable to CDB yielding 3 percent a year. In effect, the Ministry footed the bill for the bad loans, although it took a long time to do so.

What happened to the rest of the original bad debt? A remaining 21.7 billion yuan of bad debt (and perhaps more) was converted into equity, where the bank gives up its debt in return for equity in a company; this was a popular way for resolving SOE debt under Premier Zhu. Unlike the commercial banks, CDB was able to hold equity in companies—an early example of how its privileges as a policy bank allowed it to expand over other banks. In its financial statements, CDB says such exchanges were government directed, as was the valuation of the equity and the price at which the company could purchase it back at a future date. Foreign banks also got a look in for the first time at some of China's bad loans. In April 2002, the *China Daily* reported that CDB would cooperate with UBS Warburg to dispose of 48 billion yuan of debt-for-equity shares the bank held, 30 percent of the equity that had been transformed from NPLs.[60]

While the bank's profit was still minuscule by the end of 2002, its NPL ratio was 1.78, compared to 3.91 percent just a year earlier. So, in the space of a year, the ratio had improved dramatically, and Chen regained his confidence. In the 2003 *Xinhua* interview, he said that the bank had resolved 90 billion yuan of bad debt on its own.[61] As we saw in Chapter 1, some of the debt could be resolved creatively with the help of local governments. In Tianjin, for example, CDB asked the local government to clean up a bad loan to the car company Xiali in return for a hefty loan for local development. In Chongqing, CDB also worked with the local government's investment company to resolve bad debts at SOEs. That was to be the model of CDB lending to local governments: They would guarantee that the loans would be repaid, and the bank would lend to projects and urban construction. How many billions more were resolved this way?

Developing a Slogan

Chen had bigger ambitions than cutting bad debt. While China's commercial banks were still cleaning up their balance sheets, Chen brought in the international friends he had made during his decade as a globe-trotting central banker, establishing an international advisory council in March 1999 that included big names in economics and finance, such as former AIG head Hank Greenberg, former secretary of state Henry Kissinger, and economist Fred Bergsten.[62] Annual meetings of the international advisory board were prompt with "crisp presentations," according to Frenkel, the former Bank of Israel governor who is chairman of JPMorgan Chase International and a member of CDB's international advisory council. He has known Chen for more than 20 years. In early 2012, the meeting was held in the Ritz-Carlton Hotel on Beijing's financial street, followed by a dinner at the prestigious China Club. The European debt crisis was discussed, with Jean Lemierre, a BNP Paribas advisor at the time leading Greek debt talks on behalf of private creditors.[63] What better advice could you hope for?

Still, that came later. In late 2002, Chen held a meeting of his newly formed international advisory group. In one photo, then-president Jiang Zemin stands at the center, flanked by Chen Yuan and Greenberg. Chen used the foreigners to float his new idea of "development finance" and sell the role of CDB to Jiang, according to someone involved with the meetings, who did not want us to use their name. "He was kind of strategic in outlining that philosophy," they said. It wasn't the first time China had used foreigners for its own bidding. "They tutored Jiang Zemin and Zhu Rongji, that was the strategy of Chen Yuan," the person told us. "Use these people to communicate the idea to the big leaders." In the end, Jiang recited some Chinese poems and didn't seem interested in development finance. There was also a tour to Chengdu in Sichuan Province for a talk on local government financing. Chen was friends with all of the foreigners, and counted on their prestige.

Every official in China needs a slogan, so Chen had come up with the idea of "development financing." It marked a turning point for state-led allocation of capital. The bank would finance development, not just policy, and it wouldn't make losses. In that way, the Chinese government wouldn't, either. Initially Chen said CDB would be able to finance projects that commercial banks would not touch. In 2003, CDB's bond issuance overtook the Ministry of Finance's for the first time, as it started to take on a growing proportion of infrastructure projects.[64] The bank also worked with borrowers to improve their ability to pay back loans. Chen believed that using a bank to finance infrastructure would improve China's credit culture and capital markets, rather than funding everything through the budget. It would create markets, because in a country moving from communism to capitalism, there often were none. In this way, China could avoid the problems that Eastern Europe and the Soviet Union faced in building markets during their economic transitions. His views followed on in theory from Chen's neoconservative days in the early 1990s.

The bank's official history defines development finance in this way: "Development finance is an important means to fulfill the government's will by market-orientated ways, different from commercial finance." By *market*, the bank means that instead of direct allocation of state funds, it raises its funds through the bond market at market rates and lends according to the prevailing lending rate, even though in China's system, the central bank sets minimum lending rates with bond yields closely following those rates. So while risk was not completely market determined, it was better than nothing in imposing discipline on borrowers. CDB was aiming to back projects that could be commercially viable, because it needed borrowers to pay back their debts so that it could pay back its own bondholders. In fact, CDB's bond rates have sometimes been higher than commercial bank deposit rates, making its cost of funding higher. As Frenkel told us: "Under Chen Yuan they have put a lot of weight on securing high-quality professionals. The bank has not become where you park unsuccessful bureaucrats. In this day and age even the most centralized government realizes that efficiency is a blessing, not a curse."

Its experience with the Three Gorges Dam, the largest hydro-electric dam in the world and a project originally proposed by Sun Yat-sen, the first president of post-imperial China, is a prime example of how CDB found an early role for itself. The dam ended up displacing over a million people, and recently even the central government has recognized some of the environmental problems it caused. It is no wonder that international banks and the World Bank did not want to get involved. So CDB lent 30 billion yuan to help finish the dam, after construction had started in the early 1990s. According to the bank's official history, "the funding for the project was boycotted in the international capital market." CDB ended up paying some 60 percent of the project's long-term loans. In a 2009 interview with Beijing-based Phoenix TV, Chen said that once the dam started to produce electricity, it could start to pay back its loans and could list on the stock market.[65] The China Three Gorges Corp. has since sold debt at levels near government bonds and has the top bond rating from Levin Zhu's CICC. In 2011, China's Three Gorges won bidding for a stake in Portugal's state-owned energy company Energias de Portugal SA by offering a 53 percent premium to the company's share price, much higher than what other bidders were prepared to pay. A market-based outcome such as this was what made the loan different from one given by the Ministry of Finance, Chen said. CDB had *created* a market. As of 2009, the loans had already started to be paid back. Out of the 30 billion yuan, CDB had already earned around 7 to 10 billion yuan from interest, Chen told Phoenix.

CDB went on to fund the massive south-to-north water project that will bring water from China's rainy South to the parched North, also a dream of Chairman Mao Zedong, and the Ertan Hydropower Station, the largest hydroelectric project in western China. Such grand infrastructure projects have helped secure the Communist Party's legitimacy, and CDB, as a long-term lender, has been willing to take on the risks. The bank would later provide a 43.4 billion yuan loan to support the Beijing Olympic Games for stadiums and sports facilities that now stand mostly empty in the north of the city, as well as money for the 2010 Shanghai Expo, a glittering display of China's new wealth in the city where Chen's father had first become a Communist Party member in the 1920s.

Beating the Commercial Banks

Before 2007, Western banks were enjoying the fruits of a credit bubble, with stock prices high, larger and larger buyouts backed by leverage, and a fever to deregulate financial markets. China faced formidable competition. At the same time, it also had promised to open up its banking system to foreign competition under its obligations in joining the World Trade Organization (WTO) in 2001. It was a frightening prospect. According to the journalist Li Luyang, Chen had studied the fall of the Soviet Union (an almost obsessive subject among Communist Party members in Beijing) as well as the East Asian financial crisis. He concluded that banks that were not well run would not be able to survive. "After China enters the WTO and the age of globalization, if your financial system lags far behind you will become a colony of developed countries, and your currency will be only an extension of other countries' currency," Li quotes Chen as saying.[66]

The remarkable thing is that a "policy lender" could become more competitive than the so-called commercial banks that went on to list on the Hong Kong stock exchanges and attract foreign investors, including Goldman Sachs and Bank of America. As early as 2003, CDB was ranked first among all banks in China in terms of the ratio of its NPLs. Its cost of funding was higher than that of commercial banks, so it was more eager to seek a profit on its investments. The commercial banks got the deposits of the Chinese population for almost no cost (most savings accounts make less than 1 percent interest in a country where inflation recently has exceeded more than 4 percent per year) so were more likely to make policy loans. Still, given China's dearth of big, successful private companies and the fact that the state continued its ownership in all the key industries, in its funding for many projects and state-owned giants, CDB was little different from China's big-four state-owned commercial banks. How could the commercial banks be expected to find projects that weren't state backed?

The Chinese government's call for the country's companies to go global, started by Jiang Zemin in November 2002, landed right in the bank's lap as a way Chen could compete head-on with commercial banks. CDB's overseas loans started to rocket upward from 2007, overtaking Bank of China, the bank that was supposed to be dealing in foreign exchange and lending overseas, as the biggest overseas lender. CDB set up work teams to go and live in foreign countries, acting much like a surrogate diplomatic service, as well as making each branch at home look after a different part of the world, with the Shandong branch handling Venezuela, for example, and the Shijiazhuang branch in Hebei Province handling Peru, although large investments have to be sent to headquarters for review. In 2003, CDB gave its first loan backing an overseas acquisition for an SOE, with a loan to Sinochem to fund its purchase of Atlantis, a subsidiary of Norway's Petroleum Geo-Services with assets in the Middle East. In December 2003, it gave a $301.87 million loan to support the transportation of liquid natural gas into Guangdong Province, the country's first-ever import program that was signed with foreign companies BP, Shell, and Australia's Woodside Petroleum. In 2003, it also issued the first US dollar bond in China. By 2011, the bank's foreign exchange loans made up 20 percent of the market share in China, despite the fact that CDB had no foreign investors and wasn't listed overseas. Since 2001, it has also provided what became a total of $45 billion in lines of credit out of the Shenzhen branch to Huawei and ZTE, companies that today are among the world's biggest telecommunications equipment makers.

"The commercial banks at the time complained loudly about CDB to the central bank; because we can issue bonds and our burden is much lower than commercial banks, we don't have to run so many branches," the person who used to work at CDB told us. "And many of the projects are the projects for the commercial banks. So there was lots of competition. And sometimes we had some advantage, using the lower cost and better government relationship to compete for those projects. So the commercial banks said, 'You are a policy bank, you should do the other projects, not compete with us.'"

In effect, CDB was taking the money off the hands of commercial banks (the commercial banks bought its bonds) and doing a better job at lending it to key sectors, such as power, road construction, railways, petrochemicals, and telecommunications. As early as 2003, CDB funding to these areas accounted for two-thirds of the total provided by Chinese banks. A look at the prospectuses for local government financing vehicles discussed in Chapter 1 shows the rates of CDB loans and commercial bank loans. They ended up financing the same projects, the only difference being that CDB could provide longer maturities and more money. By 2010, a total of 19 percent of the bank's loans were going to highways and another 29 percent to "public infrastructure," most of it to local governments. Yet how much of that was dependent on China's monstrously huge property bubble?

As China's land and property prices boomed from 2004 onward, CDB turned more than ever to financing infrastructure in the richer coastal regions of the country, often backed by land as collateral. As Hong Kong–based analyst He Yuxin pointed out, in 2000, CDB's proportion of loans to China's prosperous East grew by 8 percentage points, while those in the western China fell by the same amount, even as the central government was trying to promote development in the West.[67] Although CDB's loans are backed by the government, meaning they are not likely to be defaulted on, can a state-led and state-guided system do any better at allocating capital when the property market starts to rise? Chen sounded very much like so many other bankers at the beginning of history's most numerous and endless property-based bubbles when he said in a 2003 interview: "Ordinarily, city land prices and city construction won't drop; at the most it will just stop."[68]

Having the best relationships with local governments, the mild-mannered banker did not fear commercial bank competition. As he told *Caijing* magazine, commercial banks would need take on the hard work of reforming local government companies to build infrastructure, including improving their governance structure. If they did this, they, too, could be as successful as CDB.[69] Chen's ambition had been secured, and his power had led to the building of a unique and unrivaled institution. Douglas Paal remembered visiting Chen in 2006. "He is quite proud of how he built [the bank]. I went to visit him in my J.P. Morgan capacity in 2006 and asked him how he was doing in nonperforming assets and he said there were none. 'We're unique in China.'"

Chen's status as a princeling had allowed him to build something almost as big as the Ministry of Finance, with little oversight or regulation. "For other government officials, they think they are the manager for the party, everything belongs to the party, so how do I get the most from this business. But for Chen Yuan, he thinks everything belongs to me and the whole clique. He has a better sense of ownership," said the person who used to work at the bank.

Still, Chen's efforts to build a first-class bank could not stop others taking from the state's coffers. Wang Yi, a vice president at the bank, was investigated and later sentenced to death with reprieve in 2010 after taking about

12 million yuan in bribes. According to the *Economic Observer*, of a 2.5 billion yuan loan provided for development of Henan's tourism industry, only 200 million yuan went to the intended projects.[70] Wang was an outgoing man who had risen rapidly, graduating from Peking University and becoming a secretary to Bo Yibo, the father of Bo Xilai, the head of Chongqing who was later fired by the party in a high-profile corruption and murder investigation in 2012. He became vice chairman of the securities regulator in his forties, which gave him confidence and arrogance, according to a person who used to work at the bank. He often bragged about teaching finance at Peking University, while he himself had only studied history. A member of China's Bai ethnic minority, he liked to compose music and sing. The person who used to work at the bank remembered listening to one of Wang Yi's songs; everyone in the bank knew them. A vice governor of the bank for almost ten years, his was the most high-profile corruption case at CDB. With all the assets belonging to the state and so many loans, how can CDB be sure the money goes where it is promised?

Gao Jian: Creating a Market for "Risk-Free" Bonds

Gao Jian, a soft-spoken man whom we met in Chapter 1, began his love affair with the bond market while at the sleepy Ministry of Finance in the early 1990s. He used a tender method for the first time to sell 1 billion yuan of bonds for the ministry in a Dutch auction, using a Hongtashan cigarette box to hold the handwritten bids. China basically had no bond market then, with the central bank using its reloan facility to control the money supply. The nation's stock exchanges had only just been founded, and there were few corporate bonds.

Until early 1999, CDB bonds had been administratively distributed to state-owned commercial banks, and CDB borrowed directly from the central bank. But six months after Chen Yuan joined, CDB started to sell bonds in market auctions. Gao helped expand that after he arrived in 1999 to work in the treasury department, garnering him the title the "father of the bond market." Now CDB is the country's biggest bond issuer, after the Ministry of Finance, and in one year it has surpassed the Ministry. Gao has handled every bond the bank has sold, both in China and overseas.

"The bond market is part of my life—it is the focus of my devotion and dedication," he wrote in his book on China's bond market.[71]

Gao's life, like Chen's, had been buffeted by the Cultural Revolution, and it was not until late in life that he discovered the bond market. "I belong to a generation whose destiny was randomly governed by various political movements," he wrote. "Prior to the reform, I was sent to the countryside for reeducation, a movement that reshaped the lives of at least two generations. Next I served in the armed forces. Later, I stepped into a public securities bureau. Such experiences were typical at that time. Like a small boat adrift on the tide of political movements, I had little freedom to select a job in which I might really be interested."

CDB is unique among Chinese lenders in that it is financed almost completely by bond sales rather than deposits. In many ways the country's bond market owes its existence to the bank. To finance such large projects off the budget, China had to keep its financial system closed, so the loans' risks could only ever be passed onto another arm of the state system.

CDB's funding relied on a unique mechanism that hides the true amount of central government liabilities. It sells bonds to commercial banks, which use people's savings to buy the bonds and earn higher yields for absolutely zero risk on their balance sheets. To this day, the banking regulator has allowed these commercial banks, among the largest in the world, to assign a zero-risk weighting on the bonds, meaning they have to set no capital against them, even as CDB has ramped up lending to a host of commercial sectors and risky countries with long histories of defaults, such as Venezuela and Ecuador. The bonds are, in effect, sovereign bonds, but the state takes no overt responsibility for the lending. For the commercial banks they are free returns. The yields on CDB bonds have been for the most part higher than the benchmark deposit rate but lower than the lending rate—that is, the commercial banks can earn a return buying risk-free CDB bonds with depositors' money rather than lending the money out and taking the risk of default. For CDB the cost of funding is still lower than commercial banks, however, as it doesn't have to bear the costs of maintaining thousands of retail branches with tens of thousands, if not hundreds of thousands, of employees. The government meanwhile ensures that the Chinese people themselves cannot buy CDB bonds and earn higher yields on their money; the bonds are sold mainly on the interbank market, only to other banks.

In China, the rate depositors receive is often below inflation, and the lending rate has been kept below producer prices, meaning that bond market rates have also been kept artificially low. This is a classic example of "financial repression," as economists describe it.[72] As Carmen Reinhart and Kenneth Rogoff put it in their book on financial crises: "Under financial repression, banks are vehicles that allow governments to squeeze more indirect tax revenue from citizens by monopolizing the entire savings and payments system, not simply currency. Governments force local residents to save in banks by giving them few, if any, other options. They then stuff the debt into the banks via reserve requirements and other devices."[73]

Still, Gao worked hard to improve China's bond market, making CDB bonds more useful to the commercial banks through innovations such as selling them at a floating rate over the bank deposit rate (China had no London Interbank Offering Rate [LIBOR] at the time); if banks believed interest rates were going to rise, they could make good profits. In this closed system, CDB bond issuance has long surpassed the bond sales of the Export-Import Bank of China and Agricultural Development Bank of China, the other two official policy banks. Gao's desire to innovate led CDB to sell, as an asset-backed bond, a $1 billion bond in New York in September 2005, and the first yuan-denominated bond ever in Hong Kong in July 2007. In the domestic bond market, CDB can now sell 20 billion yuan of bonds nearly every week. (See Figure 2.1.)

Until 2011, China's bond market mostly didn't follow market rates, but a rise in inflation and interest rates in 2011 caused yields on local government borrowers and even the Ministry of Railways and CDB to rise. For CDB, however, the spike in yields was short-lived. As most people in the bond market acknowledge, there is an unofficial cap on bond yields. Investors have little sway in demanding higher yields to compensate for risk as the banks dominate by owning 70 percent of the bonds. The control over lending rates also ensures that infrastructure is not funded at the market rate. The cost of a CDB bond rises and falls with lending and deposit rates, not with whether the bond is more risky or not.

For this reason, CDB does not need a rating to sell its bonds. When CDB bonds sell overseas, Moody's, Standard & Poor's, and Fitch rate

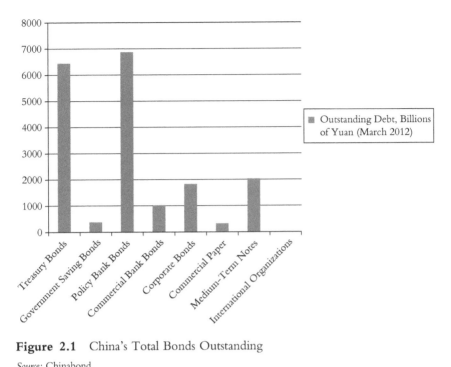

Figure 2.1 China's Total Bonds Outstanding

Source: Chinabond.

them at the same level as the sovereign bonds, assuming that the state will always bail CDB bonds out. CDB credit-default swaps, which investors use to insure against a default risk and speculate on credit-worthiness, still trade below many other global banks, despite the risk of some 2 trillion yuan in local government loans. The global market seems to be saying that the risk involved in any government bailout or recapitalization is very low.

To appreciate how little impact the bond market, domestically or overseas, has had on CDB's transparency, it is worth looking at its 2010 annual report, a glossy production audited by PricewaterhouseCoopers.[74] The report says that fully 23 percent of its lending goes to sectors classified as "other." That's a total of over 1 trillion yuan that the public, let alone the international and domestic investors who buy its bonds, has no right to know about. Buying CDB bonds, as Fan Wei, a young fixed-income analyst at Hongyuan Securities in Beijing, said, is "a political duty." The banks could earn more by lending their money out.

But if banks stopped buying the bonds, CDB would be out of business in a matter of days, and it is too big to fail.

The West Self-Destructs: The Financial Crisis

Chen wanted to be more than just a lender for overseas ventures. He wanted to own an overseas financial institution. In the early summer of 2007, just as the subprime real estate market in the United States was beginning to collapse, CDB agreed to purchase a 3.1 percent stake in England's Barclays Bank for £1.45 billion at £7.2 a share so that Barclays could increase its offer to purchase the Dutch lender, ABN Amro, in one of the biggest proposed bank acquisitions in history.[75] Singapore's sovereign wealth fund Temasek also had agreed to pump money in. Barclays' bid lost out to a consortium led by Royal Bank of Scotland (RBS) that ended with RBS and ABN Amro having to be saved by the governments of their respective countries. What for a short time had seemed like the center of global financial action had ended in bailouts. Barclays' shares had fallen 70 percent by the end of 2008, as the global financial crisis hit. As of early 2012, they are still down some 60 percent. If Barclays had succeeded, under the terms of the agreement, CDB would have had to invest a further $8 to $10.5 billion. Or, to put it another way: CDB would have invested over three times its 2007 profit in a British bank.[76] What was a policy bank from a developing country that relied on the government's sovereign state credit doing helping a British bank complete a bank merger on borrowed money? By the end of 2007, CDB was trying to acquire a stake in Citigroup, despite mounting warnings that subprime mortgages were likely to tip the United States into a recession and as banks, including Citi, began to write down billions of dollars in subprime-related loans.

The acquisitions reflected the ambition and ability of Chen Yuan and his desire to make CDB a global bank. But this time, he had taken his power over the bank a little too far. The State Council blocked Chen's bid for Citigroup. The purpose of the Barclays' stake also seems unclear. Having over 3 percent of the shares after the initial purchase gave CDB a chance to nominate a nonexecutive director to the board, but there is no sign that it ever did that. Then in June 2008, CDB paid £2.82 a share for another 47 million shares—60 percent less than it had paid a year earlier—as part of a

Barclays' funding drive that included investments by Qatar and a Japanese bank. Why was CDB helping bail Barclays out? The State Council ruled against this second investment, according to Zhang Yuzhe at *Caijing* magazine, but CDB went ahead anyway.[77] Despite the purchase, by September 2008, CDB's holdings had already fallen below the 3 percent threshold as Barclays sold more shares, diluting CDB's stake. As of mid-2012 it was at 2.03 percent, meaning CDB cannot nominate a director. For Barclays, the deal was supposed to help open the China market, but that has not happened. For CDB, staffers get to go on months-long temporary transfers at Barclays in the United Kingdom or Asia to learn from the bank, and Chen Yuan spoke to Bob Diamond, who stepped down as the head of Barclays in 2012, regularly. But that is about it.

CDB's purchases were unpopular, with the share drops coming at a time when the sovereign wealth fund had made a purchase of a $3 billion stake in the New York–based private equity firm Blackstone Group before its June 2007 public offering, when the shares subsequently dropped. Even stranger was the lack of transparency. The purchases were made by a Hong Kong special vehicle called Upper Chance Group that is mentioned only once in the bank's annual report, as having a registered capital of £1.584 billion. The same figure for registered capital is mentioned in 2009 and in 2010 on a bond prospectus. It is the exact amount of money that CDB has paid for its two stakes in Barclays, at face value. Who takes the losses on this state asset?

In the summer of 2012, Barclays was fined a record $451 million by regulators in the United States and UK for manipulating the benchmark LIBOR bank lending rate, a rate used by CDB itself for many overseas loan deals, driving Barclays shares even lower. China's government would learn to be more cautious; the requirement to get approval from the State Council, the country's cabinet, would be in the years ahead both a hindrance in global markets as well as a safety control on CDB's ambitions. Like the Citigroup deal, in late 2008, CDB's attempts to buy a stake in German bank Dresdner failed after not receiving the green light from the State Council.[78] CDB would not again bid for a stake in a Western financial institution.

Chen's relationship with President Hu Jintao and his Politburo seems less cozy than it had been with former President Jiang Zemin. At the beginning of 2007, Premier Wen Jiabao announced that all policy banks would become commercial, and in March 2008, as riots in Tibet were gripping the nation and the world, a small news item suggested that process was on the way. To many this meant listing on the stock market overseas, like the other commercial banks. On December 16, 2008, just as the financial crisis was worsening across the globe, CDB officially on paper became a commercial bank, but with one big omission: The bank would still be able to sell bonds with the sovereign credit rating to raise funds, the so-called zero-risk weighting that allowed banks to buy them and set aside no additional capital for potential losses. The government gave it a handy $20 billion injection from the sovereign wealth fund too, to "increase China Development Bank's capital-adequacy ratio, strengthen its ability to prevent risk, and help its bank move toward completely commercialized operations."[79] A decade after Zhu Rongji's reforms put a party cell in every bank, the state seemed to be bringing the bank closer with more defined ownership. The Barclays purchase had shown CDB as a powerful, global bank acting on its own like an uncontrolled sovereign wealth fund; Wen now moved to make CDB just another commercial state lender that faced formidable competition. Chen's fiefdom days looked to be over. CDB had started its life as an entity directly under the State Council. It would now be owned by the Ministry of Finance and Huijin, a unit of the sovereign wealth fund, much like ICBC, China Construction Bank, and dozens of other financial institutions and securities companies. But why would the state want to do that if Chen's strategy for development finance and his efforts at risk control had been successful?

Many at CDB, where the lunch break is two hours long, were against becoming fully commercial. Liu Kegu, the former CDB vice governor who is an advisor to the bank and spearheaded its push into Venezuela, summed up the difference with commercial banks for us in a March 2011 interview during a washroom break at the Ministry of Railways hotel in Beijing. "Because China doesn't lack banks based on savings, China's current financial organizations can absorb the capital. But they lack the ability to invest in high-risk, long-term large projects, especially overseas," he said. "CDB shouldn't be forced to absorb savings; it's enough for CDB to use a portion of savings from other banks."

It was more than an argument over principles. Should CDB lose its sovereign status, a natural result of commercialization, the market would demand a higher premium for its bonds, meaning CDB's cost of capital would rise and get even more expensive relative to that of the deposit-taking commercial banks. It would also mean that the major holders of the bonds, the commercial banks, which have some 3.9 trillion yuan of CDB bonds on their books, would have to set aside more capital to meet capital-adequacy requirements. Estimates of losses to bondholders if the bonds were to lose their zero risk-weighting status are in the billions of yuan.[80] Zhang Xuguang, head of the company's private-equity arm (more on him in Chapter 5), fretted that commercialization could undercut CDB's fundraising model. "It is a problem for CDB raising new funds after it expires," Zhang said in a December 2010 group interview to foreign media in Beijing, referring to CDB's sovereign status. "I hope it can be extended."

Fred Hu, the former Goldman Sachs China head, was even more blunt, saying in an interview that China needs its policy banks to fund long-term infrastructure projects. Commercializing them could derail infrastructure funding and the urbanization process so central to China's continued growth. "The trouble starts once they become a commercial bank; then the asset risk premium will be much higher, and then the spread will be much higher to compensate for the risk," he said, referring to the extra yield bondholders would require to compensate for the risk of buying the bonds. "I don't know why Wen Jiabao wants to push CDB into becoming a commercial bank. I don't think he really understands the consequences."

Wen's efforts at reform turned out to be half-hearted. Chen, Liu, and Zhang got a reprieve. In early 2011, CDB won an extension of its sovereign bond status through 2012. In part, CDB had been helped by the collapse of the Western financial system, which created an opening for the bank to redefine itself as a policy bank that still had important uses to the country. For China, the crisis was a once-in-a-lifetime opportunity to increase its global financial power. And luckily for Chen, at that precise moment, it needed a convenient vehicle to provide the requisite funds.

Moving Beyond Wall Street

In a Phoenix TV interview in August 2009, Chen, looking pale and scholarly, told host Wu Xiaoli that he had turned against the Wall Street assets he had once sought to buy. "The quality of Wall Street assets is very bad; they have many problems. We should think about what China really needs."[81] China needs natural gas and oil and should take the opportunity to buy overseas resource assets, he said. The financial crisis opened the eyes of Chen and Chinese officials regarding the desirability of owning stakes in US and European banking institutions, as each teetered on the brink of collapse. More importantly, Western banks that were supposed to be able to regulate themselves had totally failed to practice good risk management or allocate capital efficiently, instead piling into bonds backed by subprime mortgages that later failed. Who would want a model like that, which would require even bigger bailouts of the financial system by taxpayers? The US Treasury had effectively ended up being the backstop behind every bank in the country. The West had given China an opportunity for its state-owned financial system to flourish.

When the Chinese government launched its 4 trillion yuan stimulus in November 2008—an average of 3,000 yuan for every person in China—CDB, with its decade-long connection with local governments, was the perfect bank to help carry it out. Its loans rose to almost 20 percent of the loans of the big four banks. This was not commercial lending by any stretch of the imagination, as we saw in Chapter 1.

After his experience with Barclays in 2007 and with Citigroup a year after the financial crisis started, Chen saw the financial crisis as a failure of the market. He said that China needed to create its own financial system, according to a TV interview he gave with the confident young journalist, Rui Chenggang, in July 2009. "The government and the market will have to reach a proper balance," he said about the lessons of the financial crisis. "You can't entirely rely on the market itself."[82] China was in a stage of production and construction and shouldn't use a financial system suited to America's consumption stage, he said. His words sounded much like his ideas from the early 1990s.

Asked about his ambition to build CDB into a first-class international bank, Chen took a more measured view of that yardstick, dropping his earlier desire to be like an American bank. "The standards to measure a world-class bank should not be based on the Western standards alone. There should be an international objective standard: If we do well, we can become a world-class bank," he told Rui. Later Chen went on: "I believe the current financial crisis is an important opportunity. In the past, when it comes to the reform of financial institutions, we always emphasized commercialization and profit as the only goal, but for large wholesale financial institutions with not many employees, we have to make sure our financial targets are consistent with social targets; only in this way can we have more room to grow. We should take the opportunity of the crisis to reflect on the relationship between government and market." What did he mean?

It is no coincidence that Chen did these TV interviews just after the government had officially converted CDB into a commercial bank in late 2008. Chen seemed to be saying that CDB still could act as he wanted it to be, not a commercial institution acting on a level playing field but a state-owned hybrid bank that could compete on the world stage. Keeping it as is was the best way to serve the state, too. "China Development Bank's main business, its special status, won't change," CDB's Liu said in a March 2011 interview.

For one thing, the oil bubble had collapsed, giving China a prime opportunity to buy overseas energy and resource assets at a discount. Oil had fallen 51 percent by the end of 2008 from a record $147.27 a barrel in 2007 (see Chapter 4). The country's oil consumption had doubled in the previous decade to 8 million barrels a day by 2008, and China was importing about 45 percent of its needs. As Chen told Rui: "When we buy oil we don't need to go to Chicago and New York futures exchanges, and to buy minerals and metals we don't need to go to the London metals exchanges; we can negotiate directly, and directly cooperate. This kind of cooperation has better results." Western banks weren't going to be expanding into Africa and Latin America without capital and with little risk appetite especially when their governments wanted them to lend at home. China's foreign direct investment hit $54 billion in 2008, more than triple the 2007 figure. And CDB was behind many of the transactions and could still sell bonds to overseas investors, who saw China's sovereign credit as becoming the safest in the world. What other bank could lend such large amounts for long maturities? The banker to China Inc. had arrived.

CDB went on to back a $14 billion secret raid by Aluminum Corp. of China, known as Chinalco, to acquire stock in Anglo-Australian miner Rio Tinto in February 2008. China had been alarmed by BHP Billiton's attempts to buy the miner, creating a monopoly of the global pricing of iron ore that China depended on for its growth. The dawn purchase of shares in Rio Tinto, the largest overseas purchase by a

Chinese company in history at the time, was followed by more CDB-backed purchases in a rights issue in 2009. Even though the State Council had disagreed with CDB's investment in Barclays, it backed these deals, and CDB's board did not have a say. The bank was happy to stress more than ever before its usefulness in serving the state and helping SOEs to expand overseas. In September 2009, CDB gave China National Petroleum Corp., parent of PetroChina Co., then the largest company by market value in the world, a $30 billion loan to fund overseas acquisitions. China had already spent $12 billion in 2009 on oil fields and refining assets. The five-year loan would be provided at a "discounted interest rate," the announcement said. "The credit agreement is of great importance for CNPC to speed up its overseas expansion strategy and secure the nation's energy supplies," the corporation's president, Jiang Jiemin, said in the statement. By 2011, CDB's role was entrenched. As Chen titled an article in the central banks' magazine, *China Finance*: "Using Development Finance to Serve the 'Going Out' Policy."[83]

CDB also found a role for itself in helping the country's currency, the yuan, start to displace the US dollar in trade. A drying up of US dollars during the financial crisis had an impact on world trade, as a majority of Chinese companies settled their bills in dollars. China was fed up with the world's entrapment to the dollar. China was exposed to the US dollar but couldn't hedge that exposure in the market without contributing to the dollar's depreciation. China's international assets had increased from 15 percent of its GDP in 2004 to 26 percent in 2009, but its currency was hardly used in international trade settlements. In March 2009, Zhou Xiaochuan, the head of the central bank, called for special drawing rights (SDRs), units of value used by the IMF that are based on a basket of currencies, to replace the US dollar's role as China's reserve currency. CDB was the first bank to sell so-called dim sum bonds in Hong Kong in 2007; it was the first time a bond had been sold in China's currency outside its borders. CDB was the perfect vehicle for the experiment: It got the sovereign credit rating by foreigners, yet it could take all the risk, and foreigners' liabilities could be isolated in one vehicle. By September 2011, the bank could claim that it had lent the most cross-border loans in China's yuan, worth 61.5 billion yuan, including to Venezuela, which could then buy Chinese equipment and services in the currency. (See Figure 2.2.)

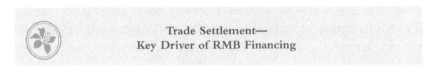

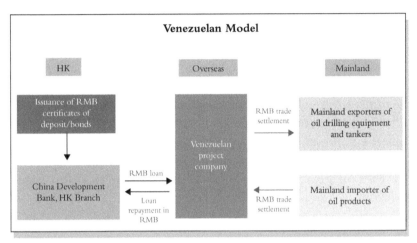

Figure 2.2   Yuan Internationalization Through CDB

Source: HKMA online presentation.

In July 2012, CDB reached another milestone: It sold the longest-maturity yuan bonds in Hong Kong to international investors, with a maturity of 20 years. At the same time it sold three-year notes to central banks in Africa who could shift their reserves away from the US dollar, the first time they had bought yuan bonds. European, African, and Middle Eastern investors made up 60 percent of the buyers, the bank said.[84] It was the beginning of the Chinese government's ability to sell debt in its own currency internationally at low interest rates, a privilege the United States had enjoyed since the end of World War II. And CDB was the desired vehicle, as all illusion that it was a commercial bank was fading from view. China had kept its financial system closed to foreign competition to build it up, and now it was using it to expand its currency overseas. China had easily quashed the view that it could be just an extension of the developed world's currency or subject to the whims of J.P. Morgan or Goldman Sachs as Chen had once feared. China had built a state-dominated financial system that was starting to spread its wings; the question was whether it would prove any better than the Western lenders who had so spectacularly collapsed. Especially as CDB started lending to Latin America and Africa, regions where foreign banks had been burned before during the 1980s.

■ ■ ■

CDB's rise on the world stage was due to the ambition and determination of Chen Yuan, who wanted to build a bank that could serve the government, yet still be profitable. In the next two chapters, we look at the bank's lending to Africa and Latin America, which has helped propel Chinese companies into new markets. The world's most powerful bank is dominating the World Bank in Africa and acquiring a level of influence with the government of Hugo Chávez in Venezuela that parallels the height of Yanqui imperialism.

Notes

1. Interview with Douglas Paal, July 2011.
2. Interview with William Rhodes, September 2011.
3. Interview with Yu Xiangdong, vice president of the Academy for World Watch, who has done research for Chen Yuan and CDB for many years. Beijing, June 2012.
4. Ibid.
5. "陈元：做一个真正的银行家." "Chen Yuan: Being a Real Banker," *Economic Observer*, October 31, 2009.
6. For more on Chen Yun's disagreements with Deng Xiaoping, see Ezra F. Vogel, *Deng Xiaoping and the Transformation of China* (Cambridge: Harvard University Press, 2011).
7. "陈伟华：读懂我的父亲陈云." "Chen Weihua: Reading My Father Chen Yun," *China Youth Daily*, September 5, 2011.
8. "Chen Yun, Who Slowed China's Shift to Market, Dies at 89," *New York Times*, April 12, 1995.
9. Ezra F. Vogel, *Deng Xiaoping and the Transformation of China*, p. 412. Chen Yun said: "Now every province of China wants to set up special economic zones. If they are allowed to do so, foreign capitalists as well as domestic speculators at

home will come out boldly and engage in speculation and profiteering. Therefore we should not do things this way."

10. Ibid.

11. This anecdote appeared in Richard McGregor, *The Party* (New York: HarperCollins, 2010).

12. www.lebal.fr/portfolio/le-bal-des-debutantes-2006/

13. Interview with Fred Hu, Beijing, October 2011.

14. Interview with Yu Xiangdong, Beijing, June 2012.

15. Liu Zhiqiang interview in Beijing, May 2012.

16. Lunch with Geoff Raby, Beijing, August 2011.

17. Sheryl WuDunn, "Investing After the Crackdown," *New York Times*, August 20, 1989.

18. Ibid.

19. Ezra F. Vogel, "Chen Yun: His Life," *Journal of Contemporary China* 14, no. 45 (November 2005).

20. Interview with Yu Xiangdong, Beijing, June 2012. The notes were called 盐业流通券.

21. Ibid.

22. "陈元：做一个真正的银行家." "Chen Yuan: Being a Real Banker," *Economic Observer*, October 31, 2009.

23. Interview with Yu Xiangdong, Beijing, June 2012.

24. Frank Dikotter, *Mao's Great Famine: The History of China's Most Devastating Catastrophe, 1958–62* (London: Bloomsbury, 2010).

25. Vogel, "Chen Yun: His Life."

26. Interview with Yu Xiangdong, Beijing, June 2012.

27. Dikotter, *Mao's Great Famine.*

28. Chen Weihua, *China Youth Daily.*

29. Vogel, "Chen Yun: His Life."

30. "陈伟华：读懂我的父亲陈云." "Chen Weihua: Reading My Father Chen Yun," *China Youth Daily*, September 5, 2011.

31. Ibid.

32. Roderick MacFarquhar and Michael Schoenhals, *Mao's Last Revolution* (Cambridge, MA: Harvard University Press, 2008).

33. "陈元：做一个真正的银行家." "Chen Yuan: Being a Real Banker," *Economic Observer*, October 31, 2009.

34. Ibid.

35. Carl E. Walter and Fraser J. T. Howie, *Red Capitalism: The Fragile Financial Foundation of China's Extraordinary Rise* (Hoboken, NJ: John Wiley & Sons, 2011).

36. *Selected Important Documents Issued Since the Third Plenum* (Beijing: Renmin Chubanshe, 1982).

37. 李璐阳, "陈元印象." Luyang Li, "Impressions of Chen Yuan," 国际金融 (*International Finance*), no. 10 (2000): 7.

38. See Chen Yuan's essays collected in "陈元集，运行，调控，发展," 黑龙江教育出版社, July 1990.

39. Joseph Fewsmith, *China Since Tiananmen: The Politics of Transition* (New York: Cambridge University Press, 2001).

40. Nicholas Lardy, *China's Unfinished Economic Revolution* (Washington, DC: Brookings Institution Press, 1998).

41. 苏联巨变之后中国的现实应对与战略选择，中国青年报思想理论部. See translation by David Kelly in "Realistic Responses and Strategic Options: An Alternative CCP Ideology and Its Critics," *Chinese Law and Government*, 29(2), Spring–Summer 1996, pp. 1–96.

42. Ibid.

43. 陈元，"我国经济的深层问题和选择 （纲要)." Chen Yuan, "China's Deep-Seated Economic Problems and Choices (Outline)." 经济研究, *Economic Research*, April 1991.

44. William Diamond, *Development Banks* (Baltimore, MD: Johns Hopkins Press, 1957).

45. Ibid., p. 23

46. Ibid., p. 26

47. Barry Naughton, *The Chinese Economy: Transitions and Growth* (Cambridge, MA: MIT Press, 2007).

48. Nicholas Hope, Dennis Yang, and Mu Yang Li, *How Far Across the River?: Chinese Policy Reform at the Millennium* (Stanford, CA: Stanford University Press, 2003).

49. Guonan, Ma, "Who Pays China's Bank Restructuring Bill?"

50. John Caparusso, "Asset Management Companies: Recovery Rates, Bad Debt Costs, and System Recapitalization," Citigroup Smith Barney, August 20, 2004.

51. Victor Shih, *Factions and Finance in China: Elite Conflict and Inflation* (New York: Cambridge University Press, 2009).

52. Source, telephone Interview, 2011.

53. "Becoming a Real Banker," *Economic Observer*.

54. Source, telephone interview, 2011.

55. *Practice and Achievements of Development Finance*, Research Academy of China Development Bank, October 2011.

56. "Becoming a Real Banker," *Economic Observer*.

57. "陈元：中国的银行不是制造不良资产的机器，" 新华社. "Chen Yuan: China's Banks Aren't Machines for Producing Nonperforming Assets," Xinhua News Agency, March 31 2003, http://finance.sina.com.cn/roll/20030331/1054326297.shtml

58. CDB 2006 annual report.

59. According to a CDB bond prospectus, CDB earned 17.4 billion yuan of interest on Cinda's bonds, which was set against the principal. The remainder of the amount was taken by the Ministry of Finance in the form of a receivable with interest of 3 percent a year. www.sfc.hk/sfcCOPro/EN/displayFileServlet?refno=0575&fname=28010517_book(e-15.35)final.pdf

60. "Banks Cooperate to Swap Debt into Equity," *China Daily*, April 6, 2002, http://www.china.org.cn/english/2002/Apr/30239.htm

61. "陈元：中国的银行不是制造不良资产的机器，" 新华社, "Chen Yuan: China's Banks Aren't Machines for Producing Nonperforming Assets," Xinhua News Agency, March 31 2003, http://finance.sina.com.cn/roll/20030331/1054326297.shtml

62. The International Board is mentioned in the 2003 annual report for the first time.

63. For a list of 2012 attendees to the Beijing meeting, see http://www.cdb.com.cn/english/NewsInfo.asp?NewsId=4129

64. CDB 2003 annual report, data from Chinabond.

65. http://v.ifeng.com/f/200908/741e885b-746f-4819-94d6-92aaf780d3e4.shtml

66. 李璐阳, "陈元印象." Luyang Li, "Impressions of Chen Yuan," 国际金融 (*International Finance*), no. 10 (2000): 7.

67. He Yuxin, *China Development Bank: The Best Bank in China?* GaveKal-Dragonomics, China Insight Companies, July 1, 2010.

68. "陈元：中国的银行不是制造不良资产的机器，" 新华社, "Chen Yuan: China's Banks Aren't Machines for Producing Nonperforming Assets," Xinhua News Agency, March 31 2003, http://finance.sina.com.cn/roll/20030331/1054326297.shtml

69. Hu Shuli, Kang Weiping, and Chen Huiying, "Interview with Chen Yuan," *Caijing*, no. 5, March 5, 2004, http://topic.news.hexun.com/detail.aspx?classid=1&id=587998.

70. "Missing Funds Spark Probe of Bank Vice President," *Economic Observer*, June 27, 2008, http://www.eeo.com.cn/ens/2008/0627/104454.shtml

71. Gao Jian, *Debt Capital Markets in China* (Hoboken, NJ: John Wiley & Sons, 2007).

72. Nicholas Lardy, "Financial Repression in China," Policy Brief 08-8, Peterson Institute for International Economics (September 2008).

73. Carmen Reinhart and Kenneth Rogoff, *This Time Is Different: Eight Centuries of Financial Folly* (Princeton, NJ: Princeton University Press, 2009).

74. CDB 2010 Annual Report. Available on their Web site at www.cdb.com.cn

75. Dealbook, "With Barclays, China Continues Overseas March," July 24, 2007, www.cdb.com.cn/english/NewsInfo.asp?NewsId=2183, http://dealbook.nytimes.com/2007/07/24/with-barclays-china-continues-overseas-march/

76. 2007 profit of 29.6 billion yuan = $4.6 billion.

77. 张宇哲, "国开行增持巴克莱被否," Zhang, Yuzhe, *Caijing*, July 16, 2008.

78. "Beijing's Caution Scuppered Bank Bid," *Financial Times*, September 4, 2008.

79. "China Taps Its Cash Hoard to Beef Up Another Bank," *Wall Street Journal*, January 2, 2008.

80. Ba Shusong estimates losses of 71.5 billion yuan if the bonds are rated AAA. See 巴曙松, 孙隆新, 牛番坤, 政策性银行, 商业化改革对债券市场的影响研究, 北京 : 经济科学出版, November 2009.

81. Interview available at http://finance.ifeng.com/video/20090808/1061220.shtml

82. Interview available at http://finance.ifeng.com/news/hgjj/20090717/956257.shtml

83. 陈元, "以开发性金融服务走出去战略," 中国金融 2011 年第 23 期.

84. CDB Web site, http://www.cdb.com.cn/web/NewsInfo.asp?NewsId=4192

Chapter 3

Nothing to Lose but Our Chains

China Development Bank in Africa

With the current financial crisis, it's very difficult to go anywhere in this world and get $3 billion.
——*Ghanaian President John Dramani Mahama, on his country's $3 billion loan with CDB, April 2012 interview, Beijing.*

In early 2012, outside Ethiopia's capital, Addis Ababa, as the sprawling city of congested traffic gave way to flat green fields beneath sloping hills, the China–Africa Development Fund (CADF) of China Development Bank (CDB), China's largest Africa-focused investment vehicle, was trying to make a return on its investment. Weekenders normally came out here to drink and to eat goat in the simple courtyard hotels, but now there were the Chinese living in a row of gray factory buildings by the side of the narrow two-lane road. Unlike China's manufacturing centers, where factories are more like small towns and migrants from villages work day and night to escape to a better life, the factory was a quiet place that emptied out after the end of its shifts, leaving nothing but the sound of the wind.

Although Ethiopia might not have oil and gas (yet), it has a plentiful supply of cows and sheep and labor, perfect for the leather industry. CDB is trying to help the country utilize this natural advantage in the brutally competitive environment of world trade, much as China did in the 1980s. It's another example of the bank's powerful influence across the globe. Besides the leather factory, the bank's Africa fund has invested in a large glass factory on the outskirts of Ethiopia's capital, as well as a cement factory, and is considering investing in a new economic zone based on China's Special Economic Zones that helped propel its growth from 30 years ago. Aided by Chinese demand for its exports and raw materials, Africa has experienced its best decade and a half of economic growth since independence from colonialism. CDB is helping to change failed development policies by stimulating manufacturing and building much-needed infrastructure that many countries require to have a chance to compete in the next stage of economic growth. Its large package loans bring Chinese companies and governments together. One example is a $3 billion loan to the West African country of Ghana, the biggest loan in the country's history, which will allow for contracts for a host of Chinese contractors just after Ghana starts to tap new offshore oil fields. Yet the ambitious glass factory in Ethiopia's capital had to cut production, and the CDB's Ghana loan has been criticized by Ghana's noisy democracy, facts that show that the bank's road on the continent, even with the best intentions, won't be easy.

In the leather factory, all of the machinery came from China, and the leather will go back to clients in the southern provinces of Sichuan and Guangdong, according to Jiang Lele, 26, one of the factory managers, an idealistic young man who had come to Ethiopia earlier to volunteer in a hospital. Wearing a tight light-brown leather jacket, he showed us inside the rows of identical buildings where Ethiopian workers clad in dark-blue overalls stood amid the pervading stench of chemicals, a few Chinese alongside them getting their hands dirty, drying the leather in large black sheets, bringing in the sheep hides, and tanning the leather in large spinning machines. All the chemicals have to be imported, too, from China and Germany, Jiang said. Each building had reminders of China— the standard red Chinese banners with white writing with slogans reminding the workers of the higher calling of their cause: "Developing China–Africa friendship and building a harmonious world," one said in English and Chinese. On the way out, Jiang pointed to two different sides of the factory forecourt: On one side, some 400 locals eat; the 24 Chinese staffers eat in another building attached to the main office. Jiang was there to work: He had been there two years and said he didn't go to Addis Ababa much. He just worked, and whiled away the evening browsing the internet. In the capital, he had four cell phones stolen by pickpockets. So he preferred the quiet of his factory to the dusty and dirty downtown of the city.

Ethiopia, Africa's second-most populous nation, has a 12 percent production cost advantage over Vietnam in leather and 37 percent over China, according to World Bank estimates from a report from late 2011.[1] Due to rising labor costs in China over the last few years, labor is cheaper, Xu Jianliang, the general manger who is in charge of the project, said, sitting in a meeting room with chairs decked with doilies, arranged around the edge in the Chinese custom, suitable for visiting Chinese officials. The staff members are mostly women from the surrounding farms who didn't know anything about factory life before, according to Xu. "Before we came here most had no jobs; they were just living on the farm and herding sheep," he said in soft-accented English. "Only one year and a half and their living standard has increased a lot." In China, workers in leather tanneries receive 2,000 to 3,000 yuan a month, which is around 6,000 to 9,000 birr in Ethiopia; whereas 1,200 birr is enough at the factory, Xu said. Ethiopia's wages are a fifth of China's and half of Vietnam's, according to the World Bank. And despite the great demand, there's a shortage of leather in China, and the quality is much better in Ethiopia, said Xu, a smart, middle-aged man in a suit jacket and glasses, who has spent his life in the leather industry and came from central Henan Province to run the factory.

Inside the office pictures of the head of CDB, Chen Yuan, sitting next to State Councillor Jia Qinglin and Foreign Minister Yang Jiechi on their visit in January 2012 line the walls, a sign of the patronage this small and remote factory has behind it. Ethiopia's government has long relied on the West for aid, with millions of Ethiopians still dependent on emergency food aid, but Meles Zenawi, a former Marxist who ran the country for more than two decades before his death in August 2012, has brought Chinese investment to the country. Ethiopia had only $8 million in leather product exports in 2010, compared to Vietnam's $2.3 billion.[2] So Meles invited

Xu's leather company to invest, and after three years of market assessment, it moved in. Ethiopia offered duty-free import of Chinese machinery and a seven-year break in income taxes as all of the business was for export. The factory took one year to construct and can process 10,000 pieces of sheep- and goatskin a day. Xu said he wants to expand into producing gloves and aims to make total profit of around $15 million a year. In a country seeking foreign exchange, such exports would be a welcome boost.

Yet the factory also highlights the difficulties of shifting China's manufacturing to Africa, a continent that for decades failed to gain any share in the global market for consumer goods. Despite Ethiopia's natural advantages, in early 2012, it was not making much of a profit. It struggled with rising prices for sheepskin, in a country where at one point in 2011 inflation was the second-highest rate in the world, peaking at 40.6 percent. "At the moment we can make profit but it's very small because of the increase in prices for materials," Xu said. Sheepskins in 2011 cost about 8 to 42 birr ($2.35); in April 2012 they were about 100 birr apiece, still "a little cheaper" than China, he said. The country also suffers from its landlocked position: It takes four days to reach the nearest port in Djibouti, almost 500 miles away along a bad road. Such delays mean it costs 60 percent more to ship to the United States from Djibouti port than from China.[3] Unable to wait a week to clear customs, the factory ended up having to fly some orders to China. Though even with that additional cost, Xu said, it was cheaper than making the leather in China. So, will the country become a manufacturing center? "It will take some time because of cultural difference and also it's very poor," Xu said.

In contrast to China, where local governments compete viciously with each other to attract foreign investment, boost their GDP, and ensure their promotion, Xu had to convince the local government of the importance of the factory. He added that it's also difficult to motivate staff members, and they are unskilled. As a result, the Chinese managers organized regular meetings to explain the notion that if they work harder they can participate in the profits of the business. Yet labor laws are also tougher than in China: The factory has to pay double for overtime and more for holidays, he said, emitting a faint sigh. "We are foreigners, so we must keep the local conditions of labor." The staff sometimes expect pay without putting in the hard work, he said. "But I think sometimes the problem is they work very slowly compared to Chinese."

Liu Jun, an intelligent young man and the head of CADF in the country, had just arrived in early 2012 to take up his post in Addis Ababa. He is also in charge of making sure the factory starts to make a profit. Like many other private equity investments made by the fund, the leather factory is an offshore company formed by a joint venture between CADF, a subsidiary of CDB, and Xinxiang Kuroda Mingliang Leather Products Ltd. CADF holds 45 percent of the company, which was set up with $37 million in capital. Liu spends his days showing officials from China Petroleum and other companies around and lives with many of the other Chinese in a hotel complex in downtown Addis that has its own Chinese canteen and Chinese cooks, where rice and sautéed bok choi are served in molded metal trays, as in the bustling canteens of Chinese universities.

Addis Ababa, a city set on the country's vast central plateau, which is the political heart of Africa with the African Union and United Nations Economic Commission for Africa stationed there, was alive with the construction of cement tower blocks, looking much like Loudi in central Hunan. An "Ethiopia–China" named street is marked by a smart black plaque. Chinese construction firms have been busy here for years: They helped build and fund the ring road in the late 1990s, and China Railway Group Limited is building an ambitious light-rail project around the city. Most symbolically, a Chinese construction firm built as a gift the massive, shiny new African Union building that consists of a tower block and silver-colored dome in the center of town. Investment in the project totaled 800 million yuan, the biggest Chinese aid project in Africa since the Tanzam Railway was built in the 1970s.[4] Chinese construction firms have a 25 to 40 percent cost reduction over non-Chinese construction companies when they compete for bids, said Gedion Gamora, a young academic in Addis Ababa who has studied China–Africa relations.[5]

Telecom firm ZTE, China's second-largest maker of phone equipment, has helped build the country's national phone and Internet network with the local state-owned provider, and Chinese help service it. Its Chinese rival, Huawei, has a big office in the center of town near the Hilton Hotel. Both are long-term clients of CDB that together have been awarded a combined $45 billion in lines of credit from the bank. Local workers dig up a trench for pipes on a road diversion in the Bole

Road area south of the city that will link it to the center; the project is funded by Export-Import Bank of China (Exim Bank) and carried out by China Communications Construction Company. Another Chinese company is waiting for the city to agree to building a 58-floor five-star hotel, according to *Capital*, a local newspaper.[6] But most crucially for CADF, China Railway Group is helping to build a railway to the port in neighboring Djibouti, an example of how other arms of the Chinese government build up the infrastructure that will help it make Chinese— and other foreign investment—profitable. China Railway has said the line will take only 19 months to complete.

When Richard Siegel, a US-based footwear consultant, arrived in Ethiopia in 2008, the biggest challenge footwear producers told him they had was the port at Djibouti, as they needed to import all the components for shoes. Ethiopia had not exported to major Western countries, despite having some of the world's best leather due to favorable climatic conditions. The country's sheepskins can be stretched "like a rubber band," making them perfect for gloves and shoes, like a custom fit, Siegel said.[7] Furthermore, footwear is a so-called cluster industry, meaning that it involves a long supply chain, from slaughterhouses, to hide traders and tanneries, to factories. This makes it one of the best-suited industries to increase employment and reduce poverty. Charged with helping out a US Agency for International Development (USAID) program to export shoes to the US market, Siegel managed to convince up to ten US footwear companies to import from Ethiopia. Then USAID moved its funding to a more agriculture-based program known as "Feed the Future," he said, just before the Chinese arrived. "Ethiopia has the biggest herds. It had over 100 million head when I got there, and they had a penetration of the world leather market of 0.9 percent. Here's the largest herds in Africa contributing less than 1 percent to the world leather market. A total waste."

Made in Ethiopia

CADF's investments in Ethiopia follow a trend that the World Bank has highlighted with increasing frequency, especially under its previous chief economist, Justin Yifu Lin, who, as a young Taiwanese military officer, defected to China in 1979 by swimming to the mainland from Jinmen Island. Manufacturing hasn't had much caché among the global elite that focuses on Africa in the West. As the leather factory shows, it can be dirty and can have an impact on the environment. As Deborah Brautigam, an expert on China–Africa relations, points out, it is not included in the United Nations' Millennium Development Goals, a 15-year plan to reduce poverty established in 2000.[8] But Lin believes that countries should focus on investments where they have a comparative advantage, such as cheaper labor costs or raw materials, as the best way out of poverty and toward industrialization. Except for a few countries with oil, no country has reached a high-income status without industrializing, and countries with natural resources or land-rich countries that achieve middle-income status cannot sustain growth without a large manufacturing sector, Lin has written.[9] "I disagree with those who assert Ethiopia and other Africa nations of similar income levels are too burdened with governance, poverty, and poor investment climates to exit the poverty trap. China and Taiwan, China—where I am from—as well as many other newly industrialized economies were just as poor a few decades ago and equally saddled with corruption and other obstacles. Many of them still rank low in various governance and business environment indicators today. I was involved in China's transformation away from agriculture and I'm confident a similar evolution can happen in Africa," he wrote in March 2012 after a visit to Ethiopia.[10] He has said that China's current growth and rising wages will lead it to dispense of as many as 85 million new manufacturing jobs. Africa currently has fewer than 20 million such jobs. In a lecture to the United Nations in May 2011, Lin said that setting up special economic zones was among six recommendations for developing countries; they were a road map for economic growth and China's influence was a "leading dragon."[11]

Under decades of lending by the West, the World Bank, and the International Monetary Fund (IMF), Africa has missed out on the global manufacturing boom. (See Table 3.1.) It contributes only about 8 percent of gross domestic product (GDP) in sub-Saharan Africa today, according to the World Bank, and has had no effect on overall growth between 2000 and 2007.[12] Sub-Saharan Africa's export growth has accelerated in the last decade, but 73 percent of it has been due to mineral exports, according to

Table 3.1   De-Industrialization of Africa (Manufacturing as a Percentage of GDP)

Decade	Sub-Saharan Africa
1960s	9.4
1970s	10.1
1980s	10.7
1990s	10.8
2000s	8.5

Source: World Bank.

the bank's 2011 Light Manufacturing in Africa report.[13] "The structure of most Sub-Saharan economies has not changed in the last half century. They continue to be dominated by agriculture or mining," according to the report. Now there is an opportunity to follow the path of China, which, before reforms began, also had no share in global manufacturing and had outdated industrial factories. Its main exports were live animals, gas and petroleum, and footwear. Having moved up the value chain, the ubiquitous "Made in China" image is changing as costs for labor rise in the country's southern and eastern manufacturing heartlands. Labor costs have risen 15 percent annually since 2005, at the same time as the currency, the yuan, has appreciated.[14]

Today China has set up economic zones in Nigeria, Mauritius, Egypt, Algeria, Zambia, and Ethiopia. The zones in Africa, like the ones that had been set up in China—those hated by Chen Yuan's father for being corrupt and inviting foreign influence—enable Chinese companies to invest in factories while other Chinese firms help build the infrastructure in the surrounding country with the support of China's state-owned banks. In many of the zones, Chinese funds from CDB are playing the crucial role of foreign capital. Ethiopia, which has a population of 80 million people, has the potential to become globally competitive in apparel, leather products, and agribusiness, according to the World Bank. "Sub-Saharan Africa is unable to benefit from the relocation of labor-intensive industries from China as some of the basic factors for developing a manufacturing base are missing: financial capital, entrepreneurial skills, links with global buyers and markets. For these countries, FDI [foreign direct investment] is a panacea," Lin wrote.[15] China itself relied on foreign capital and investment to set up its export zones and has since become the biggest exporter in the world. China's Wu Bangguo, the country's top legislator, visited Ethiopia in December 2008 and said the zone there could "let Ethiopian people share China's 30 years of successful experience of opening up and reform," according to the zone's promotional literature.

CDB's CADF is one of the leading investors behind the zones, although many have been hampered by delays and have found it more difficult to attract investors than at first thought. "The inability . . . of the African governments to move as quickly and make decisions as quickly as what some of these companies are used to in China is definitely something that holds up the process," said Hannah Edinger, an analyst at Frontier Advisory in South Africa who has studied the zones.[16] CADF has invested in the Lekki Free Trade Zone in Nigeria, and is involved in the Mauritius–Jinfei zone and the zone in Egypt with Tianjin Economic Technological Development Area (TEDA). In Ethiopia, Jiangsu Qiyuan Group, a private company from Zhangjiagang in eastern China, won the bidding for the economic zone in November 2007, from China's Ministry of Commerce. "The SEZs have had a lot of political support," Edinger said. "The nice thing about the CADF fund is they automatically bring in CDB. For all your capital needs. CADF normally provides equity financing and then CDB comes with the checkbook for debt."

Ethiopia needs to make sure it uses the capital wisely, according to Gedion Gamora, a young academic in Addis Ababa who has studied China–Africa relations. Chinese investment "has opened up opportunities for skilled labor, but only for low-level managers; high-level managers are all Chinese," he told us over coffee. "This limits the technology transfer, the skills transfer." He argued that the government needs to be sure to encourage technology transfer and joint ventures and favor some domestic firms. "The government needs to leverage the investment for local development," he said. Problems also lie in the different expectations of working hours, something Gamora mentioned during a 2011 meeting with the Chinese vice minister of commerce on his visit to the country. Chinese law favors the employer but Ethiopian law favors the employee, he said. "The Chinese working culture is very hard, working all day and all night—that is based on terms of culture, not skills," he said.

The Chinese manufacturing zones will be successful, as Brautigam points out, if they attract significant local and foreign investment, create

African employment, promote exports, and elevate industrial competitiveness in an environmentally and socially sustainable manner. However, if they end up as Chinese enclaves, do not employ Africans or only at the lowest level, fail to transfer technology, and attract industries that are more polluting, "fears about Chinese exploitation would be confirmed."[17]

Ethiopia's Zone: Exporting to the West

In the other direction from Addis Ababa from the Chinese leather factory, along the road that leads to the nearest port at Djibouti, Ethiopian workers lined up for their morning training at the Eastern Industry Zone. Kong Xianglu, 25, who had been in the country for four months, led it, responding with in Chinese "Turn left" and "Turn right." The young men and women shifted in unison from side to side responding with the Chinese numbers "*Yi!*," or one, and "*Er!*," two. It was similar to a bustling Beijing street outside a beauty salon where uniformed employees exercise every morning. Zhang Huarong, founder of the company, Huajian Group, which makes 20 million pairs of shoes a year for export to America and Europe from China, used to be in the military. "This is about attitude training before production; this is very important for the management," Kong said. The workers complete this training for two or three days before moving onto the production line in the green-and-yellow factory building, a long, clean structure where 700 local workers sitting at desks in teams make up to 2,000 pairs of shoes a day. At the other end of the factory, women's shoes were packed into boxes labeled with "Guess" and "Tommy Hilfiger" and marked "Made in Ethiopia," before being taken on the long journey to the port.

Fannie Gong is a friendly investment manager at the zone who has lived in Washington, Tokyo, and Italy and whose husband works at the United Nations in Addis. She pointed to the fancy new gate being built at the main entrance to the zone. It was the same design as the one the company built in its hometown of Zhangjiagang in eastern China. Chinese workers were putting the finishing touches on the gate by erecting a large TV set over it. Inside, a queue of young Ethiopians waited in the hot sun clutching plastic folders with their resumes. Gong said when the zone first opened, it had 1,000 applicants for 200 jobs.

Still, finding skilled labor in the country is hard, she said. "They are all Chinese putting up the TV as you can't get locals to do it," she said.

On a trip to China in August 2011, Meles visited Shenzhen, which has risen from a fishing village to a city of more than 10 million in 30 years, and met with Zhang, Huajian's founder. In September, Zhang led a delegation from Guangdong's chamber of commerce to Ethiopia, and he decided to invest, attracted by the low cost of labor, cheap electricity, and support for foreign investment by Meles's government. In October, the machinery was on its way; a month later, 90 Ethiopian workers went to China for two months to study the company's culture and technical training. Zhang, who had joined the army in 1978, founded the company with a workshop at home with three sewing machines and ten workers after he left the army in 1982. Now, thanks to the economic zone, the company is following China's call to "go global."

Inside the new factory, young, college-age Ethiopians lined up in teams interspersed with the occasional young Chinese to cut and attach together pieces of leather by hand and man the expensive-looking Italian machines, which looked like souped-up cappuccino makers. As in the leather factory, multiple slogans covered the walls—in English and Chinese on red banners. Zhang Kai, a young and energetic purchasing manager at Huajian with smart, black-rimmed glasses, had motivational slogans on the back of the name tag that hangs around his neck. "We have a company song that everybody who is Ethiopian knows how to sing in Chinese," he said. The staff are given bright-green shirts, apart from white shirts for managers, Zhang said, and the orange shirts for quality control. He was especially proud of the free lunch—large slabs of local Injera and a Chinese option for the Chinese staff. He, too, praises the quality of Ethiopian leather. "We want to use the local sources," he told us, showing the zippers to be put on the shoes. "We can use this leather, we can get a good price and control the quality. Ethiopian leather is perfect. Too many material we import from China. The customs is very trouble, too many processes in Ethiopia," he said in the English he taught himself.

Zhang also wanted to work overtime to meet customer orders. But electricity was a problem, so the company ordered new generators from China. He emphasized that the factory wanted to use only local labor. "Labor is not only cheaper, but our owner wants to help Africa," he explained. "All the technicians' jobs we want to give to them because we know in the future you need to use the local employees."

CDB's CADF signed a memorandum of cooperation with Huajian to help it expand when Jia Qinglin visited Ethiopia in January 2012, possibly investing as much as $2.5 billion, according to Huajian. They envisioned creating 100,000 jobs and as much as $4 billion in exports every year as well as building an International Footwear Institute, a hotel, smart European houses for experts, and managers' apartments. On the wall of the Addis Ababa factory are photos of its operations in China—rows upon rows of thousands of workers lined up outside, a haze hanging on the horizon, standing erect, shoulder to shoulder, with the precision of a North Korean parade. Could this be Ethiopia's future? "One hundred thousand jobs we will give them," if they get the investment, Zhang said.

China–Africa Development Fund: The State's Private Equity Arm

On a sunny day in November 2006, Beijing made an extra effort to welcome 48 African leaders: Billboards throughout the city announced Africa as "the land of myth and miracle," and high-rises were covered with pictures of elephants and giraffes, a gesture the government thought would make African leaders more at home.[18] Robert Mugabe, president of Zimbabwe, was quoted by state news agency Xinhua as saying that the summit would enhance cooperation: "We have nothing to lose but out imperialist chains."[19] President Hu Jintao promised to establish up to five special economic zones in Africa and to start a new $5 billion fund, the CADF, among other measures, to boost investment by Chinese firms and offshore some of China's manufacturing. Where would the money come from? CDB, which can get money cheaply from the bond markets, as we saw in Chapter 2, turned out to be the best answer. Despite attempts at outside fundraising, CDB has provided all the funding for CADF.

Set on the main east–west avenue in Beijing in a new glass office building just steps from the central bank—the same building as Thomson Reuters and Exim Bank—CADF's smart offices give the air of a sleek investment operation, where well-suited Africans are sometimes seen in the lobby near the Costa Coffee café. The fund was formed at a ceremony in the Great Hall of the People in June 2007, attended by Commerce Minister Bo Xilai, Foreign Minister Yang Jiechi, former foreign minister Tang Jiaxuan, and Gao Jian, vice governor of CDB.

Chi Jianxin, the head of the fund, has a large map of the world with China at the center in his Beijing office. A short, academic man with a considered manner, he sat down for an interview in late 2011 in a meeting room with a plush carpet with the logo of the fund emblazoned in the center. Paintings on the wall showed African landscapes portrayed in the traditional Chinese style of rivers and mountains. Other staff members who spoke fluent French and lived in West Africa sat around him. Chi himself has long experience with CDB. According to a photo of the event, Chi was there the night of the Wuhu financing signing that created China's local government financing vehicles. But he is relatively new to Africa: He first visited in September 2007, after becoming the fund's chief executive. Those who work with the fund consider it to be commercially motivated and professional. "It's a very gung-ho private equity fund," said Martyn Davies, head of Frontier Securities in South Africa. "I find the guys extremely helpful and very good and very professional to deal with. I wouldn't use words like shadowy. It's largely commercially driven."[20]

The fund opened its first West African office in November 2011 in Ghana, its fourth regional site in Africa. It also has offices in South Africa, Ethiopia, and Zambia and is the only Chinese private equity fund investing in the continent. A 2011 *Xinhua* article quoted company chairman Zhao Jianping as saying that the prospect for returns from its Zambian investments were "pretty good."[21] But Chi Jianxin, in an interview, was less sanguine. The fund has not so far been able to exit any of its investments, he said, although it is still seeking a "beneficial result" over the long term. It generates enough cash flow to maintain its operations and has made a small profit. When we questioned him regarding the business proposition of such a fund, he grew ruffled for a second, saying that just because it hasn't been able to exit any projects so far did not mean over the longer term the fund couldn't make a profit. "When we started, we didn't have investing experience in Africa, and we hoped to have a quite good profit in three to five years so we could exit investments," he said. "But we've seen it's not so easy as that."

Despite promising to operate on market principles, by early 2012 the fund had not raised any money from outside investors due to the risks of investing in Africa. That year, it obtained another $2 billion from CDB. "From a point of view of a money manager, the more simple the funding, the better," Chi said. "We think CDB investment is the simplest." CDB seemed to be the only bank that could take on the long-term risks, as Chi put it. "We very much hope that in the future we can raise money from the market, but from the current situation, because African investment is long term and has high risks, that is difficult." Just like the investments CDB had made in China over the last decade, the market seemed not capable of financing the initial investment needed to build up the projects. The fund hopes to reach $5 billion eventually and by 2012 had promised $2 billion of investments across 30 countries and 60 projects.[22]

The fund takes only minority stakes in projects alongside other Chinese investors and aims for Chinese firms to give capital and technology as well as experience to local partners—much as did foreign firms in China's development. "We believe our investments will benefit the local economies because we structured it as a win–win solution," Chi said, using an overused cliché of Chinese officialdom. "The project can generate benefits to the investor and on the other hand it can generate benefit to the local community. Only in this way can the project be sustainable and contribute to the local economy. We dub this as blood generating rather than blood transfusing." Because of its minority investment but strong state backing, the fund can have a multiplier effect, according to Davies. He estimates it could originate $50 billion of investment to Africa if it could get to $5 billion in size, adding in the co-investment and the debt portion. "That is investment; that's not charity, it's investment into the continent and that's wow! That's never mind other money that's in the pipeline from CIC [China's sovereign wealth fund] and all other sorts of private businesses as well."

CDB is the force behind the fund. As an article in the business newspaper, *21st Century Business Herald*, said: "If you cooperate with them, you not only get capital from the fund, you can also apply for loans from the parent company. Also they have strong connections with the business and political community."[23] The fund itself says its model is "investment + loan." Many of the Chinese partners are partners that CDB has already funded. In February 2012, for example, the fund signed an agreement with Xinjiang Goldwind Science & Technology, a wind turbine manufacturer, to develop the African market. CDB had given the company a $6 billion credit line in 2010 for international expansion and signed another agreement for 35 billion yuan in January 2011. CADF also formed a venture with carmaker Chery Auto, based in the city of Wuhu in Anhui Province, to set up factories in Africa. As we saw in Chapter 1, CDB helped the local government set up a financing company to hold its equity in Chery in 1998. No other private equity fund in the world could count on such a large state-owned bank as its backer.

The Chinese government doesn't interfere with the decisions of the fund, Chi said. The fund also does not seek to control or take a controlling stake, and the exit period is five to eight years. The fund will supervise the operations but will not be involved in day-to-day operations. For every investment, it sets up a joint venture offshore—often in the Cayman Islands, as in the case of South African miner Wesizwe Platinum—and makes the equity investment with the venture. Still, the fund maintains "direct" communication with the embassies in the African countries for investment deals and has regular briefing sessions, according to the *21st Century Business Herald*.[24] The article said that the fund steering committee is co-chaired by the Ministry of Commerce and the Ministry of Foreign Affairs, and the committee's office is under the Ministry of Commerce's West Asia and Africa division. Representatives to the meetings also include the Ministry of Finance, the National Development Reform Commission (China's powerful economic planning agency), and the financial regulators: the central bank, the banking regulator, the State Administration of Foreign Exchange, and, of course, CDB. Each can send one ministerial representative. One or two meetings are held every year and the steering committee provide policy guidance while not interfering with daily operations. "If the projects interfere with sensitive or material or economic or diplomatic policy, then they have to listen to the steering committee," the newspaper explained.

Chinese expatriates in Ethiopia are eager to have the fund make investments, because they recognize that they can take all the profit while the fund bears the losses. Although the fund is commercial, how can anyone not see the money as money from the state? In the West, there simply is nothing equivalent to CADF. The closest, according to Deborah Brautigam, is likely the British Commonwealth Development Corporation, which has been around since the 1940s.[25] (See Table 3.2.) CADF's investments are large and increasingly influential. For example, it took a 45 percent stake with Chinese metals company Jinchuan Group

Table 3.2   Other Private Equity Investors in Africa

Fund Name	Fund Size
China–Africa Development Fund	$1 billion, targeted $5 billion
British Commonwealth Development Corporation	4.1 billion (Assets: £2.6 billion, 2011)
Proparco's FISEA fund	$307 million (€250 million [2010])

Source: Company annual reports; CADF.

in Wesizwe Platinum in South Africa, a country that is the world's largest platinum producer.

Not all the fund's mining ventures have been successful. In May 2010, Chinese-listed mining company Zijin Mining and the fund offered to pay $284 million for Platmin Congo Ltd. to gain copper and cobalt assets in the Congo. The deal was called off months later when Zijin Mining was involved in regulatory probes and cleanup for acid-laced waste leakage in a river in southern China that killed enough fish to feed 72,000 residents a year, not a promising sign for Africans expecting environmentally friendly investments.

And in Ethiopia, a glass factory cut its production.

Ethiopian prime minister Meles had stood with the Chinese ambassador beneath the chimney tower and large warehouses of the factory on the outskirts of the capital Addis Ababa in May 2009. It planned to export glass throughout East Africa and create 300 jobs. Meles, wearing a dark-gray suit and sunglasses, declared: "This factory is the beginning of a glorious path of cooperation in industrialization between Ethiopia and China."[26] It was a classic example of Meles' focus on development to reduce poverty.

The factory now lies empty, next to yellow, standard five-story subsidized housing beside broken streets where workers wait for buses. It will reopen with lower production and was too ambitious, according to Chi. It was expected to produce 40,000 tons of glass per year, but that was too much for the local market, which can use only 20,000 tons a year, Chi explained. The fund considered exporting to neighboring regions, but transportation difficulties made that impossible. "I think it is possible for manufacturing to develop in Africa," Chi said. "However, the manufacturing industry should not be confined to its local market; it should integrate or incorporate a regional dimension in terms of marketing base. This is different from China. Because China is a huge country, it has a huge market with a huge population, it can consume or digest the products of its own manufacturing companies, but African countries are much smaller."

On a weekday in April 2012, the factory was quiet with no workers seen on the site. The investment was by CGCOC Group, which has mainly been involved in construction. "This project has promoted local infrastructure, housing construction, employment, and people's livelihood," according to CADF's promotional literature. Chi said that with the development of Ethiopia's economy, the demand will increase, and if the factory reaches its production target, it will make money. Was this going to be a white elephant reminiscent of the projects built by Western lenders that littered Africa in the 1960s and 1970s? Notably, when China built the new African Union building in the center of town, all the glass was flown in from China.

Rising Role of China in Africa

In December 2011, Chen Yuan sent Shanghai-based scholar Yu Xiangdong to Paris as the bank was planning power project investments in Côte d'Ivoire and Senegal, former French colonies in West Africa. Chen told the Chinese delegation to listen to the French to see what they think and find out if they are "really anti-China," Yu recalled. The French media often criticized China as being new colonialists in Africa. The CDB delegation visited three French construction companies in their imposing offices on the Champs Élysées, the city's main boulevard. The French companies said they had done business for 80 years in Côte d'Ivoire, or Ivory Coast, as it's known in English. Yet they said they couldn't find business in Africa because the Chinese companies got it, with their lower prices. "They asked us, 'What can we do about it?' " Yu said. "They said, 'Why are your prices so cheap?' " The French wanted to know what they could do. Yu decided to give them the truth: "You can never beat China; you can only turn yourselves into the IBM of construction." By that he meant that the French couldn't compete against Chinese companies in building railways and power grids. IBM doesn't make hardware anymore. The French have 80 years of experience in West Africa, but the Chinese have just arrived. He admitted that the Chinese don't understand the local society, the politics, and the environment. "Why don't you provide a consulting report about the political, social, and environmental impact of the project?" he suggested. The Chinese side would pay the French a consulting fee. "You change into an IBM and provide consulting," Yu explained. After that the French managers brought all their mid-level managers into the room, more than it could hold. They were willing to transform now, they said, but wanted to know what Chinese companies they should approach. After the meeting, Yu's delegation went to the Foreign Ministry, where it had previously struggled to get a meeting. The foreign economic studies department was very happy. It said that the European Union had five projects in Africa all undertaken by French companies. "If you want to do these five projects, we're willing to give them to you," they said. "But consulting and planning the French will do, and you give us the money."

Chen Yuan previously had asked Yu to look into the problems African countries faced after independence from colonial powers in the 1950s. Yu told Chen that one of the biggest political problems was the rule of dictators and the loss of exports. At that moment Chen stood up, Yu remembered. "Right now the situation has completely changed," Chen said, because of a large demand from China for Africa's products. China's demand would push up the prices of Africa's large commodities, such as fuels and mining minerals, with prices for metals more than tripling in the past decade. This was the beginning stage: At the same time, African countries had started to use Western aid more efficiently and were moving toward democracy. The next stage meant an increased demand for infrastructure and development of industrial production of raw materials. But the Africans don't have the skills to develop the infrastructure; nor does the West, which turned its back on that type of investment years earlier. "They [the West] don't have experience of massive urban construction in a short period," Yu said. "They need 10 years to build one road." Chen Yuan believed that the bank needed to combine China's experience of infrastructure and long-term lending. And once Africa's economies take off, the growth will create new markets and demand for China's goods. Chen believed the situation had changed forever because of China's demand, Yu said.

China now is lending more to developing countries than the World Bank, the traditional lender that has dominated development thinking for decades.[27] Its financing for infrastructure in Africa is also on a par with the traditional donors and the private sector. China has imported Africa's commodities and resources and sent it cheap manufactured goods, with Angola now the second largest supplier of China's oil. African countries have benefited from the rising oil prices that China has helped cause, with China's demand pushing oil prices up between 2000 and 2007 by up to 27.1 percent, according to the World Bank.[28] The continent has exported oil, iron ore, copper, and coal, while African imports of Chinese goods have risen over 15-fold in the first decade of this century. Over 80 percent of the lending of the Exim Bank, the other policy bank along with CDB, has been to resources.[29] Exim Bank, which like CDB relies on selling bonds to raise funds, alone has lent some $67.2 billion to Africa from 2001 to 2010, according to Fitch Ratings estimates, more than the World Bank.[30] CDB has outstanding loans to Africa of $13.7 billion, Yuan Li, the bank's vice president, said in July 2012, up from $5 billion at the end of 2010, although it doesn't release annual figures on its lending to Africa.[31] That number doesn't count CDB lending to many of the Chinese state-run companies that have invested on the continent. As CDB has done at home, much of the African lending is about creating new markets for companies. Many are those that CDB has backed for years: Huawei in telecom, carmaker Chery Auto from Wuhu, the state-owned oil majors such as Sinopec, and dam makers like Sinohydro Group. In July 2012, Chinese President Hu Jintao pledged $20 billion in new loans to Africa for infrastructure and manufacturing, as Europe was still reeling from a prolonged debt crisis. "The West has turned to poverty reduction and not used these loans to generate business," Brautigam said. "They haven't really seen Africa as a place for business, except for extraction. The Chinese see a lot of different areas have potential—extraction but other things as well."[32]

China's aid to Africa began in 1956 and grew out of Mao's ambitions to lead the developing world. In the 1970s, China provided support for national liberation movements and by mid-decade had even more aid projects in Africa than the United States.[33] Although Africa dwindled in importance to China in the 1980s, after the 1989

Tiananmen Square crackdown, the developing world and Africa became a more important part of China's policy. "China's Africa aid is characterized by no strings attached, noninterference in others' internal affairs, and focusing on infrastructure construction," according to Wang Cheng'an, former deputy director of Department of Aid to Foreign Countries of Ministry of Commerce, reciting Chinese foreign policy mantras chapter and verse.[34] Such thinking follows from the "Five Principles of Co-Existence," which was formulated in 1954 and stipulated "reciprocal non interference in internal affairs." (China does set certain conditions, however, and many countries receiving aid cannot recognize Taiwan.)

CDB has also taken its lessons from financing local governments at home, where it has gone in and built projects and a credit culture in tandem with local officials where nothing existed before. "Traditional banks would look at a project's cash flow and return," CDB vice president Li Jiping said at a conference on overseas investment in Beijing in November 2011, and decide not to do a project. CDB, however, "believes we have to cultivate a project; if we do not cultivate and create safe conditions, we can never make the project successful." Success to CDB also means a market outcome. As Chen Yuan recognized in the Three Gorges project, a dam can produce electricity and electricity can be sold. In the Congo in March 2011, CDB signed a deal that would improve Congo's road and rail networks as well as the mining, energy, agriculture, and manufacturing industries. Such package lending allows CDB to create conditions for its loans to succeed; if one project fails, the others will subsidize it. As Chen Yuan put it about local governments in China, "Package loans are aimed to balance cash flow and lessen identified risks, so as to make good projects better while remedying those requiring correction."[35]

The World Bank estimated in 2009 that Africa needs to invest $93 billion in infrastructure every year to meet national development targets, still short of what China allocated to infrastructure during the last 20 years.[36] CDB's experience building infrastructure in China, such as the Three Gorges Dam, its ability to assess a complicated project and lend for the long term, make it a perfect fit. The market for new infrastructure is available, too: CDB's involvement in lending to Africa started after a period in the 1990s and early 2000s when, under former

World Bank head James Wolfensohn, the World Bank was focused on poverty reduction, not infrastructure, a process that had started in the late 1960s and 1970s and was further spurred by the attention of environmental nongovernmental organizations. The view of infrastructure as key to economic growth is not new; Western lenders had that view after World War II. As the new lender, CDB has a chance to learn from the lessons of the past.

Fixed Capital: Western-Style Lending

In September 1950, the World Bank announced two loans to Ethiopia, its first loans for Africa. A total of $5 million was pledged for a road program and $2 million in foreign exchange was promised for a new development bank. The bank had sent a mission to the country for six weeks in March that concluded that the priorities were highway improvement, telecommunications, and the establishment of a development bank to support industry and agriculture.[37] The first telecommunications loan was made in 1951. The World Bank began much like the Chinese banks today, financing infrastructure, such as dams and other projects that could generate income. As one China Exim Bank official said over 60 years later in 2011, the bank invests in infrastructure that "directly benefits the people" on the ground, such as railways, roads, bridges, and telecommunications.[38] "The reigning orthodoxy of the time held that the accumulation of fixed capital—of factories, machinery, and roads—was the key to development," Sebastian Mallaby wrote in his history of the World Bank.[39] "Poor countries, after all, had large numbers of underemployed people, so labor scarcity did not appear to hold them back; capital scarcity was the bottleneck." Such capital scarcity was similar to the problem faced by China in the 1980s. A total of 80 percent of the World Bank's portfolio from 1948 to 1969 was for power and transportation, roughly $2.9 billion.[40]

By the time former US defense secretary Robert McNamara took hold of the World Bank in 1968, it had moved toward focusing on poverty, which meant shifting money to projects in agriculture, rural development, and social services. Africa was littered with white elephants, and the focus on growth seemed to have failed.[41] In the

1960s, the government of Ghana built a shoe factory, a sugar factory, and a glass factory that never went into production.[42]

As the World Bank turned away from its initial focus on infrastructure, in the 1970s and 1980s, Western banks went on a lending spree in the developing world, recycling oil money from the Middle East. Between 1970 and 1986, the average debt-to-export ratio for developing countries had more than tripled from 127 percent to 463 percent. African economies financed their deficits by borrowing abroad to counter the global downturn, leading to a buildup in foreign debt and then growing inflation. (See Table 3.3.) Once Mexico announced in August 1982 that it could no longer service its debt and defaulted, international banks withdrew their credit. Global commodity prices collapsed, and as developed countries raised interest rates, the cost of the loans indexed to short-term rates rose. Rising interest rates meant that most money was going to repaying debt rather than productive investments. This caused governments to borrow at home, leading to growing deficits, and forced them to turn to the IMF and the World Bank, which introduced their often-controversial structural adjustment and stabilization programs. In the 1980s, debt in sub-Saharan Africa doubled, and real per-capita incomes were lower at the end of the period than at the beginning.[43]

While Chen Yuan's father, Chen Yun, advocated that China cross the river while feeling for the stones, the West took a different approach

Table 3.3   Africa's Debt History

Country	Years of Default and Rescheduling
Algeria	1991
Angola	1985
Central African Republic	1981, 1983
Côte d'Ivoire	1983, 2000
Egypt	1984
Kenya	1994, 2000
Nigeria	1982, 1986, 1992, 2001, 2004
South Africa	1985, 1989, 1993
Zambia	1983
Zimbabwe	1965, 2000

Source: Carmen M. Reinhart and Kenneth Rogoff, *This Time Is Different: Eight Centuries of Financial Folly.*

to Africa: Countries were urged to implement austerity and liberalize prices all at once. As China's planners believed in the 1980s, excessive or too-quick market liberalization could be a disaster if countries had not built up strong enough institutions. Even though the World Bank had written the handbook on development banks in 1957, it turned against them as hindering the private sector and called for a greater role of the private sector in development.

The 1980s debt crisis and the advent of free market beliefs in Reagan-era America and the Thatcher-era United Kingdom allowed the World Bank and the IMF to dominate Africa's policy making. By 1995, 37 sub-Saharan countries had received at least one World Bank adjustment loan, and 33 had two or more loans.[44] Loans were tied heavily to conditions such as structural change, freeing of prices, and privatization as well as macroeconomic stability. The economic beliefs that underpinned such loans lasted long into the following decade. In 1997, Ethiopia and its Prime Minister Meles were engaged in "heated debate" with the IMF, as former World Bank chief economist Joseph Stiglitz recounted,[45] because the fund had suspended its lending program, despite the country's good macroeconomic results, due to worries about its budget. The IMF had also criticized Ethiopia for repaying a loan to an American bank early and not telling the IMF. "The IMF felt that countries receiving money from it had an obligation to report everything that might be germane; not to do so was grounds for suspension of the program, regardless of the reasonableness of the action," Stiglitz wrote. Ethiopia's banking system at the time was smaller than that of Bethesda, Maryland, measured by assets, yet the IMF wanted to open the country's financial markets to Western competition. "To the Fund, a liberalized financial system was an end in itself," he wrote.

Although the conditions set by the World Bank and the IMF made a lot of sense in terms of reducing debt, the African countries didn't have the political institutions to carry them out. Only in the late 1990s did many countries get rid of their debt burden, through the Heavily Indebted Poor Country initiative and the Multilateral Debt Relief Initiative. Today, 29 countries have completed the entire process, including Ghana.[46] "I think China has learned from the mistakes at the World Bank and the IMF, and I think the conditionalities often were counterproductive and were an important ingredient in the deindustrialization," Stiglitz told us in

Beijing in March 2012. Can the Chinese make sure a large buildup in debt doesn't happen again?

African Tiger: Can Ghana Escape the Resource Curse?

In June 2007, as oil prices had begun an escalation that would see them rising to over $140 a barrel, the UK company Tullow Oil and US company Kosmos Energy announced that they had discovered 600 million barrels of light oil off the coast of Ghana, one of Africa's most successful democracies.[47] Tullow's shares rose 10 percent on the news, one of the biggest oil finds of recent times in Africa. Tullow started pumping the oil in late 2010, and by 2011 output from the Jubilee field was 70,000 barrels of oil per day.[48] "Oil is money, and we need money to do the schools, the roads, the hospitals," the former Ghanaian president John Kufuor told the BBC.[49] "Even without oil, we are doing so well already. Now, with oil as a shot in the arm, we're going to fly." Later he said that Ghana would be an "African Tiger." On the fiftieth anniversary of diplomatic relations with China in September 2010, Ghana's then-president, John Atta Mills, discussed financing agreements with Chinese president Hu Jintao. And so, in April 2012, Ghana's vice president went to Beijing to sign the first tranche of a $3 billion loan with CDB, the biggest loan in the country's history and representing 8 percent of its 2011 GDP. It was also in discussions with China Exim Bank for a $6 billion loan. To put that in perspective, the World Bank's International Finance Corporation lent a total of $2.2 billion to all of sub-Saharan Africa in 2011. "This is the single largest loan Ghana has taken; actually it's the single largest credit facility to an African country," former Vice President John Dramani Mahama said in the Kempsinki Hotel in Beijing in April 2012 after signing the first part of the CDB loan.

Ghana, a former British colony previously known as the Gold Coast for its natural deposits of gold, was the hope of Africa with Kwame Nkrumah's declaration of independence in 1957. In 1964, it was where Chinese premier Zhou Enlai laid out China's theory of aid in a speech. Despite Nkrumah's efforts to build an industrial state, by the early 1980s, Ghana's economy had stagnated. Average income fell by one-third between 1970 and 1983,[50] and the country borrowed heavily in the 1980s to offset declining government revenues. Ghana's debt-to-GDP ratio was 120.5 percent in 2001; thanks to international debt relief, it fell to 17.6 percent in September 2007.[51] Agreed debt relief by the World Bank and the IMF totaled $3.7 billion, and China later forgave $24 million of debt. A 2002 BBC article announcing the relief referred to Ghana as a "poverty-stricken West African country."[52] Yet, the country has also enjoyed a remarkable turnaround. It held successful elections in 1992 and since then has enjoyed two decades of peaceful rule. Over the past 15 years, the economy has grown by 5 percent per year, with annual growth in income per person of 2.6 percent per year,, and in September 2007, it sold a bond to international investors (see Figure 3.1). It has received the equivalent of gold stars from all the multilateral institutions. But if a copy of Oxfam's 2009 report on Ghana and its oil passed across CDB's desk, the country would seem one of the riskiest places on earth to lend money to.[53]

Oil in Africa—in Gabon, Nigeria, and elsewhere—has not led to tangible benefits for the poorest people, Oxfam said, listing a litany of problems that could appear, from unsustainable public spending sprees to hollowing out of nonoil industries, known as the Dutch disease. The report called it a "difficult and tortuous journey to move from the generation of oil wealth to its proper investment." The history of oil in Africa is one of dividing people, as depicted in Nicholas Shaxson's book, *Poisoned*

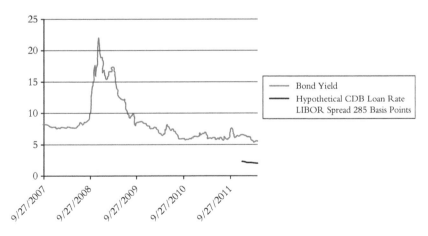

Figure 3.1 Ghana's Ten-Year Bond Yield

Source: Bloomberg.

Wells.[54] "Resources like oil and gas should be a blessing for countries that produce it. Norway and Britain seem to have done well out of their oil-fields, but in Africa the record is different. Producing oil seems to be a bit like taking cocaine: if you are already healthy it might invigorate you, but if you are weak or sick, as many African countries are, it can do you serious harm."[55] He might have pointed out that it has also not been great for debt repayment: Despite having huge reserves of oil, Nigeria has defaulted on its external debt five times since achieving independence in 1960.[56]

Similar to many African countries in the past that have found oil, the natural resource promises an easy change. Ghana's economy, which has been dependent on exports of cocoa and gold, was recalculated in 2010, pushing it into the lower-middle-income category. It is the only country in West Africa to have escaped low-income status, with per-capita GDP raised by $500 to $1,300. At a press conference in Beijing in April 2012 officials from Ghana talked about how power had constrained their development and said the loan would allow them to "relaunch their industrialization." They forecast that the oil would add $1 billion annually to their national revenues. It meant that new infrastructure could be built that needed to be built, the most urgent thing being a gas pipeline onshore, so the gas produced from the oil wells was not flared or wasted. But there was a hitch: As it had borrowed mainly from the IMF and the World Bank in the past, Ghana was still constrained by that "concessional" financing, even though it had moved up from being considered a poor country. As a result of a three-year IMF loan, or extended credit facility, given on July 2009, Ghana had to submit to a series of strict benchmark targets, including structural reform and regular reviews to continue getting the money. A limit on the amount of nonconcessional debt taken on, common to the IMF's assistance to so-called low-income countries, was included. Ghana had to ask the IMF to waive this limit for the CDB loan, which was commercial in terms.

The loan was agreed to in China in September 2010. Despite the need for the gas pipeline, it was signed only on December 6, 2011, two days after the IMF had approved raising Ghana's borrowing ceiling from $800 million to $3.4 billion, a more than threefold increase. Chinese officials, who had tried to cooperate with the international institutions, saw this delay as insulting. "I'm not sure why this loan was shelved for over one year. Ghana is now in a crucial phase of development. This is similar to China 30 years ago; they need foreign assistance to develop basic infrastructure," the Chinese ambassador to Ghana was quoted as saying in Chinese media.[57]

CDB has made sure that Chinese companies will benefit from nearly all of the loan's proceeds. The loan stipulates that Chinese contractors must implement projects worth 60 percent of the loan amount. The loan is strict in its conditions and is certainly not free money: Split into two tranches, the Bank of Ghana must pay interest every six months into CDB accounts opened in Hong Kong and pegged to the six-month London Interbank Offered Rate (LIBOR), a rate heavily influenced by what's going on in the fickle global markets. The rate is 295 basis points above LIBOR for the 15-year loan and 285 basis points for the 10-year loan, and includes a 1 percent commitment fee every year on the undrawn amount of the loan. (See Table 3.4). Ghana also has to ensure that it has a cover of 1.5 times each repayment in a debt service reserve account at all times. The country's legal fees were $400,000. The list of projects provided for by the loan is long, and Chinese companies are heavily involved. It includes the liquid petroleum gas (LPG) processing project, to be built by Sinopec and operated by the Ghana National Gas Company; a port project; a railway rehabilitation project; a western corridor gas infrastructure development project to transport natural gas from the oil fields for power generation; a free zone project to be built by China Hasan International; and an eastern corridor road project being built by a Ghana-based company and Jiangxi Corporation of China. A so-called off-taker agreement obliges Ghana National Petroleum Corporation to sell 13,000 barrels of oil a day to Unipec Asia, a subsidiary of state-owned Sinopec, for 15 years and 6 months, longer than the term of the loan, so that CDB can ensure that it gets paid. Unipec will make the payments into a petroleum holding fund in Ghana.

At the Beijing Kempinski Hotel, Ghana's vice president, John Dramani Mahama, who became president in July 2012 after the sudden death of Mills, talked with us after the signing of the first tranche and having lunch with Chen Yuan. "The process for accessing World Bank and IMF credit unfortunately has been quite tiresome," Mahama, a bulky and ebullient man in his early 50s, wearing a black-and-white thread shawl, said. "They come with a lot of strings, and the procedure for accessing the credit goes through quite a bit of rigmarole, and so it's not easy. We still continue to rely for multilateral funding on the World

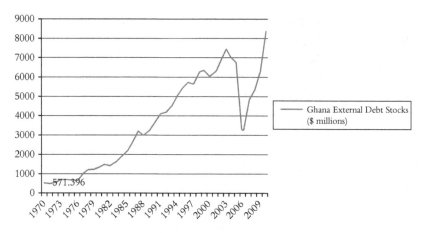

Figure 3.2   Ghana External Debt
Source: World Bank.

Bank and the IMF. But we still [need] quite some massive amount of money for investment in infrastructure and we find it's easier to go to the BRIC countries [Brazil, Russia, India, and China]." The rate on the CDB loan is competitive, he said, and it would not be possible to get the same terms on a loan from the West. "With the World Bank and the IMF you will get credit for, say, shoring up your foreign reserves, which is a good thing," he said. "Now, what we're looking for is investment in building our economic infrastructure. With the current financial crisis, it's very difficult to go anywhere in this world and get $3 billion. And yet these are infrastructure projects that we need to put in place in order to move Ghana to the next economic level." The loan would also create hundreds of thousands of jobs, he said, rising up in his chair. "Rail workers are going to be at work again, loaders, station men, signalmen are going to go back to work. Our railways have been dead for many years now."

The loan highlights the different perceptions of debt sustainability between CDB and the World Bank/IMF. CDB looks at the return of the individual projects and figures that the gas project alone can cover from 80 percent to all of the loan amount, with most of the money going to Chinese contractors. CDB pays loan disbursements directly into project contractors' accounts and does due diligence on each project, according to the agreement, ensuring that the money doesn't go through the Ghanaian government or local firms. Chinese companies undertaking the projects can feel relieved because they are getting payments from CDB. The IMF, in its debt sustainability analysis of Ghana published in November 2011, however, considers Ghana's overall fiscal and economic condition when looking at the debt, especially the fiscal revenues that the projects produce. Chinese have also countered that the IMF and World Bank don't consider the growth the loans will produce. It is as if China and Western institutions are using different baselines; China is looking at the enormous growth that its own economy has produced while Western institutions are more likely to consider Africa's recent history. And China will also get oil as collateral; as in Venezuela, it doesn't matter about political institutions if there is oil, as oil flows whether there is political strife or not. As Nicholas Shaxson pointed out, West African oil has pumped steadily since the 1950s, and new leaders don't want to rewrite contracts for fear that their assets will get caught up in foreign courts. "What we've done in this financing as much as possible is take the credit for projects that can potentially repay that credit," Mahama said. "So if you look at most of the areas where the credit is going for the port expansion, the port will be able to raise more revenue and pay the investment over time. If you look at the western railway line, it's going to move manganese, bauxite, cocoa, and other such projects and is going to earn revenue and potentially pay."

Mahama was eager to avoid the impression that it was an oil-for-loan deal, although this model of paying oil into an escrow account was used before by the Chinese and Western banks in Angola. The oil will be sold at market price, and the loan can be paid off from any other source, he said. "We could have sold it to anyone else, and they pay the amount of debt service into the escrow account. It's not like the oil is really tied to the loan in that sense in terms of collateralization." Rather, the Chinese have the right to take the cash flow produced from the oil, what is known in the industry as receivables, in case Ghana can't pay. Still, at the press conference in Beijing after the loan signing, Mahama said Ghana had the ambition to become a major oil producer. "Going forward we see Ghana becoming a significant player in the oil and gas industry in Africa. Estimates going forward in the next five to ten years are that we can potentially produce between 500,000 and 600,000 barrels a day." He paused, then added, "I hope."

The loan has been heavily debated by think-tanks in Ghana and by opposition politicians in the run-up to the country's elections in

December 2012, a sign of the strength of its democracy. CDB has released no information on the loan and held no press conference, but it risks becoming an issue in Ghana's domestic elections. The opposition New Patriotic Party has said that it would renegotiate the CDB loan and has criticized its up-front management fees and the fact that 60 percent of the work must go to Chinese contractors.[58]

Just as the IMF was about to increase Ghana's borrowing limit, Fitch Ratings said in November 2011 that the country's rising debt levels are a concern. The country's debt ratio is increasing to where it was when it got debt relief and was at 41.7 percent of GDP in August 2011 compared to 37.8 percent in the previous December, Fitch said.[59] Ghana is rated B+ by Fitch Ratings, the fourth-highest junk assessment and one level lower than other African oil producers, such as Nigeria, Angola, and Gabon. "The discovery of oil does put Ghana in a fairly positive light," Richard Fox, the head of Middle East and Africa sovereign ratings, told Bloomberg. "But until they can demonstrate they can keep their fiscal house in better order we've taken a view it's not going to join other African oil producers at the BB− level."[60] The IMF said in its debt sustainability analysis of November 2011 that a ratio of 40 percent "does not provide strong buffers against shocks."

A May 2011 IMF study that looked at 150 low- and middle-income countries from 1973 to 2008 found that the discovery of resources did not help poor countries due to their weak institutions.[61] But in countries with good governance, oil can lead to higher economic growth. Ghana, as a democracy, has time to debate how to deal with its oil and absorb the lessons of other West African nations to decide how best to use this resource—to keep it transparent and avoid making it the only cash cow in the economy. There have also been successful examples of resource use in Africa, such as diamonds in Botswana, a country that has been growing steadily since the early 1970s after the first diamond mine opened. Still, that often sounds easier on paper than in practice. We asked Shaxson whether he thought Ghana could escape the resource curse. "Direct distribution is the only solution that inverts all the power relationships. Everything else—oil funds, better management of spending, and so on— are in my view just tinkering around on the margins," he said in an e-mail. "The problem is oil wealth will tend to undermine those very institutions that are supposed to be defenses against the problems."

Western banks have provided oil for loans across Africa before, from Angola to Nigeria, but no other Western bank could provide such a

Table 3.4   Ghana B+ (Fitch) Loan Rates

Loan	CDB Loan Rate	Conditions
CDB Tranche A, 15 years	6-month LIBOR plus 2.95%	60% to Chinese contractors Commitment fee: 1% per annum. Grace period: 5 years
CDB Tranche B, 10 years	6-month LIBOR plus 2.85%	
World Bank	6-month LIBOR plus 0.7% (for loans of maturity 12 to 15 years, signed after April 2012)	Front-end fee: 0.25%
JPMorgan bond spread for Africa	233 basis points (2.33% above benchmark rate)	

Source: Ghana Government, Bloomberg, International Bank for Reconstruction and Development.

package that allowed for contracts for a whole swath of companies from the same country in one fell swoop, from oil companies to road construction firms. Normally in the West, a construction company can bring along the finance, but other actors from other countries might be involved. China also has much greater demand for oil, the product of the loans, than the West ever did. The CDB conditions, while strict, do not require the regular and detailed reporting that the IMF's lending does, such as "quantitative performance criteria" and other fiscal and macroeconomic targets since the loans go to Chinese contractors rather than the government and are secured by resources. Their purpose is different, and CDB's deal unlocks new business for Chinese firms. While CDB makes sure that Ghana's infrastructure is upgraded, its CADF opened an office in Ghana in November 2011 to provide equity financing. ZTE and the fund are involved in a project with Shenzhen Energy Investment Co., which has committed to build a 200-megawatt gas-fired plant in Ghana, and CADF will hold 40 percent of shares in the venture. And telecom firm Huawei, which CDB has long supported, is installing a cable from the capital Accra to Tamale in the north at a cost of $30 million, part of the construction of Ghana's fiber optic cable. The loan had perfectly combined CDB's strategic priorities of seeking resources, building infrastructure in the host country, and helping Chinese firms to go global. Now it's up to Ghana to decide how to best use the projects.

Fresh Capital

James Mwangi, the chief executive of Equity Bank Ltd., one of Kenya's biggest lenders, was in a buoyant mood at the World Economic Forum's "Summer Davos" meeting at a cavernous conference center the size of a small city on the outskirts of Tianjin in 2010. His bank had signed a 4 billion shilling loan agreement with CDB in May. The loan allowed Equity Bank to lend to small and medium-sized companies for half the normal interest rate in the country, he said. The bank paid 3 percent to CDB over six years for the loan, less than the 5 percent lending rate in China in 2010. "You can't get that kind of loan globally," he told us. "It was a very low-price loan. The ease with which you can get the loan is not the traditional terms and conditions. You draw as you need. We structured it that way—we match the drawing with the disbursements, so that we don't pay interest when we are not earning."

China's lenders offer a new hope to African economies, but it will be up to African leaders to leverage the capital, much as China used foreign investment in the 1980s and 1990s to transfer technology and build up manufacturing and other industries that are now taking on the world. China has also promised to increase imports from Africa and to improve the terms of trade. CDB has experience making loan deals across the globe, propelled by its state-owned connections and using experienced Western lawyers, such as UK-based Linklaters and US firm White & Case, to make sure it gets the best deal. Indeed, such is the volume of CDB's international business that the bank provides law firms with special computers to use for secure communication. As much as China talks of mutual equality, lenders have considerable power over borrowers. Can African countries ensure *their* institutions are strong enough to get them the best deal?

In many ways, Chinese capital from CDB is advantageous. CDB believes in the ability of investment to stimulate growth, after decades of the West trying to save Africa through aid and social programs. China's investments in Africa are similar to the West's in Asia in the latter half of the twentieth century, which led to decades of economic growth. China knows what it is like to develop its economy starting from nothing, with no markets. It still has a strong state sector so it is unlikely to talk about privatization and free markets. And unlike the IMF and the World Bank, there is much less chance for Africa's institutions to be hollowed out by talented people leaving to work for CDB, as the bank hires no foreigners and doesn't offer cushy sinecures in Washington and New York.

But China's noninterference policy will be tested. CDB under Chen Yuan acts like a bank, not a government agency and, as such, expects a return on its investment. As CDB's loans to Africa rise, it will have a strong interest to protect its assets, including oil and energy supplies, leading CDB to get involved in domestic politics whether it wants to or not. And in democracies like Ghana, CDB can't avoid its money entering the discourse of domestic politics and parliamentary debate. Africa loses some $150 billion a year due to corruption, according to an African Union report.[62] Can the Chinese really keep their hands clean in oil-rich states when so many have failed in the past? Increased transparency is the answer to avoid the siphoning off of money. Although it is not the way that things are done at home, transparency will help China and help Africa. CDB has no official public relations department and rarely publishes any details on its lending to Africa, including in its annual reports, even though the bank is a signatory to the United Nations Environment Programme Financial Initiative and publishes annual social responsibility reports.

Like the local governments in China, when governments of Africa and Latin America borrow from CDB, they are borrowing from the sovereign. The penalty for not paying back the loan is likely to be more difficult and catastrophic than not paying back a Western bank. For a decade, China's two main policy banks, Exim Bank and CDB, have monopolized overseas lending. When Chen Yuan travels overseas to Africa or Latin America, he sits at the front of government delegations next to the top Communist Party official—surely a visual symbol to poorer borrowers with weaker institutions that they are dealing with the might of the party, which has uncontested power over the second largest economy in the world. Many of CDB's loans are tied to short-term indices, such as six-month LIBOR, which can rise quickly, as Africa found out in the 1980s. Africa may need to broaden its sources of capital to other emerging countries, such as Brazil and India, who are increasingly offering competition to China's lending.

■ ■ ■

In Ethiopia, CDB is helping Chinese companies, from private to state-owned, shift manufacturing to Africa as labor costs rise at home. In

Ghana, it is using its experience funding local governments at home to build much-needed infrastructure so that the country can benefit from China's demand for resources. Africa faces its best prospects for growth since independence from colonial powers some 50 years ago. Still, a rise in capital inflows, combined with resources such as oil, has led Africa to difficulties in the past, and the continent will increasingly be vulnerable to changes in Chinese demand as its economy slows. Nowhere is overdependence on CDB's capital more clear than in Venezuela, where one resource, oil, has dictated an entire political relationship.

Notes

1. World Bank, "Light Manufacturing in Africa," http://go.worldbank.org/3XIDRTFJA0

2. Ibid.

3. Ibid.

4. Liu Wei, "Chinese Aid Transforms Addis Ababa Skyline as AU HQ Rises," *ChinAfrica* 4 (February 2012).

5. Interview in Addis Ababa, April 2012.

6. http://www.2merkato.com/201204251154/gcg-to-build-skyscraper-in-ethiopia

7. Telephone interview, June 2012.

8. Deborah Brautigam, *The Dragon's Gift: The Real Story of China in Africa* (Oxford: Oxford University Press, 2009).

9. Justin Yifu Lin, "Leading Dragons Phenomenon: New Opportunities for Low Income Countries to Catch Up," April 23, 2012, http://blogs.worldbank.org/developmenttalk/leading-dragons-phenomenon-new-opportunities-for-low-income-countries-to-catch-up

10. Justin Yifu Lin, "Africa Means Never Saying Goodbye," March 22, 2012, http://blogs.worldbank.org/developmenttalk/africa-means-never-saying-goodbye

11. Justin Yifu Lin, WIDER Annual Lecture 15: "New Structural Economics." Viewable at http://vimeo.com/24252747

12. World Bank, "Light Manufacturing in Africa."

13. Ibid.

14. Dexter Roberts, "Chinese Export Machine Gets Upgrade as Sany Cranes Replace Toys," Bloomberg News, April 6, 2012.

15. Justin Yifu Lin, "Leading Dragons Phenomenon: New Opportunities for Low Income Countries to Catch Up," April 23, 2012, http://blogs.worldbank.org/developmenttalk/leading-dragons-phenomenon-new-opportunities-for-low-income-countries-to-catch-up

16. Telephone interview, April 2012.

17. Deborah Brautigam and Tang Xiaoyang, "African Shenzhen: China's Special Economic Zones in Africa," *Journal of Modern African Studies* 49, no. 1 (2011): 27–54.

18. Audra Ang, "China Defends Dealings with Africa," Associated Press, October 31, 2006, www.washingtonpost.com/wp-dyn/content/article/2006/10/31/AR2006103100666_pf.html

19. Ibid.

20. Telephone interview, April 2012.

21. 穆东，"中非发展基金拓展海外业务合作双赢局面初步形成，" Xinhua News Agency, January 11, 2011, www.cnstock.com/index/gdbb/201101/1097118.htm

22. "中非基金已承诺在非投资20亿美元，" Xinhua News Agency, July 18, 2012.

23. 昝春燕，"中非发展基金这半年，" *21st Century Business Herald*, June 12, 2010, http://www.21cbh.com/HTML/2010-6-14/4MMDAwMDE4MjA4MQ.html

24. Ibid.

25. Brautigam, *The Dragon's Gift*.

26. Ethiopia Hansom International Glass Plc website, http://hansomglass.com/

27. See FT research, http://www.ft.com/cms/s/0/488c60f4-2281-11e0-b6a2-00144feab49a.html

28. Quoted in World Bank, "East Asia and Pacific Economic Update," 2012, Vol. 1.

29. Lucy Corkin, "Redefining Foreign Policy Impulses Toward Africa: The Role of the MFA, the MOFCOM and China Exim Bank," *Journal of Current Chinese Affairs*, April 2011, 61–90.

30. "The Africa-China Connection, Special Report," Fitch Ratings, December 2011.

31. http://www.cdb.com.cn/web/NewsInfo.asp?NewsId=4189

32. Telephone interview, April 2011.

33. Ian Taylor, *China's New Role in Africa* (Boulder, CO: Lynne Rienner, 2009).

34. Liu Wei, "China Continues to Assist with Africa's Development and Strives to Improve the Way Its Aid Is Managed," *ChinAfrica* 4 (February 2012).

35. Chen Yuan, "Development Financing and China's Urbanization," 2005, www.cdb.com.cn/English/NewsInfo.asp?NewsID=1174

36. "Africa's Infrastructure: A Time for Transformation," World Bank, November 2009, http://web.worldbank.org/WBSITE/EXTERNAL/COUNTRIES/AFRICAEXT/0,,contentMDK:22386904~pagePK:146736~piPK:146830~theSitePK:258644,00.html

37. Edward Sagendorph Mason and Robert E. Asher, *The World Bank Since Bretton Woods* (Washington, DC: Brookings Institution Press, 1973).

38. Zhu Xinqiang, speaking at the Latin America China Investors Forum conference, Beijing, September 2011.

39. Sebastian Mallaby, *The World's Banker: A Story of Failed States, Financial Crises, and the Wealth and Poverty of Nations* (New Haven, CT: Yale University Press, 2005).

40. Nkunde Mwase, Yongzheng Yang, "BRICs' Philosophies for Development Financing and Their Implications for LICs," International Monetary Fund, IMF Working Paper No. 12/74, March 2012.

41. Dambisa Moyo, *Dead Aid: Why Aid Is Not Working and How There Is a Better Way for Africa* (New York: Farrar, Straus & Giroux, 2009).

42. Mallaby, *The World's Banker*, p. 45.

43. Per-capita income in sub-Saharan Africa declined at an average annual rate of 2.2 percent during the 1980s while exports were stagnant; see: Mohsin S. Khan, Simeon Inidayo Ajayi, "External Debt and Capital Flight in Sub-Saharan Africa," International Monetary Fund, 2000.

44. Devesh Kapur, John P. Lewis, and Richard Webb, *The World Bank: Its First Half Century* (Washington, DC: Brookings Institution Press, 1997).

45. Joseph E. Stiglitz, *Globalization and its Discontents* (London: Penguin Books, 2002).

46. Steven C. Radelet, *Emerging Africa: How 17 Countries Are Leading the Way* (Baltimore, MD: Center for Global Development, 2010).

47. "UK's Tullow Uncovers Oil in Ghana," BBC News, June 18, 2007.

48. Ekow Dontoh, "Ghana's Jubilee Producing 70,000 Barrels a Day, Tullow Says," Bloomberg News, May 3, 2012.

49. "Ghana 'Will Be an African Tiger,'" BBC News, 19 June 2007, http://news.bbc.co.uk/2/hi/africa/6766527.stm

50. Radelet, *Emerging Africa*.

51. Martyn Davies, "How China Delivers Development Assistance to Africa," Centre for Chinese Studies, University of Stellenbosch.

52. "Ghana Gets Debt Relief," BBC News, February 27, 2002, http://news.bbc.co.uk/2/hi/business/1843958.stm

53. "Ghana's Big Test: Oil's Challenge to Democratic Development," Oxfam America, 2009.

54. Nicholas Shaxson, *Poisoned Wells: The Dirty Politics of African Oil* (New York: Palgrave Macmillan, 2007).

55. Ibid., p. 5.

56. Carmen Reinhart and Kenneth Rogoff, *This Time Is Different: Eight Centuries of Financial Folly* (Princeton, NJ: Princeton University Press, 2009).

57. 非洲向中国寻贷, 商报网, May 8, 2012.

58. William Wallis and Lionel Barber, "Ghana Opposition Says China Loan Is Poor Value for Money," *Financial Times*, April 27, 2012.

59. "Ghana's Rising Debt a Concern, Curbing Rating, Fitch Says," Bloomberg News, November 28, 2011.

60. Ibid.

61. Burcu Aydin, "Ghana: Will It Be Gifted or Will It Be Cursed?" IMF Working Paper (May 2011).

62. "Corruption 'Costs Africa Billions,'" BBC News, September 18, 2002, http://news.bbc.co.uk/2/hi/africa/2265387.stm

Chapter 4

Risk versus Reward

China Development Bank in Venezuela

The more important metric is the debt service capability, not necessarily the absolute amount of debt or debt-to-GDP. . . . Oil is very simple to drill. You drill a hole, put in a pipe and it comes out! And then you ship it. So Venezuela's debt service ability is very strong.

—*China Development Bank Advisor Liu Kegu, Interview, March 2012*[1]

The revision of the Outlook to Negative reflects Venezuela's weakening policy framework, which has resulted in increased vulnerability to commodity price shocks and deterioration in fiscal and external credit metrics as well as rising political uncertainty related to the 2012 political cycle.

—*Erich Arispe, Fitch Ratings report, April 2012*

Einstein was said to have quipped that insanity was doing the same thing over and over again and expecting different results. China Development Bank (CDB) is putting about a third of its overseas lending into Venezuela—$40 billion and counting—and drawing in with it dozens of Chinese companies that have collectively received more than $96 billion in financing or promises of future lending from the bank. All this in a country with a sovereign credit rating five notches below investment grade that Moody's Investors Service puts lower than Albania's and just above Argentina's, a country which defaulted on its international debt in 2002.[2]

China's plunge into Venezuela is sui generis. No developing country has received a greater number of loans in such a short time than CDB has provided the government of President Hugo Chávez since 2008. By way of comparison, US aid to Iraq from 2003 to 2006 totaled $28.9 billion, and its postwar aid to Germany from 1946 to 1952 totaled $29.2 billion in 2005 dollars. Although some of that money was in the form of grants, not loans, the totals give a sense of the enormity of CDB's undertaking.[3] CDB is betting that two centuries of investor sorrows in Venezuela are a thing of the past. This time will be different. That begs the question: Is CDB insane to expose itself to so much risk in Venezuela?

Chen Yuan and Liu Kegu, his gesticulating and highly expressive point man for Venezuela, might retort that past performance—in Venezuela's case, awful for generations of investors—is no guarantee of future returns. CDB, Chen says, has caught on to the secret of smart lending in developing countries—loans collateralized by the revenues from the sale of oil. We caught up with Chen at the annual summit of BRICS nations (Brazil, Russia, India, China, and South Africa) on the southern Chinese island of Hainan in April 2011 and asked him about the risk associated with lending to countries with a history of political instability. "We believe at CDB we have in place a comprehensive risk control mechanism. Most of the loans are related to the commodity trade, and as we see oil prices are rising and China as one of the major importers of oil, and we think to put in place a servicing mechanism such as oil for loans, we are effectively keeping the risks to a minimum level," he explained.

In just three days in February 2009, as Western banks were tottering on the brink of collapse and global oil demand had dropped, China signed oil-for-loan deals with Brazil, Russia, and Venezuela backed by CDB. It's easy to see why CDB is leading the charge to secure oil supplies for the motherland. Its mandate is to support the state, and it is doing just that. As China becomes an urban nation and its middle-class consumers buy more cars and take planes, it will have to import increasing amounts of oil. A projected tripling in the number of cars and trucks on Chinese roads by 2020 will only increase the demand. China buys more than half of its crude oil from overseas and is the world's second-largest importer after the United States. That has led it to seek supplies across the globe, from Sudan to Angola, Brazil, and Venezuela. The total amount potentially available from those deals in just three days was some 600,000 barrels a day, equal to 17 percent of China's 2008 imports. CDB loans are a crucial part of these deals, locking the countries into supply contracts that make them increasingly dependent on China's purchasing power and the revenue sources the commodity sales bring their treasuries. China imported $200 billion of oil in 2011, up from $12 billion in 2001. The agreements are "win-win" as long as the deals last because the countries get much-needed funds for their development and China gets fossil fuels to drive its expansion. Venezuela's oil is "at the service of China," President Chávez said in February 2009.[4]

Flattering words. But Chen and his bank would be well served by taking a close look at two centuries of Venezuela's tortured relationship with foreign creditors.

Default in Bolívar's Country

For a young man with grand ambitions, the mineral-rich nations of Mexico and the new state founded by Simón Bolívar on South America's northern tier offered a route to fortune and fame. If he could convince his countrymen of the wisdom of buying shares in mining companies focused on the region, fortune would be his. The homeland needed the resources that the nations of Latin America had in abundance, and those countries were desperate for capital. It was a perfect match. If the countries put behind them years of wars and revolution, investing in the region was prudent, the young man wrote. The speculative bubbles that plagued past investors in the region in the previous century were a thing of the past, he believed.[5]

The year was 1825. The young man was Benjamin Disraeli, future prime minister of Great Britain. Disraeli's shares in Latin American mining companies plummeted as speculators realized that the dreams of riches from the region far exceeded the reality. In a bid to prop up the share prices, Disraeli wrote a series of pamphlets—the nineteenth century's version of analysts' reports—arguing that the South American–focused investment craze that had ruined many a British punter 100 years earlier, the infamous South Sea Bubble, would not be repeated this time. To no avail. Disraeli's investment scheme ended in failure.[6]

In Venezuela, one of the nations formed when Bolívar's Gran Colombia dissolved following his death in 1830, Disraeli's lesson was learned again and again by generations of investors in the next two centuries. In 1902, President Cipriano Castro refused to pay the country's international debts, mostly to Europe, leading to a naval blockade by Britain, Germany, and Italy. The discovery of oil in 1922 only exacerbated the tension, leading to runaway spending and increasing debate on how to divide the revenues between foreign oil companies and the state. In retirement at a secluded villa in Caracas, Juan Pablo Pérez Alfonso, one of the founders of the Organization of Petroleum Exporting Countries (OPEC) in 1960, called oil "the excrement of the devil" after seeing the effect it had on the country.[7] In 1989, the International Monetary Fund (IMF), US Treasury, and commercial banks bailed out Venezuela so it could service the $33 billion in international debts it had accumulated in the spending spree that accompanied the surge in oil prices in the 1970s, made unserviceable by the price collapse in the 1980s. Canadian and US investors over the first decade of the twenty-first century have seen their investment in the country's massive Las Cristinas and Las Brisas gold deposits disappear after Chávez, who came to power in 1998, nationalized their claims.[8] In 2003, Chávez, who views founder Bolívar and his dreams for a United Latin America as his idol, moved onto the oil industry after taking control of state oil company, Petróleos de Venezuela SA (PDVSA), and using it as his cash cow for social spending. After two centuries of sovereign defaults, runaway inflation, and nationalized industries, global ratings agencies give Venezuela junk bond status. (See Table 4.1.)

China's Venezuelan Adventure

That history doesn't bother Liu Kegu. He sees the world divided between those who have resources and those who don't and need them, a chance for countries to enter complementary relationships. No more so than in

Table 4.1 Venezuela: Years of Default and Rescheduling

Period	Default/Rescheduling
1978–2008	1983, 1990, 1995, 2004
1875–1899	1892, 1898
1850–1874	1860, 1865
1825–1849	1826, 1848

Source: Carmen M. Reinhart and Kenneth S. Rogoff, *This Time Is Different: Eight Centuries of Financial Folly* (Princeton, NJ: Princeton University Press, 2009).

Latin America. "God is not fair; he gave Brazil vast land, water resources, mineral resources, and oil, but what we have is people," he said with a raspy laugh at a March 2012 interview in Beijing. "We need to be more diligent and smart." This time, Liu said, it will be different. Countries can benefit from the higher-priced commodities that China's demand creates, he said, and with its resources—the country has the world's largest oil reserves[9]—as the price of oil increases, Venezuela can easily increase production. It's hard to leave a meeting with Liu believing otherwise. Rail thin, ramrod straight, with a booming voice and sporting a close-cropped flattop, Liu could easily have been a US Marine Corps drill sergeant had he been raised 12 time zones to the west. Born in 1947, he spent five years during the Cultural Revolution of 1966 to 1976 clearing farmland in the northern reaches of Heilongjiang Province near the Russian border. After returning to Beijing in the late 1970s, Liu enrolled in Renmin University, studying economics, and after graduating quickly rose through the ranks of the government and the Communist Party, serving as a top official in northeastern China's Liaoning Province from 1996 through 2002, his last year as deputy to then-governor Bo Xilai. It was a time when the rust belt industrial area—once China's industrial heartland—shed millions of workers in the process of shattering the so-called iron rice bowl of government-endowed social benefits to state-owned companies. For the past decade, Liu has worked under Chen Yuan at CDB as a vice president, and since 2007 as advisor. In Venezuela, Chávez has given him a new title: brother.

And why not? Liu comes bearing gifts in the form of loans, $40 billion and counting since 2008, about a third of CDB's entire overseas loan portfolio and about a fifth of its foreign-currency loans, all to a country of 27 million people that can only borrow on international markets at rates that rank it among the riskiest in the developing world.[10] CDB's loans to Venezuela amount to about $1,400 for every man, woman, and child in the country, dwarfing those of any other institution. What's more, the scores of Chinese companies coming into Venezuela are almost without exception big recipients of CDB loans, with at least 10 Chinese companies having secured more than $96 billion in combined loans or lines of credit from CDB to finance their global expansion and operations inside of China.[11] Venezuela is using the loan proceeds to go on a buying spree in China. It acquired phone networks from ZTE Corp., railroads and housing complexes from CITIC Group, power stations from Sinohydro Group, and, of course, oil refineries and pipelines from China National Petroleum Corp. (CNPC) and China Petroleum & Chemical Corp., better known as Sinopec. When he first went to Venezuela in 2005, Liu said, the airplane flight was empty. Now, you have to book in advance due to the companies that have investments there. Such business will, in turn, improve the country's tax intake and fiscal income and allow it to pay back the loans, he said.

We caught up with Liu in March 2012 in Beijing, where he was attending the Chinese People's Political Consultative Conference, a collection of billionaires, academics, national minorities, and other groups that meet in the capital for ten days each year at the same time as China's national legislature. Liu leads CDB's delegations to Venezuela, often with hundreds of officials in tow, planning infrastructure projects and making macroeconomic policy recommendations for Chávez's government. In the days prior to the interview, Liu laid down one ground rule. He didn't want to talk about the politics of the loans.

Yet how could politics stay out of it? Venezuela has been ruled by a charismatic, virulently anti-American strongman who has used an oil boom to erode checks and balances on his power and Chinese money to fund social programs, as well as wean the country from overdependence on the United States. While Liu could take solace that Chávez considered him his *hermano*, as CDB increased its lending, he was both battling cancer and facing an election for a third six-year term in office, which he said would be spent "furthering the path to socialism."[12]

Chávez, a former army officer who was imprisoned for two years in the 1990s after a coup attempt, considers Fidel Castro his ideological mentor. He has led Venezuela since 1998, winning headlines for his rants against the United States—he once called former president George W. Bush the Devil—and his hours-long televised programs. He fought off a coup attempt against him in 2002, which he blamed on the United States, among others. In 2007, he moved to nationalize Venezuela's oil assets, leading to the exit of US energy giants Exxon Mobil Corp. and ConocoPhillips from the country and a flurry of lawsuits. In a speech at the time, he boasted: "Today is the end of that era when our natural riches ended up the hands of anyone but the Venezuelan people."[13]

It wasn't to be. Five years later, China's state-controlled energy giants Sinopec and CNPC are exploring for oil and building refineries and pipelines in the country, which must sell an increasing percentage of its crude oil exports to China. CNPC was pumping 200,000 barrels a day in Venezuela by 2012 and planned to increase that to 800,000 barrels a day by 2017.[14] A leaked memo from the state-run oil company shows that Venezuela must sell China 430,000 barrels of oil a day merely to service its debt. Liu seems unconcerned about the danger that nationalization may someday be used against Chinese oil assets in the country. As he got up to leave our interview, Liu praised Chávez's nationalization of the oil industry as a move to bring more of the country's oil riches to the Venezuelan people. Liu told us Chávez's focus on harnessing oil revenues to help the poor through free housing and food was "extraordinary." "What he's done is amazing," Liu said. "He's a people's president."

In early 2012, Chávez shuttled back and forth between Caracas and Havana, where in June 2011 he had surgery to remove a baseball-size tumor from his pelvic area. Should he leave power, what guarantee does China have that the country will honor its Chinese debt obligations? CDB has tried to make sure its loans benefit the whole country, not just Chávez, and has made the terms commercial so they seem fair to any post-Chávez government, according to a lawyer who has worked with the bank.[15] Still, the loan details have not been published, increasing suspicion from the opposition, and some of the money has been used for targeted social spending that boosts Chávez's support, such as slum housing. Would keeping Chávez in power be a safer route to making sure the money is paid back? Erica Downs, a scholar at Washington's

Brookings Institution who studies CDB's energy deals across the world, considers the bank's decision to devote such a large percentage of its overseas loan portfolio to Venezuela a mystery. "CDB is a bank that especially at home—and you can make a case abroad too—prides itself on getting paid back and making sure that it doesn't end up with any nonperforming loans. If that is your objective, is Venezuela the country you want to lend to?"[16]

A post-Chávez government may very well seek to renegotiate the CDB loans, Moises Naim, a former Venezuelan trade minister who is now a scholar at the Carnegie Endowment for International Peace in Washington, said in an interview. Two approaches might emerge. One is a move to renegotiate terms more favorable to Venezuela. Another approach that an opposition-led government may take is to classify the CDB lending as "odious debts." It's a concept articulated by Alexander Sack, a tsarist-era Russian lawyer who argued in 1927 that debts incurred by despotic states are not for the common good but to strengthen the state and repress opposition. The point of promoting the concept of odious debts in international law is to make lenders pay more attention to the character of the regimes they are lending to and to free new governments from the burden of paying off illegitimate debts of past despots. After Saddam Hussein's fall in 2003, the Canadian non-governmental organization Probe International argued that the more than $100 billion in debts accumulated by his regime were odious and the new Iraqi government shouldn't be expected to repay them. Iraq argued the same, and much of the debt incurred to Western nations was forgiven.[17] "There is a whole doctrine about what could happen if a successor government to Chávez comes and feels that the terms and conditions of the Chinese deal were too onerous and not aligned to the international interest but were just a Chávez government kind of trick," Moises said.[18]

Yet with politics excised from the discussion like one of Chávez's tumors, China's decision to plunge headfirst into Venezuela is simple and is strikingly similar to Disraeli's own reasoning. "We have lots of capital and lack resources, they have lots of resources and lack capital, it's complementary," Liu said. Since the loans are guaranteed by oil shipments, CDB can afford to make them at rates far below what US or European banks, which are constrained by Organisation for Economic

Co-operation and Development (OECD) rules on risk premiums, can offer. CDB, being a policy bank tasked with carrying out the goals of the state, is helping further China's goal of securing energy supplies through the deal. Even better, since so much of the proceeds of the loans is being used to buy Chinese goods and services, from Huawei phones to CITIC-built railroads, China wins twice, and CDB helps foster another Chinese goal, pushing its top companies to "go out" (走出去) and become globally competitive multinationals. Liu said the loan agreements CDB signed with Venezuela, drafted with the help of international law firms, don't obligate Venezuela to buy Chinese goods and services with the proceeds, unlike a similar but smaller 2009 agreement with Brazil and the one finalized in 2012 with Ghana that we saw in Chapter 3. About one-third of these loans are denominated in yuan, also called renminbi (RMB), and with such RMB loans, it is "convenient" for Venezuela to use them to buy from China, Liu said. China's plan for Venezuela, as carried out by CDB, is all encapsulated, Liu said, in a 600-page book written by CDB that Chen handed to Chávez at the September 2011 meeting in Caracas, which served as the opening scene for this book. CDB "is helping us a lot not only with financing but also with advice on long-term strategic planning," Chávez said after the meeting.[19] The strategic plan covered the period from 2010 to 2030; the next ten years alone would require around $600 billion in investment, Chávez said.

A lot of international bankers agree with the assessments of Chen and Liu that CDB is being prudent in Venezuela, efforts that will help ensure the loans remain in place should Chávez leave power. Luis Moreno, head of the Inter-American Development Bank, told us CDB has been "very savvy" in the way it set up its loans with Venezuela, even insuring that repayment guarantees are codified in Venezuelan law. "To my knowledge the Chinese are the only ones doing this," Moreno said. "I don't know of any other development bank that can do the kinds of things they are doing because it is both development and it is strategic for China. It's got the two angles." CDB takes "the long-term view," Moreno said. "The reserves of oil in Venezuela are very, very strong. They can weather the storm."

Even a US banker burned by bad Venezuelan debt under governments much friendlier to the United States than Chávez's has praise for CDB's approach. William Rhodes is a Spanish-speaking former top executive at

Citibank who spent years in the country at offices in Maracaibo and Caracas, married a Venezuelan, and helped negotiate the Brady Plan, named after then–US Treasury secretary Nicholas Brady, to restructure Latin American debt in the late 1980s. "They've been careful in the case of Venezuela," Rhodes said of CDB's strategy at a meeting of the World Economic Forum in Dalian, a coastal city in northeastern China. "They've been very hard-nosed in a number of cases and I think correctly so."[20]

Loans for Oil

A program that wins the praise of such seasoned bankers deserves more explanation. CDB's loans to Venezuela, as well as to Ecuador (a country with a credit rating even lower than Venezuela's), Russia, and Brazil, are guaranteed by commitments by state oil producers to sell a set amount of oil to Chinese oil companies. The Chinese companies, most often subsidiaries of CNPC or Sinopec, usually buy the oil at market rates from the national producer, in Venezuela's case, PDVSA, depositing the proceeds in the CDB account. For Venezuela, the CDB account holder is the country's development bank, the Bank for Social and Economic Development (BANDES). CDB then deducts its loan payments from that account.[21] BANDES and CDB agreed to set up a joint China–Venezuela investment fund in 2007, with China contributing two-thirds. CDB put in an initial $4 billion in 2008 and agreed the following year to inject another $4 billion. An August 2010 signing ceremony at the Diaoyutai State Guest House in Beijing, where President Richard Nixon stayed during his historic 1972 visit, was the occasion for CDB's biggest overseas loan ever. The dual-currency loan consisted of a $10 billion dollar-denominated amount as well as a portion denominated in RMB, amounting to 70 billion yuan. That agreement was followed by two more loans from CDB in 2011, a $4 billion replenishment of the joint investment fund signed in June 2011 and a loan to PDVSA in November 2011. In May 2012, CDB agreed to replenish the fund with $4 billion, bringing the total amount CDB has lent to Venezuela since 2008 to at least $40 billion.

The best way to look at CDB's lending to Venezuela is to view it as a claim on future Venezuelan oil shipments, according to Naim. "Analyzing the Venezuelan loans in comparison to other bank activities is not the best way," he said. "This is essentially a call option; this is a futures contract to procure oil. That's what it is."[22]

China isn't the first country to employ oil-for-loans financing. Japan in the 1980s had a loans-for-oil agreement with China, before China became a net oil importer in 1993.[23] The amount of oil countries commit to send to China usually generates income considerably greater than the amount needed to service the loan, especially given the 25 percent surge in oil prices from the end of 2009, a year many of the oil-for-loan agreements were signed, to the end of 2011. Prices continued to surge in 2012, topping $100 a barrel before falling back midyear to about $80 a barrel. For Venezuela, its commitment to send about 419,000 barrels of oil a day to China comes to about $15.3 billion a year in revenue at $100 a barrel, or close to half of its total outstanding loans to CDB.

Chávez's use of oil revenues to fund social programs is siphoning off investment from the country's oil revenue, however. From 2006 through 2010, Chávez directed state oil producer PVDSA to fund $53 billion to import food, construct housing, and build health-care clinics, among other projects, according to company financial statements. Oil minister and PDVSA head, Rafael Ramírez, wrote in an internal memo to Chávez in April 2011 that the country needed to restructure its oil deliveries to China, which amounted to one-sixth of production, because PDVSA was not getting any revenue from the arrangement as the funds were earmarked for loan repayments. "The 419,000 barrels of oil a day sent to China in the first quarter of 2011 represents a very heavy financial burden for PDVSA and requires a structural solution," Ramírez said in the memo, which was released by opposition lawmaker Miguel Ángel Rodríguez.[24]

As a result, PDVSA wasn't investing in the infrastructure needed to realize its original plan to boost production to 5.8 million barrels a day by 2012. As of early 2012, the goal was to pump 4 million barrels by 2014. With production languishing at about 3 million barrels a day, PDVSA, and Venezuela, were paying a price for deferring investment in the oil industry, forfeiting about $10 billion a month in lost oil revenues, more than enough to have funded Chávez's social programs, serviced the Chinese loans, and invested in new capacity.[25]

The company has piled on debt to meet its social funding goals, borrowing on global bond markets at rates far higher than CDB's loans to BANDES. Debt surged 40 percent in 2011 to $34.9 billion. In

February 2011, PDVSA sold $3 billion in bonds with a 12.75 percent rate.[26] That compares to CDB loans to the country, set at anywhere from 0.5 percentage points to 2.5 percentage points above the London Interbank Offered Rate (LIBOR; about 1.5 to 3.5 percent at prevailing one-year LIBOR rates in early 2012). In November 2011, PDVSA signed an agreement to borrow $4 billion from CDB to increase production at its Petrosinovensa joint venture with CNPC. The loan will be repaid with oil shipments of 40,000 barrels a day, Ramírez said.[27] "When a company like Petrobras takes on new debt, everyone is happy," Ramírez said on national television on February 7, 2012, referring to Brazil's state-controlled Petróleo Brasileiro SA. "But they criticize us when we do. We get loans because our company is strong. The China Development Bank, for example, has a very rigorous way of qualifying a company for a loan."[28] PDVSA, along with joint venture partners that include CNPC and Sinopec, said it will need to spend $236 billion through 2018 to develop the crude oil fields in the Orinoco belt in eastern Venezuela.

Two months later, Fitch Ratings presented a very different picture of the risks associated with Venezuelan debt, warning that the country's sovereign credit rating may be cut because of surging off-budget spending, such as the CDB-funded joint investment fund, ballooning deficits, and increasing vulnerability to a slump in the price of commodities, including oil and gold.[29] That year, Fitch already rated Venezuela's debt as junk, four notches below investment grade, the same as Bolivia and Zambia.[30] Although CDB lends at less than 5 percent to Venezuela, the country's benchmark US-dollar-denominated bonds in mid-2012 yielded upward of 10 percent.

In November 2011, Ramírez said that Venezuela had modified the structure for oil shipments to China, with PDVSA receiving around $7 billion for its deliveries there that year. The public disclosure of his letter to Chávez highlights another phenomenon: the disparity between Venezuela's reported oil exports to China and China's own imports as reported by the customs administration. The upshot: It appears that the Chinese oil companies are selling a portion of their Venezuelan crude on the world market, undercutting China's claim that CDB's loans-for-oil program was an essential part of the nation's strategy of obtaining secure energy supplies. Venezuela doesn't regularly report its oil export figures to specific countries—Chávez's government considers the information a state secret—so the figures in Ramírez's letter are revealing.

At an average 419,000 barrels a day, Venezuela shipped 37.7 million barrels in the 90 days from January 1 through March 31, 2011. China's customs figures show the import of 21.1 million barrels of oil from Venezuela during that period, a shortfall of 16.6 million barrels of oil over three months. In February 2012, Ramírez said PDVSA wanted to double exports to China from 460,000 barrels a day to 1 million barrels a day by 2015. "China's national oil companies are physically taking delivery of increasing volumes of Venezuelan oil; what are they doing with it? If you look at what PDVSA says it delivers to CNPC or China Oil for any given period and you look at Chinese customs data for that period, there is a huge gap," said Brookings's Downs.[31] "What is going on is that China is a major trader of oil in the Americas. Most of that oil is never going to China. I think it is being stored and sold in the Americas. What does that do for China's oil security?" (See Table 4.2.)

That is exactly what is happening, said Yu Xiangdong of the Shanghai-based CDB-affiliated think-tank. China doesn't have the refining capacity yet to process heavy Venezuelan oil but the United States does, so the Chinese companies have sold much of the Venezuelan heavy oil in the North American market. Chinese companies can get so-called equity oil and take delivery of the same amount of crude from other sources closer to home.[32] Why would Chinese tankers take a month to cross the Pacific with Venezuelan crude compared to supplying it to refineries in Houston? "It's crazy to supply China from Venezuela," former Venezuelan trade minister Naim said.

Table 4.2   Venezuelan Oil Exports versus Chinese Customs Figures, January–March 2011 (barrels)

Month	January 2011	February 2011	March 2011
Venezuelan exports	12,989,000	11,732,000	12,989,000
Chinese imports	8,905,476	6,269,140	5,891,337
Difference	4,083,524	5,462,860	7,097,663

Note: China measures imports in metric tons. One metric ton of Venezuelan oil equals 6.685 barrels.
Source: China Customs Administration, Ramírez memo (average 419,000 billion barrels per day).

It may not be a phenomenon unique to Venezuela. Brazil's Petrobras secured a $10 billion loan from CDB in 2009, part of its global fundraising efforts to help pay for the development of offshore oil deposits. The 10-year loan has an interest rate of LIBOR plus 2.8 percent and is tied to shipments of 150,000 barrels of oil a day in the first year of repayment and 200,000 barrels a day in following years to a subsidiary of Sinopec. As of February 2012, Brazil had never met its export commitment to China, at least for shipments averaged over a month, an examination of Chinese import figures shows.[33] The closest Brazil came was in May 2011, when China reported receiving 805,266 metric tons of oil from Brazil, just shy of the 863,510 metric tons needed to meet the 200,000-barrel-a-day commitment. (One metric ton of Brazilian crude oil equals 7.18 barrels.)

The loan also has a stipulation that Brazil will spend $3 billion to buy Chinese oil equipment.[34]

CDB's lending is supporting China's goal of securing its energy supplies, but the bank won't lend money to any country unless they can sit down and analyze its development needs. For Venezuela, as with African nations, those needs are focused overwhelmingly on infrastructure. Liu said that was the focus of the book Chen gave to Chávez. Chinese companies are winning a big share. The projects they're undertaking, from dams, to ports, to highways, to railroads, are hard to describe as odious.

Cars, Housing, and Gold: Good Business for China

Chinese Mandarins, like officials anywhere in the world, are enamored of clichés. One of their favorites that we've seen several times in this book already is "win-win" (双赢), used with nauseating frequency to describe just about any agreement between two parties. But for China, its loans to Venezuela truly are win-win. China wins twice: It secures large deliveries of oil for its growing economy. Even better, much of the money loaned to Venezuela goes right back to Chinese companies in the form of contracts. The majority of these companies are state owned, and almost all are long-term clients of CDB. China's largest power supplier, state-owned State Grid Corp., has contracts to construct power-transmission facilities in Caracas, and telecommunications firm ZTE is building an offshore underwater cable. It is in Venezuela that all the components of CDB's development model come into play, as in the case of automaker Chery Auto, nurtured by a CDB-established local government financing vehicle (LGFV) in the Chinese city of Wuhu and guided abroad with CDB loans. In all, among 19 Chinese companies doing business in Venezuela that we looked at, six have won a total of $11.6 billion in government-tied contracts since 2008, representing more than one-quarter of CDB's lending to the country, according to their annual reports and bond prospectuses.

As elections approached in late 2012, Chávez vowed to resolve the country's housing deficit, making it a pillar of his campaign and igniting a boom in construction. Chinese companies benefited. Machinery, including hydraulic truck cranes, was imported from XCMG Construction Machinery Co., a state-controlled company with ties to one of China's biggest state-owned arms makers, to carry out Chávez's target to build 2 million homes by 2017. And in early 2012, PDVSA planned an oil-backed loan of $1.5 billion from Industrial and Commercial Bank of China for housing to be built by CITIC, China's biggest state-owned investment company. CITIC said in a bond prospectus that it is building 20,000 units of social housing in Venezuela that has received "high praise" from Chávez.[35]

Such projects have also garnered CITIC access to the country's most valuable natural resources. PDVSA agreed to transfer 10 percent of the PetroPiar venture it has with US energy company Chevron in the Orinoco heavy-crude belt to CITIC, as well as a stake in the Las Cristinas goldmine. Chávez had nationalized the gold industry following the cancellation in 2011 of a license held by the Canadian gold producer, Crystallex International Corp., which subsequently declared insolvency.[36] "I give thanks to God that socialist China exists," Chávez said in March 2011 on state television.[37]

Unlike their western counterparts, the full weight of CDB financial support often stands behind the Chinese companies. Not only are they winning contracts from a government that is borrowing money in unprecedented amounts from CDB, the companies themselves depend on low-interest CDB financing for their operations in China and across the globe. In all, the companies we looked at had received loans or lines of credit from CDB totaling $96.5 billion.[38] Take Sinohydro Group,

China's state-controlled dam builder. The company won $295 million in contracts in 2010 from the Venezuelan government to build power plants, irrigation systems, and, as its July 2012 Chinese-language bond prospectus put it, a "socialist agriculture development project" in the form of an ecological park.[39] In that same prospectus, the company reported total long-term loans of 7.86 billion yuan. More than half of that lending—4.4 billion yuan—was from two CDB loans made at 5.94 percent with maturities in 2032 and 2029.[40] In another example, state-owned China Railway Group won a $7.5 billion contract from the Venezuela Railway Authority in 2009 to build two projects in Venezuela. The company is also one of CDB's biggest customers.[41] In June 2012, the company received a combined $35.7 billion in financing from CDB, split between yuan and US dollar lending.[42]

Arguably no company has fared better than China CAMC Engineering Co., a CDB-supported Beijing-based company in which the Chinese government holds a minority stake. It oversees projects ranging from power plants to irrigation systems across the globe. Its 2011 annual report showed that the company garnered two-thirds of its 5 billion yuan in revenue from agriculture and energy projects in Venezuela. In all, the company has signed $1.68 billion in contracts since 2010 with Venezuela, the biggest involving the construction of a thermal power plant.[43] (See Table 4.3).

For Wuhu-based Chery Auto, which CDB helped fund by setting up a LGFV to hold its equity in 1998 in the Yangtze River city, the factories and business in Venezuela represent the fulfillment of CDB's philosophy of opening new markets for Chinese companies. Chery moved into Venezuela in May 2006, later setting up a factory in the state of Aragua that opened in August 2011, allowing them to avoid the country's strict import tariffs. It was the first Chinese automaker to move into Venezuela. Chávez gave the company's cars Spanish names of "Arauca" and "Orinoco," after two Venezuelan rivers, and made an Internet video speech for the factory opening. With Venezuela's fuel prices subsidized by its cheap oil and a growing population, the country represents an attractive auto market. As of June 2010, CDB was by far Chery's biggest creditor; the company had a 13.8 billion yuan line of credit, about a quarter of its total, with the second biggest line coming from fellow policy bank Export-Import Bank of China.

Table 4.3 Win-Win for China: Contracts in Venezuela

Company	Contract Purpose	Amount ($ M)	CDB Customer?
Sinohydro Group	Power plants	295	Yes
China CAMC Engineering Co.	Infrastructure, agriculture	1677	Yes
XCMG Construction Machinery Co.	Construction equipment	761	Yes
China Railway Group	Railroads	7500	Yes
CNTIC Trading Co.	Medical supplies	927	No
Second China Railway Construction Bureau Group Co.	Railroads	392.8	No

Source: Chinese-language annual reports.

Ecuador

Chinese lending in Latin America has taken off from almost nothing prior to 2008 to the point where, in 2010, its loan commitments were more than those of the World Bank, Inter-American Development Bank, and the US Export-Import Bank combined, according to a study led by Kevin Gallagher of Boston University.[44] Venezuela isn't the only country in Latin America that has been the focus of CDB lending. China has also extended its oil-for-loans program to Ecuador and Brazil. The model is also used around the globe, from Russia, to Ghana, to Turkmenistan, as a means for China to secure energy supplies and for its state-owned infrastructure companies to win contracts. China's money is secured by winning business for Chinese companies, rather than setting policy conditions on the borrowing country.

CDB is so confident about the soundness of its oil-for-loans program that it agreed in 2010 to lend Ecuador $1 billion in a four-year loan at 6 percent interest, two years after the South American nation, the smallest OPEC producer, defaulted on $3.2 billion of bonds. The debt had been sold as part of a 2000 restructuring after the country defaulted on its debt in 1999. President Rafael Correa, an ally of Chavez, considered them part of an "illegitimate" and "illegal" foreign debt. "These debts were imposed by force," he said in Quito in June 2009. "We have rebelled against the system that established odious, unfair, illegal, immoral debts."[45] In 2011, Ecuador borrowed another $2 billion from CDB in an eight-year loan to fund more public works projects. The CDB loans are in addition to $2 billion in oil-secured loans from CNPC and a $1.68 billion loan in 2010 from China Exim for a 1,500-megawatt hydropower plant in the Amazon region that will be built by Sinohydro.[46] As of June 2012, research firm IHS Global Insight estimated that Ecuador had borrowed $7.25 billion from China, including $3 billion from CDB. That comes to about $520 for every man, woman, and child in the country.

The lending from China meant that Ecuador could afford to forgo tapping international credit markets in 2012, Rafael Correa, the country's president, said in February 2012.[47] Seeking funds from the international markets would have been considerably more expensive. Only two countries in the world—Greece and Belize—have lower sovereign credit ratings in the wake of Ecuador's 2008 default, according to Moody's Investors Service. Ecuador's dollar bonds yielded more than 9 percent in August 2012. That meant the country paid about 3 percentage points less for its loans from China.[48] In June 2012, the country announced another $2 billion credit line from China Exim to build dams.

As in Venezuela, an increasing percentage of Ecuador's oil, which it relies on for about 41 percent of government revenue, has been earmarked for China, or at least for Chinese oil companies. That led one analyst at IHS Latin America to remark in June 2012 that "committing such a significant amount of Ecuador's future oil production to the Chinese market via loan agreements or export deals means that Ecuador will not be able to maximize revenue by selling oil to the highest bidder in the event of a future rise in international oil prices."[49] As with Venezuela and Brazil, Ecuador's oil shipments to China, as reported by China's customs bureau, may not match its commitments. The first $1 billion loan in 2010 came with a commitment to supply 36,000 barrels a day of oil to China. Since then, the country has borrowed at least $4 billion more in loans tied to oil. In August 2011, Ecuador shipped 163,876 metric tons of oil to China, according to Chinese customs statistics, the equivalent of 36,370 barrels a day. That's enough to fulfill the first $1 billion CDB loan but nothing else.[50]

Russia

Unlike Venezuela, Ecuador, and Brazil, Russia's oil exports to China don't come via tankers, which can be diverted elsewhere to markets closer to the production source, but via pipeline. Russia's oil exports to China, as reported by Chinese customs, appear to exceed its oil-for-loans commitments. In February 2012, Russia exported an average of 600,232 barrels of oil to China. That's more than the 300,000-barrel commitment that two Russian state-owned energy companies agreed to. In February 2009, CDB agreed to lend pipeline operator Transneft and national oil producer Rosneft a combined $25 billion. That follows a $6 billion CDB loan to Rosneft in 2005. In exchange, the companies agreed to provide oil to CNPC via a Siberian pipeline spur into China. The agreement calls for the Russian companies to supply to CNPC 300,000 barrels a day from 2011 through 2030. The negotiations for the deal took more than a decade and came to a conclusion with talks between Chinese Vice Premier Wang Qishan and Russian Deputy Prime Minister Igor Sechin. Both sides wrangled over the interest rate the Russian companies would pay on the loans, settling on the London Interbank Offered Rate plus a margin that varies inversely with LIBOR; Rosneft estimates that the interest rates average 5.69 percent a year.[51] The Russian companies sell the oil to China at market rates. Now, talks are focused on inking an agreement for Russia's OAO Gazprom to supply gas to China via a pipeline. Then–prime minister Vladimir Putin and Sechin met with Premier Wen Jiabao in Beijing's Great Hall of the People in October 2011 to push forward that agreement, with CDB vice president Gao Jian looking on.[52] (See Table 4.4.)

China in the Backyard of the United States

While oil-for-loans deals have been done by Western banks, such as Standard Chartered in Angola, for decades, China can, as Liu points out, bring the government, companies, and banks together to offer much more sizable loans. Such money, unavailable from international investors without a sizable cost, has helped bolster Chávez and allowed China to secure influence in Latin America's largest oil supplier, just as the United States has withdrawn politically, distracted by Iraq or Afghanistan, or chosen to ignore Chávez's outspoken antics. In 2006, the United States put Venezuela on a list of nations that was uncooperative in the war on terror. Chávez has long subsidized Cuba with cheap oil and hosted

Table 4.4   China Development Bank's Global Energy Loans

Country	Project	Amount ($ Bn)	Date
Venezuela	Dual loan facility/BANDES	$20.6	2010
Brazil	Petrobras	$10	2010
Russia	Pipelines/Rosneft	$15	2009
Russia	Pipelines/Transneft	$10	2009
Ecuador	Oil for loans	$1	2010
Ecuador	Oil for loans	$2	2011
Venezuela	Oil for loans/BANDES	$8	2008–9
Turkmenistan	Oil-loans/Turkmengaz	$4	2009
Venezuela	Oil for loans/BANDES	$4	2011
Myanmar	Gas pipeline	$2.4	2010
Venezuela	PDVSA/CNPC	$4	2011
Venezuela	Oil for loans/BANDES	$4	2012

Source: Erica Downs, Bloomberg.

leaders such as Iranian President Mahmoud Ahmadinejad. In early 2012, it continued to supply oil to Syria, despite international sanctions imposed after the country used military force to quell civilian dissent against President Bashar Al-Assad's government. In Chávez's eyes, his relationship with China has dealt a blow to the United States. As Moises Naim puts it, for Chávez, the goal of the CDB-facilitated loans-for-oil program was to diversify away from the Americans and create a strong alliance with China. "He still feels that the United States is an enemy. He feels that there is a rivalry between the United States and China. This is his way of aligning with those that are not the United States. This is a deal that has more to do with the United States than with China."[53]

The problem, like that of the rows of empty skyscrapers now dotting the Tianjin skyline, is one of hubris. In the case of local government debt, CDB might be guilty of ignoring basic laws of supply and demand. In Venezuela, it may be ignoring history. Oil has a way of ruining a country's institutions and severing the link between the taxpayer and the government, increasing the risk of political disruption and corruption. These characteristics have been heightened under Chávez, who has consistently sought to strengthen the executive branch and disable the natural checks of a democracy.[54] Backed by a tripling in crude prices over the past nine years, since taking over PDVSA and firing more than 18,000 workers, Chávez has used the company for his own social spending schemes, including missions to the poor, hindering its ability to be an efficient global oil company. Venezuela, which relies on oil for 95 percent of export revenue, now pumps less oil than it did in 1998, when Chavez was first elected.[55] At the same time, oil-based spending by Chávez has caused inflation to surge to over 20 percent. With the world's largest proven oil reserves, Venezuela can be assured of Chinese demand for oil for years to come. But does China, with CDB as its executor, really believe it is immune from two centuries of Venezuelan debt defaults? The Chávez government is pro-Chinese, but a new government may seek new terms with China, just as it has done with American oil and other investors in the past. Chen, speaking in Hainan, waves off the question. "I think it is safe to say that we have been successful in controlling our risks," he said.[56]

■ ■ ■

CDB's oil-for-loans program to Venezuela is unique in the world, for both the volume of its lending—$40 billion and counting—and the degree of benefits it bestows on China. The nation wins a dedicated supply of oil, and its companies, especially the biggest state-owned companies, win billions of dollars in new contracts from the Venezuelan government. CDB negotiates loans-for-oil agreements with countries around the world, from Russia to Ghana, but nowhere on the scale of Venezuela's borrowing. Although money is fungible, it's not hard to see that the CDB loans to Venezuela are being recycled right back into the hands of state-owned Chinese companies. In a way, it is corporate welfare, Chinese style. The companies get contracts from the CDB-funded Venezuelan government, and they, in turn, especially companies such as Huawei, ZTE, Chery Auto, and Sinohydro, receive billions of dollars in loans from CDB to fuel their overseas expansion. As we'll see in the next chapter, the unprecedented lines of credit that CDB has extended to China's telecommunications and clean energy companies are changing the global corporate landscape.

Notes

1. Authors' interview with Liu Kegu, Beijing, March 12, 2012.
2. Moody's Investors Service sovereign bond ratings as of August 5, 2012 as found on the Bloomberg Professional Service.

3. Congressional Research Service, Report for Congress, "US Occupation Assistance: Iraq, Germany and Japan Compared," March 23, 2006, www.fas.org/sgp/crs/natsec/RL33331.pdf

4. Steven Bodzin, "Venezuela, China to Boost Joint Crude Output 10-Fold," Bloomberg News, February 17, 2009.

5. Stanley Weintraub, *Disraeli* (New York: Truman Talley Books), 1993, p. 52.

6. Ibid, p. 53.

7. Cited in Daniel Yergin, *The Prize: The Epic Quest for Oil, Money and Power* (New York: Free Press), 1991, p. 507.

8. Nathan Crooks, "Venezuela to Develop Cristinas Gold Mine with China's Citic," Bloomberg News, February 24, 2012.

9. Venezuela has the largest proven oil reserves in the world with 296.5 billion barrels, according to BP Plc's annual Statistical Review of World Energy. Saudi Arabia held 265.4 billion barrels.

10. As of August 2012, Venezuelan government bonds yielded an average of 11.92 percent, the highest among major emerging markets after Argentina, according to Bloomberg.

11. Authors' research from company Web sites and bond prospectuses.

12. Nathan Crooks, "Venezuela's Chavez Uses National Address to Slam Opposition," Bloomberg News, July 14, 2012.

13. Simon Romero, "Chavez Takes Over Foreign Controlled Oil Projects in Venezuela," *New York Times*, May 2, 2007.

14. Nayla Razzouk, "China CNPC to Invest in Venezuela to Pump 800,000 Barrels a Day," Bloomberg News, June 13, 2012.

15. Interview, Beijing, July 2012.

16. Erica Downs, Interview in Washington, DC, July 19, 2011.

17. Patricia Adams, "The Odious Debt Doctrine and Iraq After Saddam," speech at the Department of Economics, Furman University, September 27, 2008, http://journal.probeinternational.org/2008/09/27/odious-debt-doctrine-and-iraq-after-saddam/

18. Moises Naim, telephone interview, June 20, 2012.

19. "MPPRE (Venezuela) Caracas recibe asesoria de Beijing en métodos productivos," www.mre.gov.ve/index.php?option=com_content&view=article&id=16150:mppre-venezuela-caracas-recibe-asesoria-de-beijing-en-metodos-productivos&catid=187:actualidad-en-portada&Itemid=44

20. William Rhodes, interview in Dalian, China, September 14, 2011.

21. Erica Downs, "Inside China Inc.: China Development Bank's Cross-Border Energy Deals," Brookings Institution, John L. Thornton China Center Monograph Series (March 2011), pp. 50–54.

22. Naim, interview.

23. Kevin Gallagher, Amos Irwin, and Katherine Koleski, "The New Banks in Town: Chinese Finance in Latin America," *Inter-American Dialogue* report, February 2012, p. 15.

24. "Chavez Misses $10 Billion a Month Curbing Oil Spending," Bloomberg News, February 16, 2012.

25. Ibid.

26. Bloomberg data, PDVSA 11-year bond announced February 10, 2011, obtained from Bloomberg Professional Service.

27. Jose Orozco, "PDVSA to Repay $4 Billion China Loan with Oil, Ramirez Says," Bloomberg News, February 29, 2012.

28. Nathan Crooks, "Venezuela's PDVSA Had Record Revenue of $128 Billion in 2011," Bloomberg News, February 9, 2012.

29. "Fitch Affirms Venezuela at 'B+'; Revises Outlook to Negative," Fitch Ratings Report, April 4, 2012.

30. Global Sovereign Debt Ratings from Fitch as displayed on Bloomberg Professional Service.

31. Downs, July 19, 2011 interview.

32. Yu Xiangdong, interview in Beijing, June 5, 2012.

33. Chinese Customs Figures as found on the Bloomberg Professional Service.

34. Downs, p. 49.

35. 中国中信集团有限公司 2012 年度第一期中期票据募集说明书. CITIC Group First Quarter 2012 Bond Prospectus, p. 54, http://cfdocs.btogo .com:27638/servlet/CfDocument/cfdoc?id=SD000000002044752000&file size=102400000&autodwld=0

36. Greg Chang, "Crystallex International Gets Protection from Creditors," Bloomberg News, December 23, 2011.

37. Daniel Cancel, "Chavez Taps XCMG to Reach Goal of 2 Million Homes," Bloomberg News, March 15, 2011.

38. Authors' research from Chinese-language company reports, bond prospectuses, and press releases.

39. 中国水利水电建设股份有限公司 2012 年度第二期中期票据募集说明书, p. 66, Sinohydro 2nd Quarter Report.

40. 中国水利水电建设股份有限公司 2012 年度第二期中期票据募集说明, p. 149, Sinohydro 1st Quarter Report.

41. China Railway Group company announcement on Hong Kong Stock Exchange, August 3, 2009.

42. Xinhua, 中国中铁与国家开发银行签署开发性金融合作协议, June 20, 2012, http://news.xinhuanet.com/fortune/2012-06/20/c_123309898.htm

43. CAMC Engineering 2011 Annual Report.

44. Kevin P. Gallagher, Amos Irwin, and Katherine Koleski, "The New Banks in Town: Chinese Finance in Latin America," *Inter-American Dialogue* (February 2012).

45. Stephan Kueffner, "Correa Says Ecuador to Review Other Debt After Bonds," Bloomberg News, June 12, 2009.

46. Nathan Gill and Henry Sanderson, "China Bank Approves $2 Billion Loan to Finance Ecuador Budget," Bloomberg News, June 28, 2011.

47. Nathan Gill, "Ecuador Scraps Planned Bond Sale on Increased China Lending," Bloomberg News, February 16, 2012.

48. Ecuador credit ratings from Moody's Investors Service as found on Bloomberg Professional Service, August 5, 2012.

49. Juliette Kerr, IHS Latin America Research Note, June 2012.

50. Thirty-six thousand barrels a day, from Downs, "Inside China Inc.," p. 57. One metric ton of Ecuador crude equals 6.88 metric tons.

51. Erica Downs, "Inside China Inc.: China Development Bank's Cross-Border Energy Deals," Brookings Institution, John L. Thornton China Center Monograph Series (March 2011): 40–44.

52. "Putin Says Russia Nears Deal on Supplying Natural Gas to China," Bloomberg News, October 12, 2011.

53. Naim interview, June 20, 2012.

54. See Javier Corrales and Michael Penfold, *Dragon in the Tropics: Hugo Chavez and the Political Economy of Revolution in Venezuela* (Washington: Brookings Institution Press), 2011.

55. The nation pumped about 2.72 million barrels of oil a day in 2011, according to BP's annual Statistical Review of World Energy, down 22 percent from 1998.

56. Press conference, Yalong Bay, China, April 14, 2011.

Chapter 5

Funding the New Economy

We are a private company. The government doesn't tell us what to do.

> —*Yingli Green Energy CEO Miao Liansheng, responding to a question about the company's $5.78 billion line of credit from China Development Bank, June 2011*

None of the G-7 countries provide[s] levels of financing anywhere near those of the China Development Bank. That keeps me up at night.

> —*Fred Hochberg, head of US Exim Bank, speech, June 15, 2011*

A blanket of smog shrouded the North China Plain on a June day, reducing visibility to a few hundred yards. Nothing unusual for the Beijing area. It was a typical midsummer, or midwinter, or midspring, or midautumn day. An Austrian reporter on the bus hurtling southwest from the capital toward the city of Baoding was alarmed. In Vienna, these pollution levels—over 200 on the US Environmental Protection Agency particulate scale and classified as "very unhealthy"—would have sparked a national emergency, he remarked. Beijing's urban sprawl soon gave way to farmland, with the contrast between the flawless and underused six-lane expressway and poor workers tending the land by hand a reminder of the China Development Bank (CDB)–led infrastructure boom and the imbalances it helped exacerbate. The bus was on its way to a place that offered a solution to China's pollution woes—the global headquarters of Yingli Green Energy Holding Co. Ltd., the New York Stock Exchange (NYSE)–listed Chinese solar company led by Miao Liansheng, a former People's Liberation Army soldier. About 100 miles southwest of Beijing, in the nationally designated alternative energy production base of Baoding that is Yingli's home, the smog persisted.

Yingli's headquarters is the embodiment of China's state capitalism even though it is a private company. A red banner reading "Pay Attention to Politics" hanging over the Tempe, Arizona, headquarters of First Solar Inc. might possibly spawn conspiracy theories. A poster congratulating the Republican Party on its 160th anniversary most certainly would. But at the sprawling Yingli headquarters, the Communist Party's ninetieth birthday in July 2011 was cause for celebration, and a rooftop banner did indeed exhort workers to "Pay Attention to Politics" (讲政治).

One of the most unusual scenes at the Yingli headquarters that day was the furious construction of new facilities, in this case a new national solar research lab. Not that the erection of new buildings is a rare sight in China—the country is one vast construction zone, thanks in no small part to CDB loans—but for a solar company in the midst of a crushing global downturn spawned by massive new capacity from China and declining subsidies in Europe, building new facilities was at best bold, farsighted, and counterintuitive and at worst dangerously out of tune with market demands.

Miao, short, gruff, squat, and dressed in his signature blue coveralls, takes the counterintuitive tack, sounding more like a socialist planner than the chief executive officer (CEO) of a company listed on the NYSE. Declining prices for solar panels "isn't a bad thing, it's a good thing,"[1] he said. His chief financial officer (CFO), Li Zongwei, seeming out of place in Western business attire, said the company is "looking forward to what will happen after the downturn because we are well prepared for this down cycle."

The collapse in prices for Yingli's core product, photovoltaic (PV) cells, that began in 2010 hit the company's share price hard. From a high of $15.81 in December 2009, around the time of the Copenhagen climate summit, the price collapsed to $1.55 at the beginning of August 2012. The high hopes that investors had that China's renewable energy companies would benefit from the nation's subsidies and stimulus plans vanished into thin air. The company was losing money, reporting losses of $510 million in 2011 and another $45 million in the first quarter of 2012 as revenue fell even as PV module shipments increased. Those kinds of numbers, combined with debt of $2.24 billion at the end of 2011, according to Yingli's annual report, would have sunk a Spanish, German, or US company. They've fallen like dominoes in recent years as Chinese competitors ramped up production. But Miao's company can take solace in the fact that it has the backing of the world's most powerful bank.

Yingli, founded in 1998, is one of the biggest beneficiaries of CDB loans in the solar industry, borrowing at least $1.7 billion in dollar-denominated loans from CDB from 2008 through early 2012.[2] And it has plenty more money where that came from. CDB granted Yingli lines of credit amounting to $5.3 billion in 2010.[3] In all, since 2010, CDB has made available at least $47.3 billion in credit lines to support Chinese solar and wind companies, according to *Bloomberg New Energy Finance (BNEF)*.[4] Although much of the credit may not have been used, it is core to CDB's mission of supporting the state. China has a goal of producing 20 percent of its energy from renewable sources by 2020, and CDB financing is seen as key in a volatile industry where profit margins can vanish in a year.

The growth of China's economy over the last decade, when it overtook Japan to become the world's second largest, has meant environmental and energy problems of daunting proportions. The country is the largest automobile market in the world and the second biggest consumer of oil. Its growth in oil demand was 42.1 percentage points above global demand growth from 2002 to 2007, according to the World Bank.[5] About 80 percent of its power plants are fueled by thermal coal, leading to cities full of haze, coal trucks, daily mining accidents, and, despite huge natural supplies, a dependence on coal imports. But in the last few years, China also has managed to create a renewable energy industry from scratch using its cheap labor advantage to sell first to Germany, which supported purchases with subsidies for utilities in 2004, and later within China's own booming market led by its "golden sun" subsidy program for solar energy, which started in 2009. Chinese leaders see renewable energy as a strategic necessity. People such as incoming Premier Li Keqiang believe it not only will help solve the nation's energy dilemmas but also will help provide jobs and spawn companies that will move China up the value chain. And with annual power demand forecast to grow 5 percent, China needs to move fast just to keep up and avoid blackouts. In 2006, two companies from China were on the list of top-ten solar cell producers. In 2010, six made the list, according to *BNEF*. Yingli opened offices in New York and San Francisco at the beginning of 2009; by the year's end, it held 27 percent of the California market. China simply took over. In 2011, the country supplied some 72 percent of global crystalline-silicon module production, the most popular type of solar module that converts light to energy.

After China passed a renewable energy law in 2006, it offered greater support in the form of feed-in tariffs, which pay utilities the extra cost of using renewable energy over conventional sources, and national targets for installed solar and wind capacity. The feed-in tariffs were responsible for Germany's rapid development of renewable energy at the beginning of the century. But where would the money come from? At first, the solar companies sought the help of foreign investment bankers, such as Goldman Sachs and UBS, to list in New York and raise funds by creating shell companies in the Cayman Islands. In 2007, Yingli listed on the NYSE, with the help of Goldman Sachs and UBS, raising $319 million. Ditto for LDK Solar, a Jiangxi-based maker of multicrystalline solar wafers that are used to produce solar cells. LDK's initial public offering (IPO) that year was the largest US IPO by a Chinese company since November 2004. All told, there were more than $1 billion of Chinese solar offerings in the United States that year. Despite the listings, though, investors had scant access to the assets in China.

Certain that Chinese government support was behind the development of solar, CDB came along and the game changed. The year

2010 saw a massive expansion in CDB's lending to renewable energy, dwarfing anything to date and indeed anything in the world. It lent $14.7 billion in 2010 to clean energy and other energy-saving projects— a sum higher than that lent by other development banks, such as the European Investment Bank or the Brazilian Development Bank (BNDES).[6] The European Investment Bank lent €8 billion for clean energy projects in 2010, BNDES lent $3.16 billion in clean energy financing, and the US Federal Financing Bank was at $2.12 billion, according to *BNEF*. That year, Chinese companies such as LDK Solar got $9.1 billion in a credit line from CDB; Sinovel Wind, $6.5 billion; Suntech Power Holdings, $7.6 billion; and Trina Solar, $4.6 billion.[7] Such loans allowed Chinese companies to further ramp up production and drive down costs. In 2010, China invested some $51.1 billion into clean energy, the largest investment by any country in the world.[8] Soon, though, the companies would become victims of their own success.

Obama's Dream

Across the Pacific, another competitor equally wanted the jobs that will stem from the next stage of the energy revolution. When President Obama took office in 2009, renewable energy became top of the agenda, and the stimulus to combat the financial crisis was in part directed toward energy, with the government putting tens of billions of dollars in the sector. "The nation that leads the world in creating new energy sources," Obama said in April 2009, "will be the nation that leads the twenty-first-century global economy."[9] The US solar boom in the late 1970s had led to bankruptcies and disillusionment, but technological change meant that the industry was almost viable this time. The US Export-Import Bank tripled its support to renewable energy from $101 million in fiscal 2009 to a record $332 million in 2010, just as CDB was starting to lend billions of dollars.[10] In March 2009, Solyndra, a Fremont, California–based solar company, got a $535 million loan guarantee from the Department of Energy to construct a robotic factory that could build up to 500 megawatts of solar panels a year, with the name "Fab 2." Governor of California Arnold

Schwarzenegger and Energy Secretary Steven Chu, who won a Nobel Prize in physics in 1997, helped break ground at the factory, and even Obama visited. As with the Chinese companies, Goldman Sachs and Morgan Stanley also lined up to do an IPO under the ticker SOLY. One analyst even said the company could be valued at $2 billion after the stock offering. But by the summer of 2010, as CDB was going into overdrive, Solyndra withdrew its IPO registration. In November, it announced it would shut down a plant and lay off workers just seven weeks after opening Fab 2. CEO Brian Harrison said that solar module prices had plummeted as low-cost Chinese manufacturers ramped up production.[11] By September of the following year, Solyndra had filed for bankruptcy. Energy Secretary Chu said that federal aid to Solyndra had been necessary to compete in a "fierce global race to capture" a market that will grow by "hundreds of billions of dollars" in coming decades.[12]

Compare the support Yingli and other Chinese solar makers have received from CDB—the banker to the state—with that Solyndra received, whose $535 million in loan guarantees from the Obama administration became a staple of Republican Mitt Romney's 2012 presidential campaign. LDK's credit line from CDB is 16 times the loan guarantee Solyndra got. In total, five US companies were awarded $1.56 billion in guarantees through a US Energy Department program championed by Obama, a fraction of CDB's total credit lines. Still, under pressure and the threat of trade sanctions, China's solar CEOs hit back. At a gathering at Beijing's Grand Hyatt hotel in November 2011, where Chinese reporters broke into applause each time one of the executives criticized the threat of sanctions and defended the domestic industry, Trina Solar Ltd. CEO Gao Jifan said that China's solar panel makers borrow at higher rates than what the US government charged Solyndra.[13] CDB charges 6 to 7 percent, Gao had said earlier that month.[14] Solyndra paid an average rate of 5 percent on $70 million in 2011 before filing for bankruptcy protection. In the Hyatt meeting, where Yingli's Miao stood in his blue overalls, the solar CEOs said that the government gives them no special breaks and that most of the credit from CDB had not been used. Instead, China's success in nurturing its solar industry comes from "the wisdom and intelligence of Chinese entrepreneurs," who are more sensitive to market trends and use the best technologies, according to Suntech Power Holdings Co. CEO Shi Zhengrong.

In Baoding, where the streetlights are lined with solar panels, we caught up with Yingli's CFO Li to get more information about the CDB loan terms. In a hushed voice, he told us that CDB loan terms are the strictest of any of Yingli's bankers, which also include Citigroup and a host of state-owned Chinese lenders. "China Development Bank is undergoing restructuring, so they want to restructure from a policy bank to a commercial bank," Li said in English. "Every time we talk with those guys, they give more stringent requirements, and also their interest and yields is [sic] way higher than the others. But, you know, they are CDB, so if they give to us, we say, 'Okay, well, thank you. But we won't take too much.'"

But Li is missing the point, or at least omitting it. It is the *volume* of CDB lines of credit—the security that financing is available if needed—that gives Chinese new-energy companies a leg up over their global competitors, allowing them to focus on increasing their scale above all else and spawning trade litigation in the United States and Europe. More crucially, though, they provide the guarantee that makes commercial banks feel safer lending to the companies, thus bringing in billions of yuan of more loans. The huge credit lines prove to investors that the companies have enough funds, and prove to banks that the firms can pay back short-term loans. The CBD lines of credit are expensive and require the companies to give collateral and specify projects for their use. But they allow the companies to get cheaper working capital loans from commercial banks. The United States simply does not have a government-owned bank of equivalent scale or assets. "This is a competitive advantage with European competitors where they have difficulties obtaining bank loans," Beijing-based Jessica Ng, a *BNEF* analyst, told us. And by 2012, "only those with enough financial funds can stay in the market."

Default-Free Bond Market

By the middle of 2012, Chinese solar maker LDK's shares had dropped 95 percent since its IPO, with Trina Solar's shares down 76 percent. Yingli's had fared no better, with an 82 percent plunge. In April, Q-Cells SE, a German solar cell maker that was once the largest solar maker in the world and had grown to have a workforce of 2,300, filed for insolvency. By the summer, at least 14 US and European solar companies had filed for bankruptcy. In China, LDK announced it would cut 5,554 workers as plunging prices cut margins further. Since September 2011 alone, the spot price of polysilicon, the raw material used to make solar panels, had fallen by a third. Yet will these Chinese firms go bankrupt with so many loans due to state banks?

Not likely. LDK received a bailout in the summer of 2012, after reporting four straight quarterly losses, when the government of the eastern city of Xinyu said it would pay a portion of its debts. Xinyu, where LDK is based, even included the repayment in the annual fiscal budget. That a Chinese local government would actually go to bat for a solar maker with ever lower margins was probably unthinkable to the stock investors back in New York.

As for Yingli, it knew it could turn to CDB when times got tough, and there was no better way than through China's domestic bond market, where most investors are state-owned banks and there has never been a bond default since the market began in the late 1990s. Yingli sold 1.5 billion yuan of bonds in May 2012, with the lead underwriter CDB, even as global solar makers were cutting jobs left, right, and center. It priced in two tranches, or lots, to yield 6.01 percent and 5.78 percent for five years and three years. That deserves repeating.

A company that is bleeding cash, whose core product is plunging in price, whose competitors across the globe are filing for bankruptcy, and whose share price was 82 percent below its IPO valuation can borrow money at 6 percent, thanks to CDB. A bond's yield gives an idea of the extra money those who buy the bonds demand to be compensated for the risk. (Buyers receive 6.01 percent, or 5.78 percent of the total amount of the bond, in interest payments each year until it matures.) Not only was Yingli's bond yield below the prevailing official bank lending rate; it was widely out of whack with global bond yields for solar makers. (See Figure 5.1.) In China, underwriters often hold the bonds on their books if they don't sell, making them little different from loans. Bond yields give us a sense of how the market views a company, much like the movement in a stock. What price does the free market charge? At the same time, German solar company SolarWorld's bond yielded over 40 percent, and LDK's overseas bond, over 100 percent. Even if

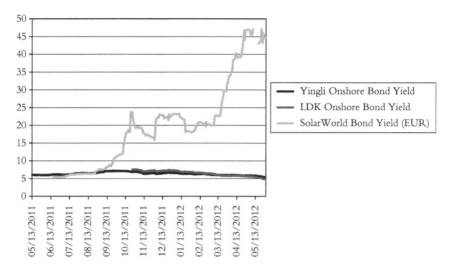

Figure 5.1 Interest Rate Subsidy: Renewable Energy Companies' Bond Yields
Source: Bloomberg.

Chinese banks lent at rates of 6 to 7 percent, as Gao Jifan insists, they are severely underestimating the credit risk. But the commercial banks know Yingli has a guarantee from CDB, even if the credit lines are never used.

The CDB credit lines and loans turned out to have other costs, however. In October 2011, a petition by SolarWorld Industries America, a unit of Germany's largest solar-panel maker, and six other US solar panel manufacturers alleged that Chinese exporters of PV cells and panels were using illegal government subsidies to sell their products in the US market. On May 17 the following year, the United States announced antidumping duties of roughly 31 percent to be applied to Chinese-made PV equipment, causing US-listed shares of Chinese solar companies to drop further. The action would make Chinese modules 27 percent more expensive in the United States than those of other international manu-facturers, according to *BNEF.* A few months later, SolarWorld went on to lead a group of manufacturers requesting that the European Commission investigate whether Chinese companies were dumping products at below-market rates. Any EU action was potentially much more serious, as it was a far larger market for Chinese goods. This time, the Chinese solar makers gathered again in Beijing to urge the Chinese government to protect their interests. In the race to the bottom, who would be the last man standing?

As prices fall further, narrowing the gap with traditional forms of energy, China's solar firms, having exported abroad for years, can sell at home or move manufacturing overseas, helped by CDB. In China, bankruptcies and defaults do not happen when the market wants them to, especially when the debt is due to domestic banks and not overseas foreign lenders. In the face of a looming trade war, Yingli said that in the summer of 2012 it planned to expand capacity at its plant in the southern tropical island of Hainan. And two months after German solar maker Q-Cells filed for bankruptcy, another Chinese renewable energy operator, Hanergy, agreed to buy a subsidiary of the bankrupt German firm. The previous year, Hanergy had received from CDB a 30 billion yuan line of credit to expand to foreign markets. LDK had offered to purchase a stake in Sunways AG, a German maker of solar panels and cells. "CDB is working with our teams very, very closely," LDK's CFO, Jack Lai, said in a June conference call with investors, and the bank had sent a delegation to Europe to visit the company's sites. CDB was also preparing a fund for LDK to pursue opportunities in Africa, he said.[15] Despite the steady stream of losses that frightened overseas shareholders, the bank had not backed away in a time of crisis, as might be expected in a more market-based funding system, fulfilling its role as a development bank. It didn't look like CDB was going to stop financing the renewable energy sector in the face of international action by the United States and the European Union; the only question was whether the Chinese government would itself get involved in a tit-for-tat trade war. But who would want to take them on?

CDB's loans are part of the package of Chinese government support that has made it the largest manufacturer of solar panels, including local government land grants, capacity targets, and its bond market where money can be raised cheaply from state banks. For LDK's hometown of Xinyu, renewable energy will bring jobs and money, helping boost their careers and giving them an incentive to ignore the strictures of the market and help flailing companies. Changing our centuries-long addiction to oil and fossil fuels is not an easy task; the costs of renewable energy and the difficulties of changing the way we live make the industry a perfect fit for development banks in the early stages. In late 2011, China doubled its 2015 solar power goal. With such political support from the top and a development bank the size of CDB, China is hugely competitive, especially since not many other countries have the stomach to support an industry in a race to the bottom. Solar has followed the course of other industries in the country: becoming cost efficient by exporting to the West, and then selling to the growing domestic market. Yet other development banks, such as Brazil's BNDES, will surely catch up to match the support. It will become a battle of subsidies. The question is whether other development banks can provide the same level of funds. With earnings for Chinese renewable energy companies dropping, the banks and local governments own the companies, as the long list of collateralized loans on Yingli's bond prospectus shows. LDK said in a filing in 2012 that CDB's loans contain covenants that if the debt-to-asset ratio breaches 75 percent, the bank "may take actions." In the end the companies become state owned through loans from the state banking system. As a result, not only are the banks in China too big to fail, but so are the companies they lend to. As China ramps up its own demand and prices drop, the Chinese firms eventually will benefit. The long-held dream of the US pioneers in the 1970s that solar would be close in price to other power sources is close to being realized, and China is leading the way, with the world's most powerful bank taking center stage. Having denied the functions of the market, though, the big question is whether these firms will ever be profitable.

Financing China's Global Company: Huawei

In a June 2011 speech at the Washington think-tank, the Center for American Progress, Frank Hochberg, the head of the US Exim Bank, which is a fraction of the size of the Chinese policy banks, pointed out what kept him up at night. One insomnia contributor was a Chinese telecom company from Shenzhen called Huawei, founded in 1987 by a retired military officer. Huawei did not export until 1996, Hochberg said, but it had positioned itself ahead of Nokia and Siemens in less than 15 years. In India, Huawei grew sales from $50 million to $2.5 billion in one year alone. "Folks, that kind of growth takes more than just good sales and marketing strategies," Hochberg said. "But what you can't see when you look at a Huawei router—and one of the central reasons the company's growth has been so dramatic—it that it's backed by a

$30 billion credit line from the China Development Bank. This backing allows Huawei to significantly reduce its cost of capital and to offer financing to their buyers at rates and terms that are better than their competitors."[16] None of the G-7 countries provided levels of financing anywhere near those of CDB, he said. "That keeps me up at night."

Huawei (pronounced *Hwah-way*) Technologies Co. is today China's largest maker of phone equipment and the world's second largest after Ericsson AB. It has sold phone-network equipment all across Africa and Europe and is now expanding its MediaPad tablet computers into the United States. In 2012 alone, Huawei expects to spend $4.5 billion in research. With 65 percent of its revenue coming from outside China it is one of China's most successful global companies. And CDB has been one of the key reasons behind its success.

CDB's credit lines are often tapped to provide so-called vendor financing. That's when equipment makers, such as Huawei, arrange funding for their customers—the telephone and data service providers—to help them buy gear. This gives Huawei and cross-town rival ZTE Corp., with its own $15 billion credit line from CDB, the means to provide competitive loans to lure customers away from Ericsson and Alcatel-Lucent.

Take Tele Norte Leste Participacoes. When Brazil's biggest land-line company was shopping for network equipment in 2010, Huawei's offer had an edge. A two-year grace period on payments and an interest rate of 2 percentage points over the London Interbank Offered Rate created an unbeatable deal, Tele Norte CFO Alex Zornig told Bloomberg News.[17] "The Chinese are filling the space left empty by Americans and Europeans," Zornig said in an interview. "They are very aggressive and they have a lot of money." The terms gave the company an interest rate of about 4 percent, at a time when Brazilian companies were paying average borrowing costs of about 5.99 percent on their dollar debt. In 2009, Mexico City–based America Movil SAB, Latin America's largest mobile phone carrier, was also seeking $1 billion to upgrade its mobile network, and CFO Carlos García Moreno reached the same conclusion as Zornig.

■ ■ ■

Toward the end of 2004, two men walked into a meeting room at the Wuzhou Hotel in the southern boomtown of Shenzhen. One, Ren Zhengfei, is an ex-military man and the founder of Huawei. The other was Chen Yuan. Ren talked to Chen about Huawei's accomplishments and the obstacles it faced in exploring overseas markets.[18] Chen sensed that Huawei had financing needs, and the two men hit it off. An hour later, the door opened, and a new chapter in the company began that would change the face of the global business. On December 27, 2004, in Beijing, Huawei and CDB signed a $10 billion agreement for overseas markets, the first of many CDB credit lines to its customers across the developing world that would allow it to gain significant market share. It also was the beginning of CDB's support of Chinese firms to "go global." "This is a brand-new business for CDB," Chen Yuan said at the signing ceremony. "And CDB is more than willing to apply and leverage the experience we've accumulated in our many years of work on development finance to serve companies like Huawei and to help these companies to grow faster and to become outstanding and global enterprises."[19] Huawei's overseas business exceeded contracts in China for the first time in 2005, and CDB ended up increasing the credit line to $30 billion in 2009.

The Huawei business was done out of CDB's Shenzhen branch, which was set up in March 1999 and was directly under the supervision of headquarters. The Shenzhen branch was languishing compared to others and wasn't growing as fast as the city's booming economy, as its funding was mainly in traditional sectors, such as energy and infrastructure.[20] So, it decided to finance large enterprises that wanted to go overseas but were short of funds and couldn't raise money on the international markets. Huawei was expanding overseas, but it faced the formidable competition of Cisco Systems, Ericsson, Siemens, and Motorola. Cisco had sued in January 2003 to stop Huawei from selling products in the United States, claiming Huawei copied Cisco software to sell data traffic switches and routers and plagiarized instructions verbatim from Cisco user manuals. The two sides settled out of court. Still, telecom equipment was expensive, and operators often would not see a return on investment for a long time. It was also difficult for buyers to offer one-time payments at the time of purchase, as they preferred to pay in installments. Such installment payments Huawei was getting weren't showing up on its bottom line and were bad for cash flow, weakening its

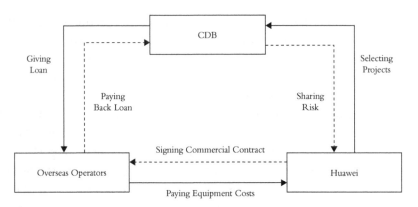

Figure 5.2   Structure of CDB—Huawei Loan

Source: China Development Bank and Renmin University, *Development Finance in China: Case Studies* (Beijing: Renmin University Publishing House, 2007).

competitiveness. The solution was buyer's credits from banks, but before CDB, Huawei couldn't meet the demand.

CDB would offer credit lines to overseas telecom operators to buy the equipment from Huawei. But how could it control the credit risk of these partners, most of them in Africa and Latin America, when it didn't know anything about them, let alone their credit history and ability to pay the money back? In early 2005 CDB's head office set up a lengthy project approval process involving many departments to work on the problem. The solution was that the Shenzhen branch would approve the loan, providing the credit through a foreign agency bank, and that it would share the client risk with Huawei. The foreign agency bank would dispense the money and help ensure it got paid back. (See Figure 5.2.) Huawei would recommend an overseas client to CDB's Shenzhen branch, after which the foreign agency bank would help dispense the money for the purchase of Huawei equipment. Huawei and CDB signed a risk-sharing "win-win" agreement in April 2005 and also agreed to share information on clients and projects after the loan had been dispensed. CDB could take guarantees in the form of assets, or a guarantee from the state-owned insurance company, Sinosure. CDB's Shenzhen branch faced an array of different legal systems across the globe, so global law firms were hired by the bank to help with English-language contracts. Still, the Shenzhen branch faced a host of cultural differences with their foreign clients, and so had a close cooperation with

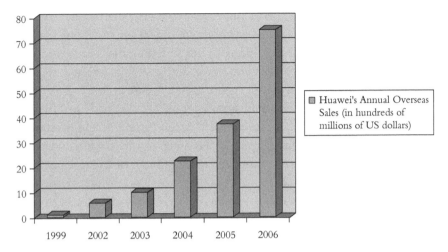

Figure 5.3   Huawei's Overseas Sales After CDB Loan

Source: China Development Bank and Renmin University, *Development Finance in China: Case Studies* (Beijing: Renmin University Publishing House, 2007).

Chinese embassies to learn more about their clients' cultures. With phone calls late at night due to the time difference, this often disrupted the lives of the CDB workers, who in the first year were often in the office until two or three in the morning.[21] The business quickly paid off for CDB, though. In the first half of 2006, the Shenzhen branch of CDB had the most foreign currency business in the city, surpassing Bank of China and other state-owned banks.

Huawei's first forays into the business didn't go well, but then its overseas sales accelerated. (See Figure 5.3.) In early 2005, its first project with Sunday Communications, a telecom operator in Hong Kong, fell through after PCCW, Hong Kong's biggest phone company, came in and bought the firm, just after CDB had hired top law firms to do due diligence. Still, in that year, CDB approved a tentative $2 billion loan commitment to 26 telecom operators including Global Com Limited of Nigeria. In 2005, CDB's Shenzhen branch gave out $836 million for some 17 projects. In December 2005, Vodafone Group, then the world's largest mobile phone company, named Huawei its first Chinese-approved supplier of network equipment, and Huawei's road to global domination had begun. A person who used to work at Alcatel-Lucent at that time remembers that at first the French company said they couldn't compete with Huawei on price, but their products were better.[22] Soon, the quality of Huawei's products improved and in some cases surpassed those of the French company. He remembers telling his chairman: "We won't die at the hands of Huawei; if we die, it will be at the hands of China Development Bank."

Yet, as with CDB's loans in new energy, CDB's loans to Huawei also caused a global backlash. In early 2012, the European Union started looking into the credit lines given to Huawei and its cross-town rival, ZTE, arguing that the companies have benefited from illegal government subsidies. In June 2012, the Intelligence Committee of the US House of Representatives took aim at lines of credit given to Huawei and specifically asked about CDB's credit lines to ZTE. In a letter to the company's chairman, Hou Weigui, the Republican chairman and the ranking Democrat on the panel asked how ZTE was able to secure its $15 billion line of credit from CDB in 2009, an amount that exceeded its annual revenue. The committee asked ZTE to provide details on which carriers obtained financing from its CDB loans.

The inquiry was part of a bigger probe the committee undertook to determine whether Huawei and ZTE should have broader access to the US market, with concerns about the ties the companies had to the Chinese Communist Party and worries that its equipment may pose a national security threat. Committee staff members made two trips to southern China in early 2012 to talk to officials of the two companies.[23] Huawei spokesman Ross Gan said in a story published in April 2011 that such vendor financing is "standard industry practice," and the amount received by Huawei's customers isn't out of line with what rivals such as Ericsson can offer through Sweden's export financing agency. Huawei is a private company that makes decisions based on market principles, he said.[24]

It looked as if a CDB loan was so good it risked becoming a global liability, likely to spark trade wars rather than global economic growth. In part, it is a result of CDB's status as a state-owned bank that can raise large amounts of funds cheaply on the bond market: No other bank can compete with its scale until CDB commercializes and raises money on its own merit rather than that of the sovereign. Only when CDB pays the proper price to get money and China liberalizes interest rates will it start to price its giant loans at a market-based rate.

The Final Frontier: Private Equity

In December 2010, in Beijing's Diaoyutai State Guest House, a group of secluded villas set back from the road in west Beijing that played host to President Richard Nixon in 1972, CDB launched its move into private equity. It was capitalism's final frontier, and another sign on the road that CDB was becoming the most powerful Chinese bank. Xie Ping, vice president of China's $332 billion sovereign wealth fund, which along with the Finance Ministry owns 100 percent of CDB, put it best. By having government backing, China's private equity funds can increase the value of Chinese companies in which they invest, Xie declared. While Western private equity has focused on being "private," China's private equity funds are based on the state system, and investors are mostly state-owned companies, he explained, pointing out that this is an aspect of the Chinese market that is different from other countries. "China's private equity industry is very particular," Xie told business leaders. "It has the imprint of the state."

CDB's private equity unit, CDB Capital, is the conduit and meeting place for channeling state capital into some of the country's most lucrative opportunities. China is the second biggest private equity market, after the United States, with about $30 billion of investments, according to the Boston Consulting Group.[25] CDB's private equity unit has a quiet office in one of the smartest and most expensive buildings in Beijing's finance street, alongside JPMorgan, Goldman Sachs, and UBS. Inside, the rooms are covered in dark wood paneling, and there are two stuffed heads of deer with antlers on the wall, giving the impression of elite and old New England money. With CNN playing in the background, the office could be in New York. But the entrance reminds you of the real owners. Its lobby sports three bronze busts of Communist Party leaders: Chairman Mao Zedong is there, and so is his eventual successor as leader, Deng Xiaoping. Then there's Chen Yun, Chen Yuan's father.

One sunny, clear day in May 2011, Jim Coulter—the founder of TPG Capital, the Fort Worth, Texas–based buyout firm started two decades ago—with slicked-back light gray hair and wearing a spotless, creaseless suit, stepped into CDB Capital's building in front of those statues, surrounded by an entourage carrying expensive-looking leather satchels, bringing a whiff of New York's Midtown into the building. The ceremony upstairs was low-key—a banner said "TPG" and a screen on TV said "Welcome Mr. Coulter." CDB Capital had agreed to buy a stake in TPG, one of the world's most successful private equity funds that has raised more for buyouts than any other private equity firm in the past ten years.[26] Coulter, too, has set his eyes on China: He said in August 2010 that industry in China should grow at least twice the rate of the world average.[27] The private equity gods of efficiency had finally met China's socialist state-owned system. Apart from a mutual love of secrecy, it was difficult to know how the foreigners would pan out.

Private equity in China was little known ten years ago, but between 2003 and 2010, it has grown at a compound annual rate of 40 percent, and CDB has been there from the beginning.[28] In December 2006, the government of the northeastern city of Tianjin set up Bohai Industrial Investment Fund Management Co., the first government-backed domestic private equity fund. Its shareholders included China Life Insurance Co., CDB (which took a 1 billion yuan stake) and the nation's social security fund. In 2009, CDB finally got its own firm, CDB Capital, which incorporated all the earlier funds CDB had put money in. Set up in August 2009 and given 35 billion yuan, CDB Capital is run by Zhang Xuguang, a smooth-looking businessman who favors striped suits and big ties and has trendy black-rimmed glasses. A splashy rollout of Guochuang Fund, its first fund of funds (funds that invest in other private equity funds) in late 2010, featured video clips from private equity legend David Bonderman and shots of the Statue of Liberty and Wall Street. It has ambitions to be a first-class commercial private equity fund, and its parent CDB's credit rating and state backing can give the companies it invests in the connections global private equity players lack. It is the equivalent of the Washington-based Carlyle Group being able to sell bonds rated the same as US Treasuries, on one hand, and then plowing that money into private equity ventures. In a December brochure for the Guochang fund of funds, CDB Capital said it "inherits CDB's primary goal of servicing the state."

As a result, CDB Capital has extended its parent's investments in local governments throughout the country in a series of urban investment funds, ensuring they get capital. "Urbanization is the core driver of China's future growth," CDB Capital wrote in its promotional literature, echoing Chen Yuan's own belief, and the fund aims to become the "one-stop solution provider for urban development in China." One such investment is in the port of Caofeidian. The city, rapidly becoming northeast China's biggest import terminal for crude oil, iron ore, and coal, stretches about six miles into the Bohai Gulf, with a six-lane highway, floating over the sea into the haze, leading to the main iron ore terminal. Running parallel to the highway, sparsely traveled on a hot day in mid-May, is a railroad bridge where a line of 100-car trains move coal into China's interior. Trucks, covered in rust-colored dust, take out the iron ore. Like the nearby "Manhattan" of Tianjin's Yujiapu district, described in Chapter 1, Caofeidian, with over 200 billion yuan in government-directed investment and counting, is dominated by state-owned companies. Instead of billboards for restaurants or autos, roadside signs have slogans touting President Hu Jintao's concept of "Scientific Development" and commemorating the ninetieth anniversary of the Chinese Communist Party in 2011. Fading posters put up at the height of the stimulus in 2009 picture a thriving city emerging from the salt plains complete with a Burger King restaurant, a Dior shop, and, oddly, a shop specializing in the sale of Kahlúa, the Mexican coffee liqueur. Instead, three years of wind and sun have almost whitewashed the posters. A lone dog barked inside a silent prefabricated compound for workers. It would seem an unnatural place for private equity. Yet, in March 2010, CDB Capital set up the CDB Caofeidian Investment Company with the Caofeidian LGFV to help fund construction projects. With a registered capital of 1 billion yuan, it marks a further step forward for the LGFV model that CDB started in the late 1990s, creating another channel through which the state can pump money to stimulate the economy.

■ ■ ■

Chen Yuan's status and power within the system has allowed CDB to be the only bank to launch a private equity subsidiary to make domestic yuan investments, approved by the State Council, as well as a securities company, CDB Securities, located in a prime position in Dongzhimen in central Beijing. (See Figure 5.4.) CDB Securities has helped underwrite the bonds of LGFVs, while another CDB subsidiary, CDB Leasing, bought the Kunming–Shilin Expressway in a 3.748 billion yuan agreement in 2009; then it leased it to Yunnan Highway, which as we saw in Chapter 1 was a heavily indebted LGFV that later said it could not pay its bank loans. CDB Securities raised a few eyebrows by becoming the top corporate bond underwriter in China in 2012, having been number 20 in 2011 and even

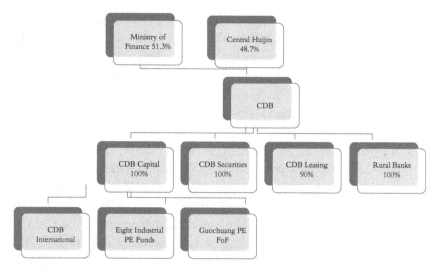

Figure 5.4   Structure of China Development Bank
Source: CDB, Z-Ben Advisors.

lower before that, according to Bloomberg data. Apart from underwriting LGFV bonds, it also has been on deals for large state-owned companies such as China National Nuclear Corp and China National Petroleum Company, the largest oil company in China. Why would a policy bank get the licenses to set up all these subsidiaries and not the more commercial banks? It was fitting that at the same time as CDB Securities became the top corporate bond underwriter in April 2012, the banking regulatory commission announced that its parent CDB's bonds would once again have sovereign credit rating for one more year, allowing it to fund these subsidiaries with money obtained from China's bond market at below-market rates.

In private equity, connections matter: former President Jiang Zemin's grandson runs a private equity fund, despite being only just out of Harvard.[29] Premier Wen Jiabao's son, Winston Wen, was cofounder of another. Jeffrey Zeng, the son of former Politburo member Zeng Peiyan, manages Kaixin Investments, a venture capital firm set up with CDB and CITIC Capital.[30] At the same time, foreign private equity funds have been constrained in China. Fred Hu, another Harvard alumnus, one of China's best-connected and most famous economists who studied under Larry Summers, thinks CDB may have overstretched its mandate by plunging into private equity. "I fully support the role of

CDB as a policy bank. A long-term lender, long-term credit, and all that. Going to private equity is a very different animal," said Hu, former chairman of Greater China for Goldman Sachs Group Inc. and now chairman of Primavera Capital, a Beijing-based private equity firm he founded, in an interview. "Honestly, I don't think they have the talent or the team to do that. CDB Capital is just an unnecessary distraction from their core mandate and core mission. They should really focus on being a very sound, reliable, quality long-term lender to finance China's infrastructure. But private equity? CDB Capital becomes a Carlyle? I don't know what they are thinking about."

Acting as a Gatekeeper

In late 2010, CDB Capital opened up the office to a group of Western media, including us, for the first time, as it launched China's first fund of funds, with sizable state investors. Zhang Xuguang, the man with the trendy suit and hipster glasses, cradled a coffee cup reading "Minnesota." A graduate of Peking University, he worked at CATIC, a state-owned aviation company, as a general counsel before entering CDB in 1998 in the investment banking department. He moved on to become president of CDB Guangxi Branch and was also the personal assistant of the chairman, a powerful position within CDB. "We don't see any conflict of interest between our parent bank's strategic policy lending and CDB Capital's profit seeking as a market-oriented asset management company," Zhang said. If this was the latest incarnation of Barbarians at the Gate, it was certainly a much more subdued one.

China's first fund of funds, the Guochuang Fund, was launched with Suzhou Industrial Park, an ambitious joint urban development project between the governments of China and Singapore that CDB had helped fund in its earliest days, and is authorized to have a capitalization of 60 billion yuan. It will invest in yuan-denominated funds. For Chen Yuan, it was another example of the bank opening up the nation's markets that would in turn bring in new funds, the perfect role for a development institution. "Sixty billion yuan compared to China's capital markets' total amount is not big, but it has quite big implications for China's private equity industry," Chen told *Caixin* magazine's Zhang Yuzhe. "This 60 billion yuan can bring with it more funds; for example, it can pry open several hundred billions of credit funds, as those companies that were invested in develop and after a few years open up the capital markets. It can again bring over a hundred billion of yuan, even hundreds of billions of yuan of financing."[31]

The Guochuang Fund turns CDB Capital into a powerful gatekeeper to the private equity industry in China. It allows both foreign private equity investors as well as state-owned firms to access private equity funds and deals that previously they would not have been able to. It also came at a good time for large state investors. In September 2010, regulators let some insurance companies invest not more than 5 percent of their assets in private equity funds. The first investors in the Guochuang fund of funds included Huawei, which invested 500 million yuan; China Life Insurance Company; China Re-Insurance Corp.; and the National Social Security Fund—all companies with good relations with CDB. The fund of funds also invited well-respected New York private equity firm Siguler Guff & Co. to provide advice. "Big investors have given us a good reaction, as they know our years of experience will give them a good return," said Deng Shuang, managing director of the fund management division, at the meeting. "What are our individual skills? Because we are backed by China Development Bank, a very important financial institution, they provide us a lot of rich resources. This is not only supporting funds, but more important is project-level resources. In the many years under Chen Yuan they [CDB] have . . . established excellent trust and cooperation with every department of the government and local governments." This was no ordinary private equity firm, but one that had the backing of all of CDB's resources that it had built up since 1994. "Many investors are very willing to take our money, as our money represents resources. One yuan is more than one yuan," Deng said. There had been support from every level of the government for the establishment of CDB Capital, she said.

CDB's move into private equity had big implications for the business in China. State-owned investors such as insurers can invest in funds screened by CDB Capital rather than putting money straight into foreign private equity firms or other offshore firms, which would likely involve more government red tape. As Shanghai-based fund information company Z-Ben Advisors put it, CDB Capital had become an "800-pound gorilla" in the alternative asset business. For foreign firms, it could also provide an in for the first time. "While investing in an FoF [fund of funds] may not be the first choice for many, it will provide exposure to the types of deals that have so far been entirely off-limits," according to Z-Ben.[32] This, too, will affect the distribution of capital in China: Since CDB Capital is a creature of the state, it is likely to prefer investing in industrial private equity funds, or government-guided funds, according to Cindy Qu, an analyst at Z-Ben Advisors. Small- and medium-sized funds would find it harder to attract investment. "CDB Capital will be one of the largest domestic LPs [limited partnerships] in China because of its very huge capital capabilities and its government background," she said in an interview. CDB Capital would be able to attract investment from institutions like the $136 billion National Social Security Fund. If the other private equity firms don't have the strong networks with those kinds of government institutions, "it's very hard to survive. . . . It will be very good platform for some SOEs [state-owned enterprises] and some insurers for them to invest in China's PE industry," Qu explained.

Imprint of the State

The expansion of state capital into private equity in China has coincided with a drop in investments by foreign firms, who face growing amounts of red tape. Investments by Chinese firms rose to $7.8 billion in 2011, exceeding for the first time the $7.4 billion put in by US and other foreign funds, according to the *Asian Venture Capital Journal*, which tracks the industry.[33] While the number of foreign-currency funds in China fell to 25 in 2011 from 44 in 2008, domestic ones increased to 129 from 70, according to data from consulting firm Bain & Co. In an attempt to catch up to local firms, foreign private equity firms have launched yuan funds. Carlyle, the world's second largest private equity firm, was among the first to announce that it had raised a yuan fund. The company raised 2.4 billion yuan in the first round of a fund with Beijing's municipal government in July 2010. In February 2012, TPG said it raised 4 billion yuan in a first round of fundraising for its yuan fund, with 90 percent coming from private investors in China. Still, foreign funds face considerable difficulties investing in the country. The powerful National Development and

Reform Commission said in April 2012 that local yuan funds that contain foreign-source investment capital (i.e., funds that have been converted from foreign currency) will be classed as foreign funds and therefore face limits investing in industries such as media, education, telecommunications, the Internet, and technology.

This provides a perfect opportunity for CDB and CDB Capital to move out, acting as a link between China's domestic markets and overseas investors. Along with CDB's African private equity fund, the only African-focused private equity fund in China (as seen in Chapter 3), CDB Capital launched its international investment platform, CDB International Holdings, in Hong Kong on December 6, 2011. Present at a ceremony were the previous chief executive of Hong Kong Tung Chee-hwa; Laura Cha, who served on the board of HSBC; Zhang Xuguang; and Li Jiange, the chairman of China International Capital Corporation, China's first investment bank. The last speaker was Chen Yuan, who said that CDB International could use Hong Kong's position as an international financial center combined with CDB's advantages as a development finance institution to become an "international first-class investment institution and asset management platform."[34] After he reached the stand, the audience clapped again. Journalists were not allowed to ask questions, and the invitation email said the event was low-profile. Also, "there will be no interviewing for the whole of the event," it said.

To get its international platform, CDB Capital took over Hong Kong–listed New Capital International Investment, a Cayman Islands–registered investment company with nine employees, as a vehicle in May 2011 for $0.40 a share, while the shares were trading near HK$1.90. The company mentions only three holdings on its reports, and it lost $11 million in 2011, according to its filings. Zhang Xuguang became chairman of the new company, and it moved into CDB's Hong Kong's offices in the smart International Finance Center, a tall glass building that is the preserve of international global banks and has spectacular views over the city's harbor. Now it was ready to take on the world. In March 2012, Zhang was back down south, this time in Macau, the former Portuguese colony that was handed back to China in 1999, at the MGM Grand Hotel. CDB Capital launched a $1 billion fund that would invest in the Portuguese-speaking countries of East Timor, Brazil, Cape Verde, Guinea-Bissau, Angola, São Tome and Principe, and Mozambique. The fund is going to target infrastructure, transportation, and telecom industries as well as energy and natural resources, according to local media. It could offer equity investment and, of course, loans from the parent CDB.

The international platform is there to serve CDB. As the announcement for the launch in Hong Kong said, it will "undertake CDB's original investment foundations, rely on its strong financial strength, wide range of resources, deep customer relationships." And it would use "CDB's brand" as well as its strong project and government resources to help Chinese companies go global and allow foreign capital to enter China for investment. It will cooperate deeply with top foreign financial institutions, it said.[35] After the ceremony, CDB International signed strategic cooperation agreements with TPG, KKR & Co., and the European private equity fund Permira, as well as the Hong Kong land developer, New World Development Co., a company controlled by billionaire Chen Yu-tung, who was rated among the top 40 richest people in the world by Bloomberg in August 2012. It was a long way from CDB's roots in the China of 1994, when the bank was lending to local projects that would never turn a profit. Now CDB had the platform to direct some of the world's most prestigious and experienced foreign money into domestic projects that would determine the next phase of the country's growth.

The move by CDB into private equity, along with other state-owned companies such as the conglomerate CITIC Group, whose private equity subsidiary is also a powerful player on the scene, ensures that the state holds a stake in this lucrative business as it generates increasing amount of profit. The opposite situation is found in the United States, where the state taxes private equity companies at a lower rate than most working people. The hope is that CDB Capital can deploy state capital more efficiently: It is helping the national pension fund, which took a 10 billion yuan stake in its parent, CDB, in 2008, gain access to greater investment deals. Private equity is still in its infancy in China, but CDB Capital is ensuring that the state plays a crucial role in its development: in getting access to foreigners' cash as well as options to invest in some of China's most successful companies. It marks the culmination of Chen Yuan's dream of making CDB a globally successful bank; beyond that, it ensures that CDB remains relevant in the face of greater competition from commercial banks. Yet it bears asking whether CDB has gone beyond its original mission and has monopolized too much of China's vast resources of capital. It will be tough to control all the bank's subsidiaries and make sure they don't morph into their own little investment banks. And at what point in the long investment chain that CDB now controls, from private equity, to leasing, to underwriting stocks and bonds, does the state give up control? Could a state-owned private equity investor help a state-owned company downsize in the face of market competition to improve economic efficiency? For China, shifting investment toward truly "private" equity and private capital may mean cutting CDB's ambitions down to size.

■ ■ ■

CDB is changing the face of two of the world's most visible industries: alternative energy and telecommunications. CDB does it at a scale only the world's most powerful bank—the banker to China Inc.—can pull off. The massive financing CDB provides for companies such as solar panel maker Yingli and phone equipment maker Huawei gives them a decided leg up against their global competitors. Yingli and other Chinese solar makers remain in business as global competitors shutter their factories, raising production even as profits and share prices collapse amid a massive worldwide glut. In China, NYSE-listed Yingli sells bonds at rates enjoyed by state-owned companies, such as the LGFVs discussed in Chapter 1, while its European and US competitors struggle to raise cash from skeptical capital markets. Huawei and ZTE use their CDB funds to win new customers, providing vendor financing that Swedish and US export financing banks struggle to match, as evidenced by the testimonials of Mexican and Brazilian telecom executives.

But CDB's success in breeding global giants in both industries comes at a price, as lawmakers in Brussels and Washington increase their scrutiny of the bank's financing methods.

Notes

1. Press conference, Baoding, China, June 19, 2011.
2. Bond prospectus on Chinabond, http://www.chinabond.com.cn/d2s/index. html

3. Stuart Biggs, John Duce, "Yingli $5.3 Billion Loan May Boost Solar Panel Supply," Bloomberg News, July 9, 2010.

4. Jessica Ng, "Shining Fresh Light on China Development Bank's Credit Lines," *Bloomberg New Energy Finance*, October 6, 2011.

5. Quoted in World Bank, East Asia and Pacific Economic Update, 2012, Vol. 1, p. 14.

6. See Jessica Ng and Vandana Gombar, "China Development Bank—How It Came to Be a Giant Lender to Clean Energy," *Bloomberg New Energy Finance*, March 11, 2011.

7. Converted from original yuan figures into US dollars.

8. Vandana Gombar, March 11, 2011.

9. The White House, Office of the Press Secretary, "Fact Sheet: President Obama Highlights Vision for Clean Energy Economy, Underscores Urgent Need to Pass Comprehensive Legislation," April 22, 2009, http://www .whitehouse.gov/the_press_office/Clean-Energy-Economy-Fact-Sheet

10. Vandana Gombar, "Fair Play: US Exim Bank Gears Up to Offset China's 'Exceptional Financing,'" Bloomberg New Energy Finance, October 4, 2011.

11. Todd Woody, "Solar-Panel Maker to Close a Factory and Delay Expansion," *New York Times*, November 3, 2010.

12. Jim, Snyder, "Solyndra Decisions Mine, Chu Tells Republican-Led Inquiry," Bloomberg News, November 17, 2011.

13. Michael Forsythe, "Chinese Solar CEOs Say Government Gives Them No Special Breaks," Bloomberg News, November 30, 2011.

14. Natalie Obiko Pearson, "Chinese Loans to Solar Companies Not Subsidized, Trina Says," Bloomberg News, November 2, 2011.

15. LDK Solar Co. Q12012 Earnings Call, June 26, 2012.

16. Fred P. Hochberg, "How the US Can Lead the World in Exports: Retooling Our Export Finance Strategy for the 21st Century," remarks at the Center for American Progress, Washington DC, June 15, 2011, http://www.exim.gov/ about/leadership/hochberg_20110615.cfm

17. Edmond Lococo, "Huawei's $30 Billion China Credit Opens Doors in Brazil, Mexico," Bloomberg News, April 25, 2011.

18. This account from: 国家开发银行，中国人民大学，"开发行金融经典案," 中国人民大学出版社，2007. China Development Bank and Renmin University, *Development Finance in China: Case Studies* (Beijing: Renmin University Press, 2007) (in Chinese).

19. Ibid, p. 257.

20. Ibid. This section taken from the account in the book.

21. Ibid.

22. Interview in Beijing, June 2012.

23. "Rogers and Ruppersberger Intensify Investigation of Huawei and ZTE," June 13, 2012, http://intelligence.house.gov/press-release/rogers-and-ruppersberger-intensify-investigation-huawei-and-zte

24. Edmond Lococo, "Huawei's $30 Billion China Credit Opens Doors in Brazil, Mexico," Bloomberg News, April 25, 2011.

25. Cathy Chan, "China Kicks US Private Equity Aside as Renminbi Funds Dominate," Bloomberg News, May 15, 2012.

26. Cristina Alesci and Jason Kelly, "TPG's IPO Prospects Dim Even as Caryle Heads to Public Exit," Bloomberg News, June 21, 2011.

27. "TPG Sets Up 5 Billion Yuan Fund in China's Chongqing," Bloomberg News, August 24, 2010.

28. Zhang Yuzhe, "600 亿母基金杠杆了谁," *Caixin* 1, January 3, 2011, http://magazine.caixin.com/2011-01-01/100213223.html?utm_source=news.sohu.com&utm_medium=referral&utm_content=sohu_news_indexlink&utm_campaign=sohu

29. Interview with someone who met him Beijing, April 2012.

30. www.kaixininvestment.com/en/index.asp

31. Zhang Yuzhe, 600 亿元母基金杠杆了谁

32. "The Gatekeeper: An 800 Pound Gorilla in the Alt-Asset Space," February 14, 2011, www.zben.com/sites/default/files/Investors/Institutional%20Investors/The%20Gatekeeper-An%20800%20pound%20Gorilla%20in%20the%20Alt-Asset%20Space(February%202011)pdf

33. Cathy Chan, "China Kicks US Private Equity Aside as Renminbi Funds Dominate," Bloomberg News, May 15, 2012.

34. Press release emailed to authors, December 2011.

35. Ibid. Also see article by Xinhua News Agency on CDB's Web site, http://www.cdb.com.cn/web/NewsInfo.asp?NewsId=3900

Chapter 6

The Future

Following the financial crisis, there will be an overall contraction
of the financial sectors in developed countries, especially in the
US and Britain. The situation in China is the exact opposite—our
financial sector has the potential to expand tremendously.

*—Guo Shuqing, former head of China Construction Bank, writing
in the* South China Morning Post, *January 22, 2010*

The carmaker Chery Auto from the central city of Wuhu has
benefited from the power that China Development Bank (CDB)
can muster. In 1995, members of the Wuhu government learned
during a visit to Europe that a Ford UK assembly line was for sale, so they
brought it back to the sleepy town in central Anhui Province, one of
China's poorest. Chery was set up in 1997, and CDB helped the local
government transfer its equity in the tiny car company into four
local financing vehicles, creating the model that thousands of local governments across the country would use to raise funds. Chery began
exporting in 2001. By the middle of 2010, CDB was by far the company's
biggest lender, having provided a total of 17.7 billion yuan of lines of
credit. Later the China–Africa Development Fund helped the company
expand in Africa, forming a joint venture, Chery Overseas Industrial

Investment Co., to invest in factories and new markets across the continent. CDB loans also helped fund construction of a $200 million factory in Venezuela, the first Chinese auto company to start manufacturing there. By 2011, the Wuhu local government had stakes in a company with assets of over 50 billion yuan, with factories in Egypt and plans for more in Brazil and Myanmar. In May 2012, it announced a 12 billion yuan venture with Tata Motors' Jaguar Land Rover in China. CDB had succeeded in opening up new markets and allowing Chery to expand much faster than otherwise would have been possible. Chery exported a record 160,200 vehicles in 2011.

CDB, unlike other banks, provided Chery with "strategic long-term" support rather than just working capital, Liu Kegu, former vice governor at the bank, recalled in an interview. CDB worked with the local government to provide the financing for the company to develop the land for factories and workers' houses and later used the money to acquire patents and intellectual property and build brand awareness, he said. "When the company became stronger, it created more job opportunities on the value chain" for local small businesses as well as in the service sector, Liu said. "In China, a company needs a lot of approvals to do business and because of the government support, the efficiency of getting approvals was achieved, so Chery was able to grow rapidly. This is a very good example of combining urbanization and industrialization, the development of the private sector as well as social spending and employment."

Chery is a perfect example of how CDB has helped transform China's economy and increased its competitiveness. From its work with local governments to its investments and lending overseas, the bank is now one of the most powerful in the world. Even though development banks, such as the Brazilian Development Bank, have long existed to finance political projects, infrastructure, and favored industries that private investors would not be willing to risk their money on, never before has an institution existed with so much capital and growing financial expertise in the hands of one political party, the Communist Party. This century will be dominated by the rise of Chinese capital overseas, and CDB has been the handmaiden of this trend. From Poland, to Bosnia, to Australia, wherever Chinese companies are investing, CDB is at the forefront, helped by a phalanx of international lawyers and a war chest that comes from China's supplicant bond market. After the financial crisis that started in late 2008 led large self-regulated institutions in London and New York to turn to their governments and taxpayers for bailouts, the political and economic power of financial institutions outside of the West has grown, as have the markets and ideologies that they represent. In March 2012, in India's capital, New Delhi, Chen Yuan proposed setting up a development bank for the BRICS nations of Brazil, Russia, India, China, and South Africa, following his life's ambition to make CDB into a bank that would both serve the Communist Party's goals and be profitable. China, with its financial base in Hong Kong, now has a chance to spread its capital, currency, and influence. For money and power have long gone together and likely always will.

The combination of state backing and state-led investment has long been a powerful one. Development banks have helped countries such as France and Germany catch up to the industrial development of Britain. In China, CDB provided the capital and investment for China's economy to catch up from a starting point without a modern banking system, small stock and bond markets, and with rusty Soviet industrial equipment and bloated state-owned enterprises littering the landscape. The country had a great need for capital, but neither the institutions nor the skill to invest people's savings productively. Chen realized the importance of a powerful development bank to overcome bottlenecks in financing and create markets across the country, turning what were local government fiefdoms into companies that could borrow money and sell bonds. The result has seen China expand infrastructure like never before in its history, creating cities such as the bustling port of Tianjin and the megacity of Chongqing on the banks of the Yangtze. "Investment lies at the heart of economic development," William Diamond, a World Bank expert, wrote in his 1957 book about development banks, in a view that CDB would later share.

At the same time, before other commercial banks became involved, CDB backed the central state-owned enterprises to become internationally competitive and acquire resources and investments overseas, with loans to Venezuela and countries in Africa helping to bring in new contracts and business. Dealing with new countries and governments was clearly a steep learning curve. But Chen Yuan's familiarity with the West and his ambition has made CDB one of China's most international banks. Staff study at Barclays and at Bradford University in the UK, and work with some of the globe's top-flight lawyers. To get a sense of the bank's reach, in only a few months in 2012 CDB was backing China's top companies, such as Alibaba with a loan in Hong Kong, providing loans to help a San Francisco housing project, and a Bosnian power station, and offering a 1-billion-euro credit line to Portugese power company Energias de Portugal SA, or EDP, in which state-owned Three Gorges Corp. had bought a 21 percent stake the previous year. CDB had supported the Three Gorges company from the very beginning, when no bank would lend to the dam maker. Now China had clearly caught up.

Yet CDB's assets and lending are a large black hole in global finance: Few other banks have been as unwilling to answer questions from the public, whether it is Chinese taxpayers whose money the bank indirectly uses, or researchers from countries where it lends heavily, inquiring about the impact on the environment from dams and roads. Its annual reports mention little on local government debt or lending to Africa and Latin America. When CDB sells bonds domestically, it releases no information to bondholders, and overseas investors get little more than annual reports and the same sovereign credit rating that Standard & Poor's and Moody's assign to the Chinese government itself. CDB remains both a bank and a political institution, and as such answers to its state shareholders. With no official PR department, it reacts slowly, if at all, to reports about its lending in countries such as Ghana and Venezuela, where the money is heavily enmeshed with local politics. In part this is due to the bank's uneasy position at the nexus between policy and commercial lending, with deals often straddling the divide. As much as it pushes into commercial, international deals for top-tier companies, it is held back by its origins; it still operates with a top-down hierarchy and an often time-consuming approval process. To some of those who work with the bank it can move at the speed of a government department rather than an international bank.

To the credit of the strength of democracies of many African countries, the only disclosure of any CDB overseas loan comes from the countries themselves, their parliaments, or their media. Often the information is unconfirmed, comes out in snippets, and spreads on the Internet. There is no other way. The China–Africa Development Fund, which is funded only by CDB, with no outside investors, has little disclosure, no environmental assessments available to the public, no reports assessing the risks of projects to communities, or any invitations to work with local nongovernmental organizations. The only information it releases are descriptions of its projects for propaganda purposes.

Still, in many cases, China's capital might seem more attractive. The World Bank, the world's preeminent development institution, appointed an American citizen again as its head in 2012. What kind of message does this send to developing countries? Without political conditions attached to its loans, China, with CDB help, has sewn up political support in Latin American and Africa. There is no doubt that Zimbabwe cannot borrow from Western banks. Yet lending without any political conditions remains unproven. And in many cases CDB loans are no different from the money Africa has taken in the past: The money is linked to the London Interbank Offered Rate, it has conditions and requirements, and it is not free money. The same problem that confronted the International Monetary Fund and World Bank will haunt China: Without government reforms, effective institutions, and civil services, the money will not be paid back. It is in China's interests, too, to promote a stable Africa, whether that is through democracy or other means.

CDB is an extension of the Chinese state and the Communist Party, but it's also the reflection of one man. Through the power and connections of Chen Yuan, CDB has managed to preserve enough independence from the government to make investment decisions and function at times as a commercially driven institution. But since it is owned by the Chinese state and in turn the Party, and has its capital cheaply provided by them, there is no doubt that China's government will have a say in its future. Some of the questions China faces are these:

- Is CDB stimulating enough private investment in the economy? Or has it monopolized capital?
- Is it the most effective way to put people's savings to use?
- Has it outlived its use, and can it commercialize?

China has so far not been able to control the rise of CDB and has not been able to make it fully commercial, responsible for raising money using its own credit rating. Since Chen Yuan hasn't rotated through the party apparatus as other top bankers have, CDB has become its own fiefdom that can be regulated only by the State Council. It will be hard pushing the bank away from its killer combination of cheap money from the bond market and commercial returns from projects. China's bond market has never experienced a default, which makes its price of capital woefully inadequate.

In January 2007, the *China Daily*, a state-owned newspaper, said that reform of China's three policy banks—Exim Bank, CDB, and the Agricultural Bank—was "on top" of the agenda for China's National Financial Work Conference.[1] Four years later, Premier Wen Jiabao, in his last year in power, promised in a radio address to end the monopoly of state-owned banks. There is no doubt that the West can learn from what a strong development bank can achieve. It is a fallacy that financial innovation can be achieved only by private banks and a free market: CDB has been innovative in its deals with local governments and companies like Huawei. But China has decent infrastructure and can afford to move toward a more market-based system where consumption is better promoted and capital is freed up to follow the best, most innovative returns. China's state-owned companies have over-benefited from the country's controlled interest rates that have enabled the state banking system to make an easy profit out of depositors' money without considering the returns of projects, hindering many of the desirable functions of a market economy. While local government financing vehicles backed by CDB have been able to raise money for highways and stadiums, private companies have had to turn to unregulated underground banks. CDB also hires some of the country's best graduates who have studied overseas at Harvard and the Massachusetts Institute of Technology, sucking up some of the country's best talent. Changing CDB would be political, held up by state-owned companies, and involve breaking the bank up into less influential portions. But reform of the financial system is long overdue; although Chen Yuan has built a successful bank, the political pressures to lend to favored clients and powerful vested interests will bedevil his successor, too. Will someone without the red lineage of Chen Yuan be able to take control of that process, with the fantastically rich resources CDB has at its disposal?

Note

1. Lu Zhang, "China Exim: The Bank That Is Banking on Reform," *China Daily*, January 29, 2007, www.chinadaily.com.cn/china/2007-01/29/content_794942.htm

About the Authors

Henry Sanderson has been a reporter for Bloomberg News since April 2010. Prior to that, he was a correspondent for the Associated Press in Beijing and worked at Dow Jones Newswires in New York. While at Bloomberg, he has covered corporate finance, focusing on the bond market, China's banks, and the emergence of the yuan as an international currency. Before that he covered China for the AP, reporting on the Olympics, Chinese politics, as well as the country's environmental problems. He is a graduate of Leeds University (with bachelor's degrees in Chinese and English literature) and Columbia University in New York (with a master's degree in East Asian studies).

Michael Forsythe has been a reporter and editor for Bloomberg News since 2000. Prior to that, he was an officer in the United States Navy for seven years, serving on ships in the US Seventh Fleet. The highlight of his career in Washington was overseeing Bloomberg's coverage of the historic 2008 presidential election. Since returning to Beijing in 2009, Mike has focused on policy and politics, with particular emphasis on the international impact of "China Inc." He is a graduate of Georgetown University (with a bachelor's degree in international economics) and Harvard University (with a master's degree in East Asian regional studies). He is married and has two young boys.

Index